CHARIOTS
FOR APOLLO

CHARIOTS FOR APOLLO

THE UNTOLD STORY BEHIND THE RACE TO THE MOON

CHARLES PELLEGRINO
and JOSHUA STOFF

AVON BOOKS  NEW YORK

CBS News excerpt © CBS Inc. 1969. All rights reserved. Originally broadcast July 11, 1969 over the CBS Television Network on the *CBS Evening News with Walter Cronkite*. Reprinted by permission.

NBC News excerpt courtesy of The National Broadcasting Co., Inc. © 1969. The National Broadcasting Company, Inc. All rights reserved. Reprinted by permission.

Excerpt on page 290 from *Aviation Week and Space Technology*. Reprinted by permission.

AVON BOOKS, INC.
1350 Avenue of the Americas
New York, New York 10019

Copyright © 1985 by Charles R. Pellegrino and Joshua Stoff
Authors' Notes and Afterword © 1999 by Charles R. Pellegrino
Astronaut on moon cover photograph: NASA/FPG International
Moon cover photograph: George B. Diebold/THE STOCK MARKET
Published by arrangement with the authors
ISBN: 0-380-80261-9
www.avonbooks.com

Library of Congress Cataloging in Publication Data:

Pellegrino, Charles R.
Chariots for Apollo.
Bibliography:
Includes index.
1. Lunar excursion module. I. Stoff, Joshua.
II. Title.
TL795.P38   1987   629.47   87-14434

First Avon Books Trade Paperback Printing: June 1999

AVON TRADEMARK REG. U.S. PAT. OFF. AND IN OTHER COUNTRIES, MARCA REGISTRADA, HECHO EN U.S.A.

Printed in the U.S.A.

OPM   10   9   8   7   6   5   4   3   2

TO THE MEN AND WOMEN WHO MADE IT WORK

After a great human change, another is at hand. The great engine reneweth with the ages. In the heavens shall be seen a running fire with long sparks. They will be propelled in contraptions of flying fire. And they will go to the moon. He will come to take himself to the corner of Luna, where he will be taken and placed on a strange land.

Nostradamus, 1570

Oh yes, we shall get to the moon—but of course I daren't tell Hitler yet.

Wernher von Braun, 1941

CONTENTS

ACKNOWLEDGMENTS

Many individuals gave generously of their time to provide documents, personal accounts of life during the dawn of the Space Age, criticism of individual chapters, and incomparable advice and assistance. For helping us to get this project off the ground, we are particularly indebted to Milt Radimer, Russ Galen, Tige (Chuck) Pellegrino, Pamela (Buck) Rogers, THE Don (Peterson), Neil Nyren, Ann Keniston, Barbara Campo, Devera Pine, Stephen King, Jack Devine, George Skurla, Deloris Nicoli, Lisa Vazquez, D. R. Woods, General Tom Stafford, Herman Schonenberg and his staff at the Grumman History Center. We would like to acknowledge, in order of the dates on which they were interviewed, Bob Ekenstierna, William Kaiser, M. (Doc) Dzialakiewicz, Chet Senig, Bob Watkins, Joe Kingfield, Joseph Gavin, Al Beauregard, John Coursen, Harry Walther, Bob Mullaney, Manning Dandridge, Tom Kelly, George Titterton, Jesco von Puttkamer, Lynn Radcliffe, Frank Messina, Frank Mangro, Bill Voorhest, Tommy Attridge, Leon Gurinsky, Ozzie Williams, John Dickenson, Ralph H. (Doc) Tripp, Al Munier, Robert Kress, Ross Fleisig, Arnold Whitaker, William Bischoff, Mel Friedman, Howard Sherman, Mike Solan, Myrtice Holland, Tom Gwynne, Artie Falbush, John Logalbo, Paul Dent, Don Markarian, Ted Moorman, John Hussey, Chuck Kroupa, John Strakosch, Fred Haise, Isaac Asimov, Howard Edelson, Dick Barton, Tom Hennessy, Patrick Raineri, Joe Staff, Peggy Hewitt, Joel Taft, Greg Benoit, Bartholomew Nagy, Buzz Aldrin, Michael Collins, Neil Armstrong, James Lovell, Arthur C. Clarke, Gregory Grechko, Donald K. "Deke" Slayton, Harrison Schmitt, and Scott Carpenter. John

Papin regards his role in the LM program as part of a team effort and requests that he remain anonymous (his name is not John Papin). He wants no more recognition than has been granted to the thousands of individuals whose names do not appear in this book but who worked just as hard. For similar reasons, Don Peterson's name is also fictitious.

On a project of LM's magnitude, it is impossible to name everybody who has made a contribution. More than six thousand people were directly responsible for "one small step." To you, those six thousand plus, whether or not your names appear in these pages, we want to say thanks.

AUTHORS' NOTES

A great deal has been written about the men who first set foot upon the moon. They have, in fact, been interviewed nearly to death. But those first, hesitant steps on a world that was not our own were made possible by the efforts of designers and technicians who would never venture into the near-vacuum of outer space. These were not an elite minority of test pilots. These were men and women who had carried a machine through a long evolution—struggled to make it do what they wanted it to do and then stood on the ground as it took the sky, knowing it would work (*praying* it would work) and knowing, also, "I built that and it's going to the moon." Nobody has asked them what it felt like. Theirs is an untold story. It is a story that includes firsthand accounts of the *Apollo 1* fire, previously unavailable plans for the Soviet manned lunar-landing effort, and revelations that the *Eagle* almost exploded—only minutes after the first moon landing. Never-before-released logbooks provide glimpses of what life was like during the minute-by-minute construction of *Eagle*, and during the world's first space rescue mission, *Apollo 13*.

This is a book about people—everyday people—propelled into an historic situation, where they found themselves building, with their own hands, one of the most important machines in human history: LM, as it was affectionately called; the Lunar Module.

Astronauts are often asked what kind of courage must have been required to sit on top of a fully fueled *Saturn V* rocket. Few people ever take pause to think about the men who fueled the rocket, or climbed on top of it to perform last-minute repairs on the LM's fuel lines—*with soldering tools*—as Artie Falbush and

John Logalbo did only days before *Apollo* 11 lifted off for the moon. Given the opportunity, many of us would gladly ride a rocket to the moon, but how many would take on the responsibilities that the unsung heroes of America's space program accepted? How many of us would be willing to give up virtually all social life for six years, and miss our children growing up?

The events and personalities described in this book are real. All correspondence and dialogue has been re-created to the best recollection of the people involved (a spectrum ranging from sheet-metal workers to Wernher von Braun's closest aides) and sometimes from surviving tapes and documents. We saw no need to conjure up meetings that never took place or to enlarge events beyond what they actually were. The realities are so astonishing that, even to those of us who grew up after the dawn of the Space Age, they have the flavor of science fiction.

And strange, too, to understand finally that history really does have a tendency to repeat itself. The first edition of this book appeared simultaneously with (and immediately went out of print with) the explosion of the rocket ship *Challenger*. As with the loss of *Apollo* 1 (as with the loss of the *Titanic* nearly seventy-five years earlier), complacency and arrogance had bitten down with all the awful force of mortality. As with *Apollo* 1, there followed Congressional investigations, attempts to derail the space program and, behind the doors of NASA and its prime contractors, a paralysis born of fears that to touch anything or to design anything may lead to disaster. As with *Apollo* 1, a new generation of test pilots and engineers, not at all unlike Tommy Attridge and George Skurla, took the reins and put the space program on the path to recovery.

We have also seen a repeat of the *Apollo* 13 scenario, this time aboard the Soviet space station *Mir*. As with *Apollo* 13, the engineering challenges of a near-catastrophe proved to be the ship's trial by fire, ultimately demonstrating its true spaceworthiness, and becoming more triumph than tragedy. As with *Apollo* 13, Americans and Russians rediscovered their common humanity in the frontiers of the night.

And strangest of all, to step outside at night, to look a quarter million miles overhead and to know that there are machines up there, and footprints, and that after all these years they remain virtually unaged. Decades have passed since humanity last set foot upon that alien world, and decades more may pass before anyone returns; but to those of us who draw plans for Asimov Arrays and relativistic rockets, that world is a jumping off point to the stars. And we know, we who dream of great machines. We know that the next time people go to the moon, they are going to stay.

This is what civilization (indeed, what life itself) has been coming to, all these millennia. We will go into space—to the moon and to worlds beyond—for the simplest reason of all: We belong there.

It is as if we are, in a very real yet inexplicable sense, responding to a homing instinct.

Nothing more.

Nothing less.

(*We belong there . . .*)

Charles Pellegrino
Joshua Stoff
New York, New York
April 1998

1. STORM WARNING

It was scary.

Four and a half billion years of natural history had spawned creatures with brontosaurian appetites for competition. Now a contest spanning "only" the last few hundred centuries had spread human beings from pole to pole and put two giant nation-states in the running for first place. Whatever advantages big brains had been exapted* to some 250,000 years ago, they were certainly being put to higher use today. The same frontal lobes that once fashioned stone tools and herded mammoths into waiting traps could also plot the overthrow of governments, or probe geometry and the realm of atoms. Given the right incentives, there seemed no limit to what human minds could do.

And there were incentives.

Both the Soviet Union and the United States sought almost instinctively to establish a universal empire. But neither could do so without moving the other out of the way, and neither could move the other out of the way without first incurring a

---

*In an attempt to rid evolutionary biology of such improper words as "pre-adaptation," Harvard's Stephen Jay Gould and the Transvaal Museum's Elizabeth Vrba introduced the term "exaptation" in 1982. It defines features that now enhance fitness in new, almost unexpected ways, though they were never "built" by natural selection for such new roles (or possibly for any "role" at all). Feathers, for example, might have evolved first to prevent the loss of internal body heat, just as hair has. While retaining this original function, they became exaptations for flight once birds took the sky. Similarly, big brains, which made us better able to pursue food, and to avoid being pursued as food, have now been exapted to build computers; and computers—the products of big brains—were designed first to digest scientific data but have been exapted to do income-tax returns and play video games.

great loss, and each had too much to lose. The result of all this was a whole new brand of competition called "cold war." And so, inevitably . . .

Down there on Earth, a point of light appeared suddenly in the east, rising vertically and depositing behind itself a column of vapors that stood away from Earth like a white-hot needle. Blazing there, the upshooting light flung itself toward Alaska, its trail becoming horizontal and running parallel with the curving Pacific skin. It began to look as if it might fall back upon the atmosphere, but no, it stayed there in the farther sky, a piece of the planet detached.

On the Saturday morning of October 4 in the otherwise uneventful year of 1957, *Homo sapiens* had become adult.

It was scary.

They'd come from Mars, or somewhere, and they were a particularly nasty lot, too. They damned near flattened Washington—mummies in space suits! But Hugh Marlowe kept his head and came through. Undaunted by the fact that *they could get here and we couldn't get there* (an argument that might have persuaded less clever men to throw in the towel), he sought their weakness, and found it. Simple sound waves. That's all there was to it. So, as the people fled and the army came to pieces and the Capitol burned, Hugh drew his sonic cannon and began to raise all sorts of mischief with the invaders' guidance computers. Flying saucers tilted and swayed as if driven by drunkards. One skidded right through the Washington Monument. And then, the screen went blank.

If you stood outside the old movie house in downtown Stratford, Connecticut, that afternoon, you would have heard hundreds of kids screaming and clapping and making ghost noises in the dark, their hooting carrying right through the brick walls. The projectionist had really goofed up, and he was paying for it. As the theater lights came up to full strength, the unendurable noise rose in a steady crescendo until—uh-oh, now they'd done it. They'd brought the theater manager striding down the center aisle, and, boy, did he look mad. They knew they'd made too much noise. Knew it. It looked like the matinee was over for today. The manager mounted the stage, and, boy, did he look— Mad? No. He looked too pale to be mad. And he was trembling. Something must *really* be wrong.

He waited for silence. He didn't have to wait very long.

"I want to tell you something," he said. "I want to tell you that the Russians have put a space satellite into orbit around Earth. They call it *Sputnik*."

The silence was unbroken for a moment. Then for another. At last, an enraged voice cried out, "Oh, go show the movie, you liar!" And the film did come back on, and Hugh Marlowe did wage interplanetary war, and a ten-year-old Stephen King, who loved nothing better than to scare the living daylights out of people, sat alone and depressed and afraid, because he knew the manager wasn't lying.

On the screen ahead, alien spaceships menaced Washington, while somewhere on the other side of the sky a Russian machine flew where no plane could possibly intercept it, loaded, for all Steve knew, with atomic bombs. At any moment, the plutonium fist could come down on the real Washington, D.C., or on Stratford. He did not like the connection between that and what he was seeing on the screen. Science fiction and reality had touched, intimately, and they kept on touching.

"*Look to your skies,*" the aliens said threateningly. "*A warning will come from your skies. Look to your skies.*"

Mike Solan was scared.

His new boss at Baltimore's Martin Marietta Company was one of those German rocket scientists, and Mike somehow got the impression that the man was using him to get even for the way World War II had turned out. He was a sour personality, all right. He had little patience for anything, especially all the red tape—mountains of paperwork that the U.S. government was forever sending his way. And then Mike's draft notice came across his desk. Here was a young bachelor working in a comfortable office, one who had never been in the military and was counting on the company to get his "Renewal of Deferment" every year, as usual, and this German had shrugged at the piece of paper that meant nothing less than Mike's whole future, then scribbled "engineer" in the space marked "Job Description" and sent it off to the draft board. Fine job, Mike thought. You just don't do things like that in America. The guy had been around long enough to know better, to know that what you did with draft notices was submit a ten-page report saying that your employee was working in every program the company had, and if he went into the service, everything would come to a screeching halt in Baltimore, and that would cause a major crisis in the national defense and—Christ! Where did he think he was? This was America, man. And he just wrote "engineer." And the draft board read it and said, "Well, obviously we can draft this guy." And now the bureaucratic machinery was taking over. It was out to get Mike. It really was. When he appealed the draft's decision, the machinery said, "Sorry, kid. You're not allowed to submit any more information to the appeal board than was submitted to the original board."

"But all it says on that report is 'engineer.' "

"Sorry, kid, but you're not allowed to recolor the story. Appeal denied."

And now, trembling and alone, Mike found himself facing the Federal Court. He'd lost locally. He'd lost at the state level. And this was it. He was going to basic training. "We can only listen to the old facts," the machinery said.

Basic training. The words prepared his mind for reception of the idea.

". . . and it says here that you are an engineer."

"I *know* what it says. Now, if you'd only let me explain—"

"There's nothing to explain. We've just been told that the Russians have put this thing in space. It's called a 'Spootnik.' We were thinking of doing something like that ourselves, but they beat us to the punch. Awfully rude of them, don't you think?"

"Yes. Yes. Very rude. Very rude indeed."

"Right. Now, we're going to have to teach them a thing or two. And to do that we're going to need young engineers like you. So go back to Baltimore and get to work."

That night, Mike, like so many millions around the world, searched the skies for the "new star." For many Americans, it was a fearful sight, but for Mike—well, he felt like buying a drink for anyone having anything to do with launching *Sputnik*. Then he'd like to move on to cover the rest of Russia's population, buying drink after drink after drink, until all his money ran out.

2. SCIENCE FICTION

"I'm very glad to meet you," said Ross Fleisig, president of the American Astronautical Society, to the Russians, "because I believe you have something important to tell us."

This was the first International Astronautical Federation Congress that the Russians had attended, and getting them there to Barcelona, Spain, had put the federation knee deep in red tape. There were no diplomatic relations between Spain and Russia in the autumn of 1957, so there had been a last-minute scramble to get four Russian scientists to Barcelona on French visas; *Sputnik* had been circling the earth for four days, and the federation members were eager to hear what the satellite would do and to learn some of the technical details. But the Russians . . . that damned, tight-lipped foursome. Ross was bitterly disappointed. The federation had been able to get them to the meeting—after, he might say, a good deal of effort—and though they overwhelmed scientists and engineers with the importance of the data that would be collected from outer space, it turned out to be *them*, the Russians, who were doing all the listening and learning.

They told the federation nothing about the satellite itself, or about the vehicle that had launched it. Absolutely nothing.

Three weeks later, on November 3, 1957, *Sputnik 2* carried a German shepherd named Laika into orbit. Her pulse and respiration were beamed down to Earth from the automobile-size capsule. The signs remained normal for a full week, and then the oxygen tanks began to run out. Someone on the ground sent up a signal that squirted a massive overdose of sedatives into the intravenous food supply. Fortunately, he remembered to switch off the on-board camera. Unseen, the body began to putrify eerily at zero-gravity, staining the cabin walls with deposits of dark matter. Five months later, the unbreakable laws of celestial mechanics would bring Laika back to Earth, splashing her to pieces against the atmosphere. Meanwhile, one important fact had been learned: Space itself did not kill Laika. It did not convulse her heart or directly impair her breathing, and to the world the implications of the Laika experiment were clear. Sooner or later, a man would follow.

Two Russian moons. Jesco von Puttkamer was impressed. Only two years earlier, when asked by the Presidium of the Academy of Sciences what they thought could be conducted in space, some of Russia's foremost engineers had said, "I do not see what practical use artificial satellites could have." . . . "I do not visualize a space shot before the year 2000." . . . "I am not interested in fantasy." And yet, there they were. Jesco could go out into his back yard any evening, right after sunset, and see them racing across the heavens, clean and bright and beautiful. But the Sputniks were nothing new to him. In his own way he'd gone out there ahead of them. Some ten years earlier, as a schoolboy in postwar Germany, he was already living in space. He drew spaceship designs, and he talked often about artificial satellites and ideas he got from stories and articles by science-fiction writers, including Arthur C. Clarke, who had advocated putting aluminum moons in orbits so high that they could turn *with* the earth, hovering forever over the same bits of land and relaying television and other radio services all over the world. At eighteen, Jesco had started translating English-language science fiction for German publishers and had earned enough money that way to put himself through school. Then, while talk of satellites continued to bring yawns from Russian and American scientists, he began writing novels about moon rockets and expeditions to Mars and beyond. Publishers bought them, and, more important, young people bought and read them.

Now, at twenty-four, he drove a Mercedes to Germany's Technical University at Aachen, and he raced cars for a hobby and flew in gliders and, of course, wrote a lot of science fiction. But his tales of space travel were only dreams, and to Jesco von Puttkamer, dreaming about something was not enough. One should try to *do* something about it. And he did, always. He was just that way.

He remembered the day his affection for jazz had grown too strong. No longer could he just listen to Louis Armstrong's trumpet. He had to try it. *Had to.* So he bought himself a trumpet and learned how to play.

Dream a Little Dream . . .

It was all a dream, wasn't it? All this rocket stuff? Perhaps. But it obsessed him.

I'm Falling in Love Again . . .

Yes. It was happening again. The same thing that had happened with jazz was happening with space. Studying for a master's degree in engineering wasn't enough. Writing science fiction wasn't enough. He decided to do something about it, and Wernher von Braun, the "Wizard of Peenemünde" himself, struck him as being the only way of getting into the thing.

Dear Professor von Braun,
I have been following your work with great interest, and I believe with you that multistaged rockets and permanent platforms in space will be mankind's pathway to the planets.

I have some ideas I would like to discuss with you, particularly with regard to the possibility of lunar exploration. . . .

The first televised launch of an American satellite missed the moon by almost 250,000 miles, give or take two feet; but nobody could deny that the rocket's performance had been spectacular. On December 6, 1957, *Vanguard TV-3* lifted a few inches off the pad, hesitated for a moment, then settled back and broke open and blew up. The grapefruit-size *Vanguard* satellite rolled under a bush, dented, with its four antennae snapped off. It was still beeping away pathetically when a fire crew reached it.

Kaputnik, the press called it.

Bad taste, Don Peterson called it. "We told the White House back in October that the TV-3 flight would only give us an indication of what Project Vanguard's chances of success in future launchings might be. But Eisenhower's press secretary came out and told everybody we were launching a satellite, and all of a sudden the news cameras were there, and we found ourselves working in a fish bowl on a highly experimental project. Back in 1955, when we began work on *Vanguard*, there was no space race with the Russians. In those days, the state of the art in rocketry was such that we planned for about five launches, because rockets were always blowing apart, and if one of those five launches put a satellite in orbit, we would have achieved our objective. But then *Sputnik* happened, and—crack!—we had to succeed the first time. And it was not in the cards. The government knew we were only doing an experiment, and they were certainly an understanding customer. But the public reaction . . . Oh, brother! They saw us standing in front of the Russians with our pants down on the eve of the anniversary of Pearl Harbor—and *that's* what you call bad taste. They did not understand it. They were not used to failure when compared to another country."

But there was a brighter side of disaster, and Don had found it. If there had been no *Sputnik*, the public would have accepted the *Vanguard* failure. Not now, though. Now there was shock and anger and the world's biggest inferiority complex. And sud-

denly there was a memo from the Army that spoke of more funding and an acceleration of America's rocket program. And there
were whispers of things he'd only permitted himself the luxury of
imagining during the incessant budget crises that had gnawed
Vanguard nearly to death. Now, just maybe — could it be true? A
real space program? No, not true, he thought. It was going to
take more than *Kaputnik* against a dog in space to fire up the
guys who held the purse strings. (Oh, yes, Don did begin secretly
to hope that the Russians would embarrass America again.) Then,
with a little luck, we might actually do a few of the things Arthur
C. Clarke had been writing about, and von Braun, and that von
Puttkamer fellow.

Jesco von Puttkamer held the envelope for a long time. It was
from Huntsville, Alabama, and he dreaded the possibility that it
would contain the Rocketmaster's polite response to his ideas:
"Thank you very much for your kind letter, but no thanks." At
last he tore open the side of the envelope in one quick stroke,
pulled the letter out, and read:

> *Dear Mr. Von Puttkamer,*
> *Thank you very much for your kind letter. I was pleased to*
> *read about your work, and I liked your book that you were*
> *kind enough to dedicate to me. Now, about your ideas. They*
> *interest me. In fact, we are developing some plans along*
> *those lines. . . .*

And he thought, A human change is coming. A great wind is
going to blow, and von Braun will be in the middle of it, and I
will be there, too, I know. I am embarking on a fantastic
adventure.

3. HIGH HOPES

On January 4, 1958, *Sputnik 1* dipped into the atmosphere. At four miles per second it touched air and shattered as glass would against concrete. Twenty-seven days later, an American Redstone rocket hurled *Explorer 1* into the far sky and made it stay there. On the ground Ernst Stühlinger, one of von Braun's associates, pushed the button that circularized *Explorer's* orbit. It was a tricky maneuver. Space-tracking stations, on-board programming, and ground-support computers did not exist as yet, so Stühlinger worked it all out in his head. He held a stopwatch and did quick mental adjustments, and when he thought the Redstone had reached the apex of its long, parabolic curve, he depressed the SEND button and ignited the second stage, which threw the spinning *Explorer* up into the radiation belt. It will be flying round and round up there for the next three hundred years.

And the year wore on . . . February 5, the *Vanguard TV-3* backup veered off course and tore itself apart less than four miles above the pad . . . March 5, *Explorer 2* escaped the atmosphere, but the fourth stage failed to ignite, and gravity yanked the machine back, brutally, to burn up like a meteor over the Atlantic Ocean . . . March 17, *Vanguard 1* went into orbit, carrying a solar cell. It would still be transmitting a quarter of a century later . . . March 26, *Explorer 3* reached temporary orbit, returning radiation and micrometeor data . . . April 14, *Sputnik 2* reentered the atmosphere . . . April 28, *Vanguard TV-5* crashed in the Atlantic . . . May 15, *Sputnik 3*, weighing almost one hundred times as much as America's largest satellite, *Explorer 2*, reached orbit . . . May 27, *Vanguard SLV-1* crashed . . . June 26, *Vanguard*

SLV-2 crashed . . . July 26, *Explorer 4* reached orbit . . . August 17, U.S. *Able 1* flight was bright and noisy, lasting about two seconds . . . August 24, *Explorer 5* flew in the wrong direction and crashed . . . September 26, *Vanguard SLV-3* crashed . . . October 11, U.S. *Pioneer 1* was launched at the moon but stopped moving away from Earth at an altitude of 70,717 miles, from which it returned important radiation, magnetic-field, and micrometeor data.

EXCERPTS FROM GRUMMAN SPACE STEERING COMMITTEE NOTES

Date of meeting: October 15, 1958
Place: Bethpage, New York
Chaired by Al Munier
R. Houghton was not present at today's meeting. He was at a NASA briefing concerning a manned recoverable vehicle (for the proposed Project Mercury).

NASA Program Planning Projects were discussed. It was noted that the model chosen by our eight member committee, a lunar manned observatory vehicle, did fit in with some of the contemplated NASA projects. Committee members will outline the areas in which their groups will work and estimate the effort required in man hours.

Objective: The design of a lunar, manned, exploratory space vehicle system is to be undertaken utilizing equipment available by 1965 (?).

Description: The mission of the system is to gather information necessary to the founding of a permanent lunar station. Landing on and the mapping of the moon's surface will be of primary concern. Physical data will be collected continuously and relayed to Earth as the mission proceeds. The total elapsed time between the departure and return of the space vehicle's crew to the earth's surface shall not exceed two months. A vital part of the system will probably be manned, recoverable ferry vehicles to transport men and material to and from the space vehicles.

The performance of various propulsion systems, and combinations thereof, will be used in the parametric study of trajectories satisfying mission requirements. The result will be the first approximations to desirable flight paths and to provide boundaries within which the mission will be feasible. On the basis of propulsion systems available in 1965 those trajectories yielding maximum payload will be selected. Detailed design analyses will include lunar vehicle construction and assembly techniques (perhaps in orbit), in-flight vehicle and equipment maintenance and repair, and developments in long distance communications.

The proposal was almost beyond the fantastic, and Al Munier, a former bridge engineer for an obscure aircraft builder called Grumman, knew it. It was the beginning of Project Mercury, which meant that the week-old NASA organization was just thinking about putting a man in orbit, and here was Al, looking at sending people off to the moon. "So what?" he said.

He packed up the committee notes and drove to NASA headquarters to see what was on *their* minds. At that time, NASA worked out of a brownstone not far from the White House. Al remembers, "We had lunch and I said, 'We've been putting this moon mission together on paper.' And they said, 'You know, we've been doing the same thing.' So we sort of talked back and forth and decided we'd continue with the planning. And that's how it started.

"There were tentative studies made. Not under contract. It wasn't that formal. We—this little group—just started an outline of what we thought should be worked on. Then, as 1959 rolled around, we were having regularly scheduled meetings, but I had my doubts about whether or not the thing would actually be funded."

Then again, there's nothing certain in Washington. When Al chaired the Space Steering Committee meeting of October 15, if somebody had told him that John F. Kennedy was going to be elected president in 1960, he'd have shouted, "Go away! Never!" And if that same person had gone a step further and said, "He's not only going to be president; he's going to put up twenty billion dollars for a lunar landing," he'd have seriously questioned the man's sanity. But you can never tell.

So, for Al, it was simply a matter of expecting nothing, yet planning for something just in case. Besides, it was all rip-roaring fun. "That's what preliminary design is all about. You look ahead at, well . . . What are the possibilities? What do you see? How much does it cost? What is the state of the art to accomplish something like this? And, above all else, make sure you don't violate any physical laws. And from there on it's all high hopes. And you never can tell, which is just as well, because, if you could, you'd probably never bother to show up."

4. DOING IT

On the same day *Sputnik* 1 broke the gravitational bond between *Homo sapiens* and Earth, a lawyer-turned-revolutionary hid from soldiers in Cuba's Sierra Maestra mountains and scrounged for whatever food the trees could provide. His name was Fidel Castro, and he too was destined for an association with rockets, though not in the same manner as Al Munier and Jesco von Puttkamer. By the time *Explorer* 1 went into orbit, Castro's army of twelve fugitives had grown: Mountain farmers came gradually to support him, and word of the Fidelista movement was filtering out into the slums of the cities.

As *Sputnik* 3 took the sky, dictator Fulgencio Batista declared that he would put an end to that crazy lawyer once and for all. He napalmed the Sierra Maestra . . . but missed the Fidelistas. He sent in twelve thousand soldiers . . . but they joined the other side. On New Year's Day, 1959, Batista hauled stakes and fled to the Dominican Republic. A week later, as the Russian satellite *Lunik* 1 shot within 4,660 miles of the moon, Fidel Castro marched into Havana and took over Mr. Batista's job.

He'd done it. The crazy lawyer had actually done it.

"We can do it," Al Munier told the committee later that month. "We can get a man to the moon without having to make any insurmountable technological breakthroughs." The six-member NASA team was now dubbed the Space Task Group. Their meetings were held at Langley, Virginia, in what Al guessed to be an old hangar, and they were headed by a man named Robert Gilruth, who reported directly to NASA's first administrator, T. Keith Glennan.

Thus far, Americans had been launching satellites roughly the size of grapefruits. Clearly, sending a man into Earth orbit (not to mention sending one to the moon) was going to require rockets with weightlifting abilities far beyond those of the Vanguard and Explorer programs. Glennan turned his attention immediately to Wernher von Braun's Army Ballistic Missile Agency. "Yes," he said, "I can see. We must move in on von Braun's team in the strongest possible way, bring them into the NASA family, because it is becoming increasingly clear that we will soon desperately need this or an equivalent competence."

Competence. Applied to the von Braun team, the word was a masterpiece of understatement. Already they had developed a rocket capable of lifting a small Mercury capsule into space. And von Braun's assistants, Ernst Stühlinger and Heinz Koelle, had been peering deep into the next decade. Koelle predicted, "[By the spring of 1967] we will have developed the capability of putting man on the moon. And we still hope not to have Russian Customs there. The man in space effort dovetails with lunar and cislunar activities because you simply can't land a man on the moon before you have established a man in space capability; that is quite clear."

"The main objective in outer space," Stühlinger added, "should be man in space; and not only man as a survivor in space, but man as an active scientist, a man who can explore out in space all those things which we cannot explore from Earth."

"More to the point," von Braun said, "man is still the best computer that we can put aboard a spacecraft—and the only one that can be mass produced with unskilled labor."

To Al Munier it all made perfect sense, and he found it encouraging that Congress was beginning to ask what America should be doing in space during the 1960s. To many, the answer "a trip to the moon" was no longer a question of technical feasibility but a question of time. Al saw that it was in fact neither. The real question was *economic* feasibility. What on Earth could make the president or Congress put up all that money?

Nothing on Earth.

(Nothing on Earth?)

Right, Al thought. So be it. We've got Project Mercury to work with. And I guess half a loaf is better than— But why not go on with the planning just in case? We can look at the requirements for a moon rocket, propose a work breakdown, and maybe . . . just maybe . . .

On February 17, *Vanguard 2* returned the first cloud-cover photos of Earth. A month later, the U.S. space probe *Pioneer 4* passed within 37,300 miles of the moon. On April 13, America launched two satellites. The first came to pieces on the way up. The second orbited for a few days and then fell into the Arctic Ocean. At about the same time, the first Mercury astronauts were being selected.

By August, as Hawaii became America's fiftieth state and Fidel Castro annexed property and equipment owned by foreign compa-

nies, NASA's George Low began calling for a manned lunar landing. At a meeting intended to look beyond Project Mercury,
everybody's attention seemed to focus on putting a permanent
manned laboratory in near-Earth orbit. "But we can do better,"
Low said. "The technology for flying to the moon can be applied
directly to near-Earth space stations, but not vice-versa."

"Sorry, George," chairman Harry Goett* said. "When it
comes time to decide on whether or not to land on the moon,
and how we will land on the moon, you and I will both be retired
and we won't have to worry about it."

In Huntsville, the von Braun group were clearly worrying
about it. Only six months earlier they had announced plans for
the development of a 1.3-million-pound-thrust rocket called Project Saturn. Now they were reported to be designing a three-stage
version, almost twice as powerful and called *Saturn 2*. The Germans had something big on their minds, and, as if to confirm it,
the Space Task Group had sent NASA director T. Kieth Glennan
a memo calling for the immediate development of an advanced
version of the *Mercury* capsule. It would carry three astronauts
and would be designed to reenter the atmosphere at a velocity
nearly equal to that required to escape the earth's gravitational
influence and to fly off into . . . deep space. You didn't have to
be a rocket expert to guess where such a capsule might be returning from. It was an exciting idea, but one that saddened the
NASA director. He knew that he could not commit the space
agency to any specific long-term project, especially a moon rocket.
The big crunch was coming, he was sure. NASA might put a
man in orbit, but that would be the end of it. With the economy
in a slump, and President Eisenhower determined to balance the
budget, "come hell or high water," Glennan resigned himself to
the fact that the hopes of von Braun and the Space Task Group
were merely that: hopes.

---

*Harry Goett, an engineering manager at the Ames Research Center, was appointed
chairman of the Research Steering Committee for Manned Space Flight, which met
three times at Langley, Virginia, between April and December 1959, to study and
propose long-range NASA objectives.

Still, American rocket scientists, more and more of them, were raising their sights on the moon. Half a world away, Kremlin eyes narrowed on the same target. On September 14 the Soviets scored a bull's-eye. Loaded with scientific equipment and weighing about 860 pounds, *Luna 2* successfully beamed a flood of new information back to Earth, right up to the moment of impact.* At twenty miles per second, it dove through dozens of feet of lunar bedrock, excavated a ninety-foot-wide crater, and scattered pieces of itself for miles in every direction. Three weeks later, the two-thousand-pound *Luna 3* sent back the first photographs of the moon's far side.

In 1960 America scored with the first two communications satellites, *Echo 1* and *Courier 1B*, and the first weather satellite, *Tyros 1*. The Russians, meanwhile, launched *Sputniks 5* and *6*, two prototype-manned spacecraft, each carrying two dogs and returning them live from orbit. In the same year, Jesco von Puttkamer received his master's degree in engineering. He wrote again to his new friend.

Dear Professor von Braun,
I have completed my graduate studies and hope to one day join your fine team in Huntsville, Alabama. I do, however, feel that I need a little bit more experience before I am up to your qualifications, and therefore I should go into industry first. I have had an offer from Boeing in Seattle and Convair in San Diego, and so I am preparing to fill out the applications, emigrate to the U.S., start working in industry, and then later on join your rocket development team, if you feel that you can use me.

Yours sincerely,
Jesco von Puttkamer

The telegram arrived a few days later.

---

*According to Soviet sources, *Luna 1* "failed in flight."

DON'T GO TO INDUSTRY STOP COME TO HUNTSVILLE
STOP WE ARE GOING TO THE MOON STOP WERNHER
VON BRAUN

5. HUMAN RACE

Except for those optimists in Huntsville, few would have believed
that in the summer of 1960, Congress would add one (a capsule
able to take two Russian dogs—or one man—into orbit) and one
(pinpoint targeting of heavy payloads to the moon) and get two.
When simple logic showed that a manned flight around the
moon—a Russian flight—was not only possible but likely, there
came a chorus of "Me too"s. So, on August 30, more than a
thousand representatives of government, industry, and higher education were invited to Washington, D.C., where NASA announced plans for development of a *Saturn* rocket and a space
capsule able to orbit the moon and return to Earth. Space Task
Group leader Bob Gilruth spoke of preliminary-design contracts
that would be awarded to three companies. He wanted the atten-
dees to think in terms of an Earth-orbital and circumlunar spaceship that could, if the need ever arose, directly support a future
moon landing. He was talking about Project Apollo.

When Jesco von Puttkamer arrived in Huntsville, he was relieved to learn that the locals accepted and even welcomed German rocket scientists. They seemed to him to be surprisingly
open-minded, considering that Huntsville was, at the time, a cot-
ton village with a population of sixteen thousand. "It had not
always been so good," he says. "The old-timers, the first wave,
had come to Huntsville from Fort Bliss, Texas, where they lived

in barracks behind barbed wire. Von Braun called this group the 'Prisoners of Peace.' They were not exactly war prisoners. They had government contracts; but, maybe to protect them from the outside or whatever, they were not allowed off base. So they were very unhappy. They spent all of the late 1940s just waiting, and then in 1950, with the Korean War firing the interest of the Army, they were transferred to the former poison-gas manufacturing plant in Huntsville—the Redstone arsenal, which was closed and covered with dust. They didn't live in barracks anymore. They then had to start building their own homes. And they contributed to the entire mushrooming history of Huntsville itself. That little black cloud about having worked for the Nazis, building V-2s and so on—that applied to Fort Bliss. But when they came to Huntsville, I must say that the locals really were extremely hospitable, and they were glad that we brought new work and new economy into the town."

But farther afield, people referred to the town as *Huns*ville. This was, after all, America in 1960. This was the heart of KKK territory, which meant that you could do much worse than have a German accent. You could, just for a start, be like poor Charles Drew, M.D., who in 1940 perfected blood-preservation techniques and organized the nation's blood banks and ten years later bled to death after an accident because they wouldn't let him into a "whites only" hospital.

It was easy for von Puttkamer to put most of these things out of his mind. At center stage, the man he'd admired from afar had caught up with and surpassed his expectations. "Wernher von Braun had a great way of designing on the spot of the moment. For example, when I came to Huntsville, the team was working out the technical concepts of cryogenics. This meant very low temperatures—liquid hydrogen and liquid oxygen—which had never been done before. We wanted to burn these liquefied gases for propellant in the boosters. The last stage, which would push the ship out of Earth orbit and toward the moon, would also be a cryogenic stage. Now we had to figure out how—after an hour and a half of orbiting in weightlessness around the earth—how do you restart a cryogenic stage when you've got propellant just floating around in the tanks, probably nowhere near the fuel lines at the tank bottoms? So we had to first create some kind of artificial gravity. Before you start the main engine, you vent some hydrogen gas out into the vacuum of space, which causes a little thrust by just going out through the nozzles and pushes the fuel to the bottoms of the tanks, much like when you hit the gas pedal in a car and it pushes you back against the seat. It's that simple, and von Braun put it into the design. What amazed me was how he could come up with things like that on the quick, using only the blackboard. He often made engineering decisions, which more often than not turned out to be correct decisions, right there, listening to his intuitive feelings more than his analytical knowledge. Just looking at designs, he then started conceptualizing space vehicles by turning around to us and saying, 'Well, guys, shouldn't that be that rather than this way?' And then we had to go back to our laboratories changing and redesigning."

By October, as the presidential race between Richard M. Nixon and John F. Kennedy built up to full steam, all the planning and redesigning seemed to be for nothing. The future of Apollo, and even Mercury, had come unhinged. With the imminent change of administrations, the only thing certain about the space program was its uncertainty.

As all the world knows, Kennedy won the November 8 election. Two months later, Glennan was still waiting for some member of the incoming administration to get in touch with him. He waited in vain.

Then, one day:

Vostok 1 shot out of the atmosphere at 4.7 miles per second. Inside, a Soviet test pilot named Yuri Gagarin became the first man actually to see the curve of the terrestrial globe. Racing east, he watched Siberian dawn in reverse, then plunged through the line of shadow that bisected Japan. In total eclipse, Gagarin's ship crossed the tip of South America, emerging into daylight again as it approached North Africa. Two hundred miles below, a thin film of clouds was marching before the winds. With a single finger, Gargarin could trace the glittering Nile from its delta to the elusive tributaries for which Stanley and Livingston and scores of others had searched so hard for so long. Foreshortened in the distance, misty and vague and rolling toward him over the curve of the earth, was home. He beamed down revolutionary greetings to African nations, and shortly thereafter the automatic retrofire kicked on, nudging his capsule down toward an encounter with the atmosphere.

The ship's parachute could slow it down to only some sixty miles per hour. At that speed, a landing on the Russian desert would be anything but comfortable, so the pilot was obliged to fire his ejection seat and abandon ship at twenty thousand feet. He touched down an hour and forty-eight minutes after the flight began.

Even as Gagarin sailed over Africa, the Tass News Agency was joyfully shocking the world:

THE WORLD'S FIRST SPACESHIP, VOSTOK, WITH A MAN ON BOARD WAS LAUNCHED ON 12 APRIL, 1961. THE PILOT SPACE-NAVIGATOR OF THE SATELLITE SPACESHIP VOSTOK IS A CITIZEN OF THE USSR, FLIGHT MAJOR YURI ALEKSEYE-VICH GAGARIN. THE LAUNCHING OF THE MULTI-STAGE SPACE ROCKET WAS SUCCESSFUL AND, AFTER ATTAINING THE FIRST ESCAPE VELOCITY AND THE SEPARATION OF THE FIRST STAGE OF THE CARRIER ROCKET, THE SPACE-SHIP WENT INTO FREE FLIGHT ON A ROUND-THE-EARTH ORBIT.

It was 4:00 A.M. when the news reached Washington. Minutes later, John "Shorty" Powers, the public-relations officer for Project Mercury, was awakened by his phone. A reporter on the other end wanted his opinion of the flight. He looked at his clock, too groggy even to understand what the man was going on about, and said, "We're all asleep down here," then hung up. By lunchtime, those very words appeared as subheadings on the front pages of newspapers all across the country, heralded as an apt answer to how America had once again been beaten in the space arena.

Within a week, a second hard lesson was driven home: The United States had seriously misunderstood and underestimated the Cuban revolution. When Castro came to power, Americans had turned their heads in revulsion as some two hundred "war criminals" were executed, many for running what amounted literally to Batista's concentration camps, in which as many as twenty thousand people had been tortured and killed. Cuban-American relations soured at the outset, despite the fact that the Cuban takeover had been one of the history's least bloody of "bloodless" revolutions. The rapidity of the souring was surprising. Airship pilot William Kaiser recalls a beautiful lighthouse on the far-eastern tip of Cuba. It was surrounded by a village of about eight houses, and every few weeks, as he drifted overhead, the people came out to wave and cheer. One week they came out to throw rocks.

On July 6, 1960, in retaliation for Castro's seizure of American-owned sugar mills and oil refineries, a trade embargo was imposed. Castro retaliated by freezing *all* American assets, and the United States retaliated in turn by breaking off *all* diplomatic relations.

Up to that time, Castro had no ideological or political alignment with the Soviets. The Cuban Communist Party had in fact resisted him at almost every step. But when Russia offered to buy several tons of sugar from Cuba, the state of Cuban-American relations (none at all) produced the only alignment possible.

Out of what must have been sheer panic, fourteen hundred anti-Castro Cuban exiles were sent on April 17, 1961, to a place called the Bay of Pigs. They had been trained by the CIA, shipped off on American boats, and were to have been supported by American planes, which, for the most part, never showed up. They were expected to instigate a counterrevolution, but apparently nobody felt like revolting, and instead the United States ended up paying Cuba $50 million in private donations for the return of 1,179 very angry survivors.

Only three weeks earlier, a somewhat less humiliated President Kennedy had dismissed proposals for an acceleration of the U.S. rocket program. Now he looked at the sky a lot, perhaps in prayer (who knows?), and became suddenly convinced that space would emerge as the symbol of the twentieth century. "Space is the new ocean," he said. "And we must sail on it." He decreed that America should not take the back seat to anyone, especially the Russians, and he asked the question that led ultimately to the thing called "Bug" or "Spider" or, more properly, LM (for Lunar Module): "Do we have a chance of beating the Soviets by putting a laboratory in space, or by a trip around the moon, or by a rocket to land on the moon, or by a rocket to go to the moon and back with a man? Is there any other space program which promises dramatic results in which we could win?"

On May 5, 1961, Alan Shepard rode a Redstone booster out of the atmosphere in his *Freedom 7 Mercury* capsule. He splashed down nearly three hundred miles downrange after a flight that lasted fifteen minutes.

A good start? Yes.

Impressive? Not really.

Gagarin had, after all, flown *around* the Earth—25,000 miles against Shepard's 297. *Vostok* outweighed the Mercury capsule by a factor of five—and it went into orbit. Gagarin experienced about an hour and a half of weightlessness, against Shepard's five minutes. America's booster capability seemed pitifully small, as Kennedy was so painfully aware. "We are behind," he said. "The news will be worse before it is better, and it will be some time before we catch up."

(we are behind)

By that time, Russia was falling behind, though neither Kennedy nor von Braun nor anybody else in America knew that the momentum was indeed shifting. According to NASA technician and space historian James Oberg, Field Marshal Mitrofan Nedelin had been directing preparations for an unmanned flight to Mars.

Three rockets were constructed for the mission. The first came apart in midair, and when a Mars probe was put atop the second, it too failed. The third refused even to ignite.

The biochemist Zhores Medvedev, who defected from Russia in 1975, describes what happened next with great bitterness: "Khrushchev's misuse of space research to boost Soviet political prestige led to an irreparable catastrophe."

Pressured by Khrushchev to get on with the launch, Nedelin became eager to isolate the source of the problem and to start again, so eager that he ignored several rules of caution, including the one that states *Always drain the one-million-pound fuel tanks before you start climbing around and under and in the rocket,* and the equally important, *Never, never tap a fully loaded rocket with a screwdriver.* Nedelin and as many as sixty rocket scientists died in a tornado of exploding gases and splintered steel.*

(we are behind)

"We must move ahead," the president announced to Congress on May 25, 1961. "Now it is time to take longer strides, time for a great new American enterprise, time for this nation to take a clearly leading role in space achievement, which in many ways may hold the key to our future on Earth. . . . Recognizing the head start obtained by the Soviets with their large rocket engines, which gives them many months of leadtime, and recognizing the likelihood that they will exploit this lead for some time to come in still more impressive successes, we nevertheless are required to make new efforts of our own. For while we cannot guarantee that we shall one day be first, we can guarantee that any failure to make this effort will find us last. . . . But this is not merely a race. Space is open to us now. . . . We go into space because whatever mankind must undertake, free men must fully share. . . . I therefore ask Congress . . . to provide the funds which are needed. . . . *We choose to go to the moon in this decade.*"

At that time, NASA was on the threshold of manned orbital

---

*Until Medvedev's disclosure in 1975, not even the Soviet public had heard of the Nedelin disaster of October 24, 1960.

flight, which was in itself mind-boggling. A program to put a man on the moon—a quarter of a million miles away—and to bring him back in one piece and still taking in air sounded like pure Vernean fantasy. But they were serious about it. Truly serious.

Bob Gilruth was now charged with transforming concepts drafted by committees and study groups into actual hardware. To date, NASA's total man-in-space experience was limited to five minutes outside the earth, and Gilruth was being asked to sustain men during a two-week venture to the moon—*to the moon*. He awoke one night from uneasy dreams, with voices crying in his brain, "Get us out of here . . . get us out . . . get us out . . ." A second later, he screamed.

6. HOW DO YOU DO?

One thing President Kennedy had failed to mention was *how to get there*. Von Braun favored a multiple-rocket approach, in which as many as fifteen rockets would be put in orbit around the earth, there to rendezvous and be assembled to produce a 420,000-pound spacecraft. This giant could then push off to the moon, dropping empty fuel tanks along the way. The whole thing would then arrive directly on the moon's surface. Von Braun viewed plans for orbiting the moon before landing as an unnecessary maneuver. William Pickering, of the Jet Propulsion Laboratory (JPL), agreed: "You don't *have* to go into orbit; you just aim at the moon and, when you get close enough, turn on the landing rockets and come straight in." Maxime Faget, chief assistant to the Space Task Group and one of the prime designers of Project Mercury, said quickly, "That would be a pretty unhappy day if when you lit up the rockets they didn't light."

Nuh! Al Munier thought. The moon coming up at you like a giant flyswatter. That won't do.

But Von Braun kept pushing for a big ship: the first stage of his "Project Horizon," which called for the establishment of permanent outposts on the moon with interchangeable crews. Horizon was a military endeavor that justified its existence in terms of the "traditional military need for high ground."

In the midst of all this, any lunatic (pardon the pun) proposal that surfaced immediately found an open ear. One such proposal became known as the "poor-slob plan." It called for a relatively lightweight spacecraft to be landed on the moon. The only catch was that it and its occupant would have to stay there. Once on the moon, the astronaut could perform valuable scientific work while he retrieved supply rockets shot at him and waited patiently, possibly several years, for NASA to build and launch a ship that could bring him back. This was an inelegant solution to the Soviet challenge, whose only virtue was that it was "cheaper, faster, and perhaps the only way to beat Russia."

Equally outlandish, at least at first glance, was NASA engineer John Houbolt's plan for Lunar Orbit Rendezvous. At a May 1961 meeting held in Washington, D.C., he outlined the following scenario: Send *one* rocket, insert a "mother ship" in lunar orbit, and let the mother ship dispatch a lander to the surface. "A rendezvous around the moon is like being in a living room," he said. "Why take the whole damn living room down to the surface when it's easier to go down in a little tiny craft? It becomes a chain reaction of simplifications: development, testing, manufacturing, launch and flight operations. All would be simplified. Don't you see! This is it! If there is any idea we must push, this is the one."

But the U.S. had only fifteen minutes of manned-spaceflight experience. Houbolt's proposal seemed a good way of reducing the total weight of the spacecraft, but a rendezvous around the moon? So far from home? That was a terrifying thought. What if you missed your rendezvous when you came up from the surface and went into a deadman's curve around the moon, turned your spacecraft into an orbiting coffin . . . forever? Von Braun listened quietly to the plan and then dismissed it. "No, that's no good," he said. "Won't work."

Something had to work. It was time for the government to start giving contracts to designers and builders of the moon ship. The contractors would be private American businesses. Companies were invited to compete with one another to produce the best possible design, and the winner would be paid to build the ship for NASA. It was at this stage that General Electric approached Grumman Aircraft Engineering Corporation in Bethpage, Long Island, and asked the company to come abroad as a subcontractor on their design study.

"Now, as far as what it was about," says Al Munier, "the ship was intended to make a direct shot from the earth to the moon. And it meant that you had to land a vehicle that contained an upper stage that would bring you up from the moon to Earth. And I remember, when we were working on the proposal, one of the problems was, here you had a moon lander and an Earth-return module stacked on top of it, and the ship was about eighty feet high, which meant that you had to land a ten-story building on its tail. Okay, let's say ou can do that. Then what? How the hell do you get out of the upper stage and down to the ground? Maybe you could use pulleys and a chair to lower yourself down the side of the ship, but that's the least of your problems. Do you know what kind of booster you'd need to put a monster like that outside the earth? The *Saturn V* would have been tiny compared to its first stage. We're talking about a rocket as big as the Empire State Building. So that started some new thinking on our part. Two options came up: Earth Orbit Rendezvous, which was proposed by von Braun, and Lunar Orbit Rendezvous, which came from a chap named John Houbolt."

The publication of Houbolt's paper on Lunar Orbit Rendezvous (LOR) brought sneers from Huntsville, but in Bethpage, a soft-spoken Grumman engineer named Tom Kelly, who would one day be called the "father of LM," liked what he read. "We were doing our design studies and along came Houbolt's paper.

We agreed with what he was saying, and went down to talk with him, and it was very pleasant, because we all agreed with each other. We decided that the proponents of the other views were terribly misguided. Then, as it turned out in General Electric's proposal [for the Command and Service Modules], Grumman was given the assignment of studying the Lunar Orbit Rendezvous approach, probably because we had become very interested in the idea. The scheme was simple: You entered an orbit around the moon and climbed into another specialized vehicle that would land on the moon. The lander then came back into lunar orbit, but never came back to Earth. That's what frightened people. You were going down to the moon in a ship that couldn't, on its own power, get you back to Earth, and you really had to have faith that you were gonna be able to get back again to the ship that was gonna take you back into the earth's atmosphere. The idea of coming up from the moon and getting these two vehicles together again in space was at that time considered to be *Buck Rogers*. And much of the work that we did in that period was to show both by analysis and by simulation that rendezvous in lunar orbit was really pretty easy, and that there were many different ways you could navigate and determine your position. You could do it with radar. You could do it with infrared seekers. You could do it optically. We even had a scheme where you could do it just with a telescope and a stopwatch. You *could* do it."

Assigned to write the rendezvous section of the proposal, one of Tom Kelly's advanced systems engineers, Arnold Whitaker, recalls, "The part dealing with return of the lander—just think of the layman's view of the world. The idea of rendezvous out there in lunar orbit, a quarter of a million miles from Earth—it looked like a near-impossible task. We'd never even done an Earth orbit, much less a lunar orbit. But no matter how we did our studies, it all came out the same way: This really wasn't a difficult thing to do. And I can remember writing the first section on that proposal, and Tom Kelly came over and said, 'You've got to do that all over again, Arnold. No way can you convince anybody that

that's not going to be difficult.' The whole study showed it was totally within our capability of doing, a number of different ways, with off-the-shelf hardware.

"Nevertheless, we really had to rewrite that whole section of the proposal to make it sound quite difficult, and when I made the first presentation to the President's Scientific Advisory Committee, they just couldn't believe that it was not going to be an impossible thing.

"I guess it was Houbolt who had the hardest time, though. He really aggravated everybody in the whole organization, partly because he became very annoyed with anybody who didn't grasp his ideas the moment he presented them. He was sometimes a difficult personality to deal with. But he was very brilliant. I've read almost everything he's ever written. And he was usually right. His original calculations were just on the back of an envelope. He put it together with just straight, logical physics."

In mid-July 1961 Houbolt was invited to give a lecture at an Apollo technical conference. During a practice session, when he and other speakers presented their notes for final approval, his supervisors told him to restrict his discussion to rendezvous in general and to "throw out all that LOR crap."

In mid-November Houbolt went over the heads of his supervisors and contacted NASA associate administrator Robert Seamans, who was then facing the dilemma of recommending a set of booster rockets for the moon effort. "Somewhat as a voice in the wilderness," Houbolt's letter began,

I would like to pass on a few thoughts on matters that have been of deep concern to me over recent months. . . . I am convinced that man will set foot on the moon through the use of ideas akin to those expressed hererin. . . . Regrettably, there was little interest shown in LOR. I have been appalled at the thinking of individuals and committees. Do we want to get to the moon or not? *If so, why not develop a lunar landing program to meet a given booster capability instead of building vehicles to carry out a preconceived plan? Give us the go ahead and we will put men on the moon in very short order—and we don't need any Houston empire to do it.*

Seamans liked the letter, and passed it along to NASA administrators with instructions that LOR be given the same impartial consideration as von Braun's Earth Orbit Rendezvous or any other approach. He wrote to Houbolt two weeks later:

I agree that you touched upon facets of the technical approach to manned lunar landing which deserve serious consideration. . . . It would be extremely harmful to our organization and to the country if our qualified staff were unduly limited by restrictive guidelines.

By May 1962, some of Houbolt's severest critics at the "Houston empire" had taken a second glance at LOR and begun to change their minds. When von Braun visited Washington, Joseph Shea, systems director of the Office of Manned Space Flight, broke the news to him: LOR seemed to be emerging as the best method.

"That might well be a wise choice," von Braun admitted.

"I'm afraid your Marshall Space Flight Center will lose a good deal of work if NASA adopts LOR," Shea warned. "It just seems natural to me that you guys ought to start getting involved in the lunar base and the roving vehicle and some of the other spacecraft stuff."

Shea remembers, "Wernher kind of tucked that in the back of his mind and went back to Huntsville. Then, on June 7, von Braun dropped a bomb that, as far as internal arguments at NASA were concerned, laid to rest the Apollo mode issue. To the dismay of his staff, he announced publicly that it was the position of his center to support LOR."

"When von Braun changed his mind about LOR," Houbolt recalls, "I figured that the last hurdle had been cleared. And I admire him greatly for it."

"Of course, we in Huntsville had proposed Earth Orbit Rendezvous, or EOR," says von Puttkamer. "This would have required tanker flights and a larger ship, which would have been assembled from modules in orbit around Earth, something which comes pretty close to building a space station. We had designed a tanker ship, and there were already concepts of a space shuttle. We would have had to develop refueling techniques in Earth orbit, but we didn't see any problems in doing that. However, some other people in Houston decided to go to LOR for no real clear reason. If you wanted to rendezvous around the moon or around the earth, it didn't make too much difference in terms of safety. I think one of the arguments was that the LOR ship would have taken less time to build—eight years they projected. Kennedy, of course, wanted us to land on the moon during his second term.

"So all we had was eight years, and LOR stood a better chance, in our estimate, of being achievable in that time. But EOR would probably have given us more continuity to the future. The reason some of us wanted EOR was not just to go to the moon but to have something afterwards: orbital operations, a space station, a springboard. LOR was a one-shot deal, very limited, very inflexible. But if you developed an Earth-orbiting space station first, you would have had the flexibility to keep ships going to the moon, to land there and stay there, or to go to Mars, or just to exploit the capability of Earth-orbital operations. After the close-down of Apollo, we began to pay the price. We are trying to fill that gap, which we jumped over, and are having a tough time coming up with a convincing justification to do it. Sometimes I wish we had done EOR. Then we would probably have a space station already. Then we wouldn't have to go back and rejustify something that looks to many people like a step backwards. And in a certain sense it is. We've been to the moon already, history knows, and now all of a sudden we're trying to fill this empty space.

"When von Braun changed his mind about EOR, I figured that, well, von Bran was always very flexible, the born diplomat. When he saw that he couldn't get his opinion through, he was the first one to change. He came back from a meeting in Washington and told us, 'Hey, guys, we're gonna do it the other way.' A few of us may have been a little bitter at him and said, 'Here he goes again, yielding to the Manned Spacecraft Center in Houston.' He yielded to authority often in his life. He never was really locked in on his own ideas. In this particular case I guess some of us were a little mad at him for having been too flexible. But later on, the Apollo program proved LOR to be a right way to go. It was done in time."

It was Houbolt who later stumbled upon records of the Russian-born Yuri Kondratyuk, who had predicted some fifty years earlier not only that rockets could be used for space exploration but that a lunar-orbit rendezvous was the best approach to landing men on the moon. Nobody took notice of his plans, and in frustration and obscurity he died. My God, thought Houbolt. He went through the same thing I did.

While the infighting still raged over EOR and LOR, a Grumman/RCA team realized that planning for LOR hardware and mission requirements might improve their chances of securing contracts in the wake of an impending shift to Lunar Orbit Rendezvous. At about this time, NASA realized that if Houbolt's "little tiny craft" were left on the moon with its spent fuel tanks—if pieces of the ship were discarded as they were no longer needed—the mission became simpler yet.

"The proposal to NASA for a moon lander was an example of ignorance in action," Kelly says. "At least on our part. None of us at Grumman really knew what NASA wanted. Sometimes I wasn't sure that NASA knew what NASA wanted. Their request for the moon-lander proposal was, well, a very interesting approach in that it was sort of like an examination paper. They asked a certain number of specific questions that we had to answer, mostly technical questions about what your approach would be to this aspect or that aspect of the design. They made it clear that they were not buying a design. In other words, it wasn't a classical government approach, where you'd propose a design and they'd buy it. They were really giving you a test to see how much homework you had done and how knowledgeable you were and how ingenious you could be. The design we had on our proposal was a buggy, spindly thing with windows all around the upper stage. And for whatever reasons, we came out first."

On November 7, 1962, NASA announced that Grumman would build the LM. According to NASA, a major factor in Grumman's selection had been its facilities: spacious engineering-design and office accommodations, ample manufacturing space, and a dust-free complex for vehicle assembly and testing.

According to Al Munier, "It's just a personal feeling. After working with them on the Command and Service Module (CSM) proposal, I felt that General Electric just didn't know too much about the subject matter. I was not impressed with their knowledge of going to the moon. They approached it differently. We were aircraft engineers, and we got into trade-off studies of things like propulsion systems: coming up with different types and then trying to find out which one was the most efficient. Three major contractors were *paid* by NASA to work out a design study for the CSM. Our little company was not one of them, but we decided to go ahead and do our own study in parallel, on our own funds, because the idea of going to the moon looked so interesting and we wanted a shot at it. Our smallness helped; I'm convinced of that. General Electric put together this big team, which was pretty clumsy. They had Douglas Aircraft on board. They had us on board. They had TRW and a whole bunch of others, and how do you ever manage something like that?"

Grumman retiree Milt Radimer has a simpler explanation: "Somebody made a mistake, I guess. Years ago we were more or less told that we were a nickel-and-dime operation because we never were much for publicity. McDonnell would go down there and Boeing would go down there and give presentations, and they'd have these elaborate sound movies. Grumman would go down with ordinary black-and-white photographs of the things we were building. Then this moon-lander thing came along. It was such a complete change of design. I don't think anybody else really wanted to build it. So they said, 'We'll get Grumman to build it.' If you ever saw the first drawings of that thing . . . Now it's acceptable, but when we saw the first drawings . . ."

What the hell is this?

A cross between a praying mantis and a spider?

This is going to fly?

"Nobody on the shop floor believed it at the beginning," Radimer remembers. "Nobody believed that it was gonna fly. It's a crazy-looking thing, but it turned out to be the most beautiful ugly thing in the world. That *dumb thing* we were going to build. Back then I would call it a 'dumb thing.'"

7. DANGEROUS VISIONS

While Houbolt and von Braun squared off for their fight over the lunar-mode issue, Fidel Castro was busy proving the adage that power corrupts, and absolute power corrupts absolutely. Promises to restore democratic elections and a free press were broken, and when Cubans protested, he refilled Batista's death camps, this time called "rehabilitation centers." It's all the same. As many as five thousand people had been permanently rehabilitated. For an encore he brought the world to the brink of nuclear war.

This time, young Stephen King's fears about *Sputnik* were realized. This time rockets *were* aimed at Washington and Connecticut; and this time they *were* loaded with atomic bombs.

And it *was* scary.

And it was also strange. In the main hall of P.S. 23, in Flushing, New York, during the height of the Cuban Missile Crisis, a bronze statue of Fidel Castro stood beside the American flag. It stood there because two of Castro's nephews were attending the high school across the street. (Or something like that. Something strange.) The statue terrified an eight-year-old refugee named Carlos, who had seen nearly half his family killed personally by Mr. Cuba. "Castro is coming," Carlos would say in a shrill, unforgettable voice. "*Castro is coming. Castro has big guns. I saw them. Big Guns.*"

He had big guns, all right. The teachers told the second graders about a bullet powerful enough to empty New York Harbor and send a tidal wave rushing over the school. They told their pupils, during what must have been hourly air-raid drills, "There will be a bright light. It will come from the city. You will put your head to the wall . . . duck and cover . . . duck and cover. . . . When you walk home, don't look in the direction of the city. There will be a siren drill at four o'clock, after you get home — Who is laughing over there? Be quiet!" Right. We must always remember that: no laughing during a nuclear holocaust. And there, down the hall, Castro stood smiling. There, on the floor, at age eight, many children were beginning to believe that grown-ups were a little bit nuts. In a few years they would begin to say as much.

Into the confusion of 1962 was added a new voice, a voice that warned of deserted roadsides lined with dying vegetation, of streams no longer visited by anglers, for all the fish were gone. It was springtime, yet in large areas of the United States no robins sang. *In the gutters under the eaves and between the shingles of the roofs, a white granular powder still showed a few patches; some weeks before it had fallen like snow upon the roofs and the lawns, the fields and the streams.*

Was this World War III?

"No," the voice said. "No enemy action had silenced the rebirth of new life in this stricken world. The people had done it themselves. . . . As man proceeds toward his announced goal of the conquest of nature, he has written a depressing record of destruction, directed not only against the earth he inhabits, but against the life that shares it with him. . . . Although modern man seldom remembers the fact, he could not exist without the plants that harness the sun's energy and manufacture the basic foodstuffs he depends upon for life . . . defoliants . . . insecticides . . . Dioxin . . . for the first time in the history of the world, every human being is now subjected to contact with dangerous chemicals, from the moment of conception until death."*

Few people might have recognized Rachel Carson's voice, if not for the simultaneous addition of other new voices: "Zero-G. I feel fine. Capsule is turning around . . . Oh! *That view is tremendous*. Roger, turnaround has started. Capsule is turning around and I can see the booster doing turnaround just a couple of hundred yards behind me. . . ."†

At a time when mankind was first seeing the earth from afar, Rachel Carson was telling us how small and fragile our little bubble of air and water really was. And you didn't have to conceptualize the earth's smallness anymore. You could *see* it. The pictures were right there in *Life* magazine and *National Geographic*. The Disney song had been right all along: "It's a small world after all." Terrifyingly small. And so vulnerable. With the view from space came an awareness that there was something called a biosphere. And a new worry began to spread and take hold, especially in America, as both men and machines probed deeper and deeper into the vacuum and, looking back over their shoulders, beheld a diminishing blue-white disk, and, looking ahead, discovered that it was the only one displaying those colors, the only biosphere we had.

Ironically, the view from space, which gave power to pleas for cleaner air and water, and to the idea that the world should be viewed as one human family, would ultimately help to strangle the U.S. space program. "We've so much to do on Earth," went the familiar cry. "Look down here. Get your heads out of the clouds, fellas. What do you see? They're using the oceans for sewers. There's an arms race. There's famine. So much work to be done right here. We don't belong out there, in space."

---

*Rachel Carson, *Silent Spring*. Boston: Houghton Mifflin, 1962.
†John Glenn's broadcast from *Friendship* 7, February 20, 1962.

In Russia, the politics of space didn't look much better. Even as the Gemini team was ironing out details for America's first dual manned spaceflight, cosmonauts Andrian G. Nikolyev in *Vostok III* and Pavel R. Popovich in *Vostok IV* beat America again to the punch.

(we are behind)

Reporter: "What do you think American astronauts will find when they land on the moon?"

Wernher von Braun: "Russians."

(the news will be worse before it is better)

On the surface, the Vostok missions put the Russians in the lead. It seemed as if they had accomplished one of Gemini's main objectives: a rendezvous in space. But it only seemed so. If NASA planners had looked a little deeper, they could have easily noticed that *Vostok III* and *IV* approached within no more than three miles of each other, and from this they might have guessed that something had gone awry, that the Soviets could not yet control their rockets precisely enough to maneuver and rendezvous. Not knowing this, the Gemini and Apollo teams worked round the clock, steamed full ahead, hoping to catch up with the Russians.

With Nedelin dead, Sergei Korolev now came under Khrushchev's pressure. Korolev had been present at the Nedelin disaster and had emerged as one of its few survivors. As Russia's leading rocket engineer, he'd thought discretion to be the better part of valor when he saw workers prying the shells off a loaded rocket and, after whispering the Russian equivalent of "No way, Ray," ducked into the nearest blockhouse.

In a way, he wished he'd stayed outside, because now he felt like choking the Russian premier, and that could get him into *real* trouble. Khrushchev didn't like the idea that the Americans would soon be orbiting two men in one capsule. He wanted to top their act by sending three in one ship.

"But the new *Soyuz* capsule won't be ready in time to beat the Gemini flights," Korolev protested.

"Then you will use a *Vostok*," Khruschchev demanded.

This was a terrible decision, but there was no changing Khrushchev's mind. *Vostok* was designed to carry only one passenger, and to modify it for three required that all scientific equipment be stripped out. The ejection seat, space suits, and reserve parachute were also removed. Now three passengers could be crammed in sideways with enough oxygen, water, and food to sustain them for a single day. They renamed the ship *Voskhod*, and while *Voskhod* developed, the more advanced *Soyuz* project went into limbo for nearly two years.

Not until Aleksei Kosygin and Lenoid Brezhnev took over would the Soviet space effort get back onto the track of true science and true progress. By then it would be almost too late.

8. THE WORK BEGINS

"Grumman? Who the hell is Grumman?"

Mike Solan, the man whom *Sputnik* had saved from the draft, had spent nearly a year working on Martin Marietta's moon-lander proposal. Everybody in Baltimore had been quite certain that Martin would build the lander, and then word came that NASA was giving the contract to some little outfit up on Long Island.

Who are those guys?

Mike had grown up in Brooklyn, New York, and in all his life he'd never even heard of Grumman. That was fast changing. It so happened that Mike's contribution to the Martin proposal had been concerned with flight simulation, and simulation just happened to be the portion of Grumman's proposal that NASA had criticized.

"Grumman desperately tried to put together a program to move out in this area," Mike remembers. "And they essentially went out and hired quite a few people. They ran almost continual open houses and snatched up people just about as rapidly as they could. Then a friend of mine got an invitation to Long Island, and he asked me if I wanted to go along and I said, 'Fine. I can have a nice weekend up in New York, and Grumman will be footing the bill.'

"They offered me a job. They didn't offer my friend one. But the pay was entirely inadequate, and I told them so. I wanted ten percent more.

"Grumman didn't budge.

"And neither did I.

"What I didn't realize was that with the loss of the moon-lander contract, Martin Marietta was going out of business in Baltimore. And even though to some people the writing was on the wall—that Martin was going to Orlando, Florida, and Denver, Colorado—I kept insisting that we were in good health in Baltimore, and people around me were flying out the doors right and left, like rats abandoning a sinking ship. I sat there, and I finally came to understand that I'd better take the Grumman offer."

More engineers. Always more engineers. Grumman's senior vice president, George Titterton, was asked almost every morning to hire new people, and it bothered him remotely. It was beginning to look as if NASA related progress on the moon project to how many engineers you had working on it, which was a funny way of getting things done, as far as he was concerned. And finding people wasn't easy. The company was advertising coast to coast for critical skills, flying people in from as far away as Hawaii and trying to talk them into coming aboard. But the technical experts had already been scooped up by Apollo and were now working on the launch vehicles, or on North American Rockwell's Command Module and Service Module. In 1963 even a shoe salesman could become a rocket technician (and at least one did).

Grumman's program manager on the Lunar Module, Bob Mullaney, became suddenly and frightfully aware that the reasons NASA had given his company the job in the first place might never be fulfilled. "We'd been chosen, in part, for our highly skilled technicians and engineers and mechanics, and when the LM contract was actually awarded, we found ourselves in direct conflict with building the Navy's new fighter and reconnaissance aircraft. There was an in-house scramble for resources, namely our most skilled, talented people. It was up to us to man the LM program with whomever we could steal away from the Navy programs, plus our ability to hire new people. And nobody ever told NASA, in the beginning of 1963, that the average tenure of the worker in the shop was six months."

Mike Solan's first duty, when he arrived in Bethpage, was to help Bob Kress and the other project designers rewrite the mission-simulation proposal to NASA.

"When I came aboard, they had pulled together a good team of people with a good background, but their depth in the field of simulation was not very great. They had to hire some of us who had more experience, and the team grew in time as we began to understand the problems of getting to and from the moon."

Mike started by breaking the lunar mission down into pieces— rendezvous, landing, docking—and each of these pieces could be cut up into smaller pieces, which could be handed out to individual study groups. And when the study groups got a handle on two of the pieces, you could join them together, then plug in a third piece, and a fourth, and so on, until eventually you put the whole thing together. One of the key pieces involved building a Lunar Orbit Rendezvous simulator. Mike wanted to practice methods of getting the Lunar Module back to the Command Module if you lost on-board navigational computers. The crew would have to use star sighting, and to test the feasibility of stellar navigation around the moon you had to build a 360-degree planetarium with stars displayed floor to ceiling. Mike noticed a giant blue ball on top of a Grumman building called Plant 5. It was an old radar dome, being put to no better use than storage space, and the inside was a hollow sphere: perfect. They put stars on the walls and a fake moon in the center and installed two television cameras that could be maneuvered "in lunar orbit" via off-stage hand controls. The cameras represented views from the two modules, projected on screens that were supposed to be windows, through which the "pilots" could make measurements using various optical devices that would allow them to calculate how fast their positions were changing relative to the moon's horizon and certain stars. Then, with radio communication between two "pilots" sitting at two different consoles, they slowly adjusted their trajectories until both saw the same stars winking out at the same time behind the curve of the moon, at which point the two ships (or, rather, television cameras) were flying shoulder to shoulder again.

"Daddy? Now that we got the contract, when are we going to the moon?"

"It will be about five or seven years, hon."

"But that's . . . that's . . ."

Arnold Whitaker smiled. His little girl could not comprehend a ship that would require more than her lifetime to build. It must have seemed like forever to her. It was beginning to look that way to Arnold, too. The ship just wouldn't stay still. It kept mutating, pulling out here and there, growing a new leg, then dropping it. The planetary scientists up at Cornell were imagining all sorts of hostile things on the moon—traps in waiting—everything from molten lava to hidden ice, from deep dust to bug-infested craters (lunar ticks?), even antimatter. The problem was that half of these hazards would have to be taken into account in the ship's design. But which half? We can forget about antimatter, Arnold supposed. The Russians have already dropped an eight-hundred-pound ball of steel on the moon, and if the moon were made of antimatter, we'd have felt the explosion all the way down here on Earth. The dust was a legitimate worry, though, and as a result the lander's feet had spread wide and flat, become giant saucers, for fear that without them the ship might sink up to its nose or disappear altogether.

There were other rapid-fire mutations. The ship just didn't

want to be symmetrical (and aircraft were by tradition symmetrical). LM wanted to be lopsided. On one side was a tank full of low-density fuel. On the other side of a tank of high-density fuel oxidizer. To get the center of gravity in the center of the ship, through which the thrust of the rocket engine would be directed, one tank had to be balanced off to the side, giving the ship a distinctly lopsided appearance.

But in space appearances didn't matter. "We'd been designing airplanes for years in shapes that were previously dictated by aerodynamics," says preliminary designer Will Bischoff. "Aerodynamics said you had to have a certain shape. You then stuffed the engines and fuel tanks and everything else inside that shape. LM could be any shape it wanted to be. Its only dictate was its functional requirements. There was no external force acting against it, no air rushing over its surface, and the realization of this was slow to come for some of us, slow to come that it didn't have to be round-edged and smooth, that it could be square. It could have corners on it. Things could stick out at odd angles, it didn't make any difference. So we were designing a vehicle whose shape couldn't be conceived of before you started. If you wanted to design an airplane, you had a pretty good idea, before you put a pencil to paper, what it was going to look like. You might change the shape and angle of the wings, but an airplane still looks like an airplane. What does a moon lander look like? Suddenly we were in a very, very free-form world of engineering. There wasn't any precedent. And we developed a shape that at first looked ridiculous, and looked more and more ridiculous as we worked on."

A great deal of time went into the debate over what the pilots should be able to see as they went down to the moon's surface. Most designers perceived the lander as a helicopter with rockets instead of rotor blades, and had subsequently designed a vehicle with two pilots seated behind a hemispherical shell of glass. All that glass, hundreds of pounds of it, would severely tax the ship's fuel reserves and, farther down the line, enlarge the size of the boosters needed to nudge it away from Earth, which led to the

question, What is the optimal field of vision for the pilots and
how do we provide it for the lowest possible cost in weight?

"Good question," a young engineer said. "Perhaps you should
answer this one first: We're landing on a world that has only one
sixth the gravity we're feeling in this room right now. Why do we
need seats in the cockpit?"

From that moment, the astronauts were no longer helicopter
pilots. They had become trolley motormen. Designers stood the
two men up in the LM, provided straps to restrain them from
any shocks or movements, then carved deep angles into both sides
of the ship's face, which brought the front panel almost into direct
contact with the astronauts, and put the windows right under
their noses for the maximum field of view. The windows became
small and triangular, and gave LM a scowling, jack-o'-lantern
aspect.

During the first weeks of 1963, after the actual construction
began, Al Munier bowed out of the LM program. He was a
preliminary designer, and when the government finally bought
the idea—well, building the thing was somebody else's problem.
Preliminary design was the fun stuff.

Al began to look at possibilities for a roving laboratory called
MOLAB, to be landed separately near a LM, then driven perhaps
hundreds of miles from the landing site during a lunar mission
lasting up to a month. (A full-scale operational model would
eventually be built but never used.) Thinking about extended
stays on the moon led logically to permanently manned habitats,
and there went Al, walking into the next future.

He worked on proposals for a nine-man Earth-orbiting laboratory that could grow year by year through the addition of new
compartments. They called it *Skylab*. Even Al could now believe
that perhaps von Braun's optimism was not such a crazy thing
after all. There was a widespread feeling that Apollo was only a
beginning, and, caught up in this feeling, Al began drawing up
plans with TRW for a manned Mars mission, while von Braun
wrote:

Planning of future projects and advanced space transportation systems deserves a great deal of of emphasis today. The technology now available will enable us to accomplish the manned lunar landing in Project Apollo. And immediately beyond the moon, we shall be concerned with exploiting the tremendous capability in launch vehicles, spacecraft, tracking networks, control centers, and trained personnel built up in Project Apollo. For really serious manned exploration of the planets, however, nuclear or electronic propulsion will be required. And I would personally prefer a nuclear stage for the manned fly-by missions to Venus and Mars. And a manned Mars landing, which could be achieved by the mid-80's, would very definitely require nuclear propulsion. The highly successful test firing program of the Nerva I Engine* lends confidence to the belief that a nuclear rocket stage can be designed. A manned Mars landing could be achieved by a nuclear propulsion module concept. Standard nuclear stages, each powered by a single nuclear engine, could be used singly and in clusters to form a Mars-mission vehicle for launching from Earth orbit. In addition to manned planetary expeditions, nuclear rockets are potentially useful for a wide variety of advanced space missions, including post-Apollo direct flight to the Moon, extended stay-time lunar missions, lunar base logistics, and heavy unmanned solar system probes.

High hopes were at work again. A nuclear ferry vehicle was anticipated before 1980, a permanent lunar base by 1979, men would land on Mars between 1977 and 1986, and actual colonization of the red wilderness should begin as early as 1984. Robots driven by fusion-pulse engines would be capturing asteroids (for industrial use in space) around 1990, and unmanned flybys of Jupiter and the other outer planets would commence in 1987.

---

*Whereby liquid hydrogen is thrown onto a hot nuclear reactor and ejected forcefully into space through an engine nozzle.

Ahead of these dreams was the Apollo Applications Program. Al was called to Washington to talk about using a future version of LM as a taxi between space stations, or as an attack ship. Yes, the military had satellite killing on its mind. "The idea behind this vehicle was to go and inspect the enemy's satellites (or the proposed enemy, or whatever you want to call it: the unfriendly ones) and decide whether they were carrying hydrogen bombs or were just innocent spacecraft as described in the press (their press). And we did a study on converting the LM into that kind of inspection vehicle. They were talking about using rockets and lasers and things to put hostile equipment out of operation. I thought that the most effective thing, if you didn't like somebody else's satellite, was to get some black ink and spray their solar panels. They wouldn't know what happened. All of a sudden the thing would have no power. It's the best weapon: Spray it."

Few people heard so much as a whisper about LM's military potential. Peggy Hewitt, for example, who started working for Grumman at the beginning of World War II, had been building and testing aircraft electrical systems ever since: the F4F, F6F, F7F, F8F, F10F, TBF, the Mallard. And what attracted her to LM in the first place was the fact that it would do nothing more (or less) than land on the moon. "I guess my main motivation for wanting to work on the LM program was to get away from war weapons. *Really*. Even before Grumman got the contract I started maneuvering, manipulating. You can understand that feeling if you'd worked on machines of destruction for twenty years. It's about time to stop it, isn't it?"

And the work continued.

9. BEFORE HAL

Ross Fleisig, who some years earlier, in Barcelona, Spain, had been frustrated by four tight-lipped Russians, was now Grumman's project leader for space trajectory, guidance, and control-system analysis. Aside from providing him with an impressive comeback to the inevitable cocktail-party query "So, what do *you* do for a living?" the title put him in charge of more than one hundred people, all of them engineers and scientists devoted to the task of developing mathematical models from which you could come to terms with such questions as, How do you decelerate LM from lunar orbit to landing speed and then get it to come back up from the surface to rendezvous with the Command Module? Answers to such questions would enable Ross's group to calculate fuel usage and to size the propulsion systems: *that* would determine what the weight of the vehicle had to be, and what kinds of engine burns you would perform to accelerate or decelerate the ship, or to change directions.

Ross met regularly with some half-dozen Grumman people and a lot of NASA people at MIT's instrumentation labs. At one of the first lunar navigation and guidance meetings of 1963, an MIT professor walked to the blackboard and began to explain.

"Now, this is how we're gonna do it. We've worked out some techniques, and we've proved these techniques by writing computer programs and actually solving the equations for the Command Module and Lunar Module rendezvous. We can come up from the moon and dock the two vehicles strictly automatically. The astronauts won't have to play any role in the operation."

Alan Shepard was sitting next to Ross Fleisig, and Ross could see that he was getting frustrated. Someday his life would depend on that rendezvous. If it wasn't successful, that would be the end of it. And some Ph.D. in electrical engineering was standing up there telling everybody how a computer was going to perform the whole rendezvous and docking maneuver, and was supporting this claim with drawings of ellipses and fine curves and solutions to detailed nonlinear differential equations. Finally he stopped, put down his chalk, and said, "Are there any questions?"

Alan Shepard shot his hand up, and, without waiting to be called on, said, "I just have one question that's been bothering me. When you design this system for rendezvous, will there be a button that I can press to take over manually?"

"Why do you want it, fella?"

"Because I want to make sure, no matter what you say about automatic techniques, that in the final analysis I can take over the ship. Like any pilot, I don't trust computers. I want a manual-control capability, and when *I* decide, it will go into automatic."

"But you don't need manual control. The ship can do it all by itself. Believe me. The ship *will* do it."

"This will change."

Ross was amused. Grumman, being a manned-aircraft company, was sensitive to a pilot's needs. His people worked with test pilots every day, and he knew that the professor's attitude was the antithesis of Shepard's. Whether LM had the world's best automatic pilot or not, it would also have manual controls. You could bet on that.

Alan Shepard wasn't the only one who didn't trust nascent computer technology. Peggy Hewitt found herself in charge of forty engineers who would be working the checkout equipment for LM. "We were essentially ground support. This was probably the first of the fairly sophisticated electronics to be used in testing space vehicles. It had the capability of storing what your readings should be, telling you how to test it, comparing your test results to what the results *should* be, and then telling you how much you were off by. If you wanted to check fuel pressure in a tank, for example, you would send the appropriate signal through a black box and the machine would tell you that you were, say, two pounds below acceptable limits. However, people were still not completely confident in machines. They wanted to push the button and see the reaction and check the list and see for themselves what the acceptable limits were.

"It was supposed to be automatic checkout equipment, and we did use it, but it became only semiautomatic, because my people were always double-checking the machines. That's a pretty understandable unwillingness. It was, at that time, a really big step forward. People just didn't trust computers, even after all the practice sessions on dummy tanks were over and the real LM hardware started coming in—especially then. Computers were capable of all kinds of mischief, and they'd prove that, sure enough, once we began taking them out into space."

10. THE IRONWORKS

Milt Radimer started working for Grumman in 1941. His first assignment involved manufacturing parts for the Wildcat fighter planes.

Milt always liked to build things. As a child he'd watched his grandfather hammer pennies and scrap iron into sheets of metal, from which he constructed a small-scale stream-driven locomotive that still works. Milt treasures the intricately detailed machine, treasures it so dearly that he included a special place for its display in the house he and his wife, Kaye, designed and built. In 1962, this man who loved to build things was appointed assistant plant manager in charge of the LM descent stage. This was the part of the ship that would be left at the *Apollo* landing site, with its spent fuel tanks and the engine that spent them.

"We had about twenty departments in Plant 2. And then we had about five supervisors. Each supervisor had about four departments, and then each department had a foreman and an assistant foreman, and under them ran a hierachy of lead men and workers. So it all boiled down to about twenty-five hundred people in the plant, of which maybe seven hundred were working on the LM. My job was to oversee the descent stage's day-to-day construction.

"We started actually building the pieces and putting things together in 1963. You know, the stuff was so light! There was nothing to it. You picked it up and it was like a piece of paper. 'It's not gonna work!' the others were saying, 'That's gonna break!' 'It's not gonna break,' I said. 'There's no atmosphere up there! This won't be opened up until it's in space, until it's in vacuum. It doesn't need any weight or streamlining.' One guy said, 'Look at these drawings. Look at the shape of this silly thing! Everything sticks out here and there.' But as we started building, the more we got into it and the more things we learned, the more we became sure that it would work. You know, there were no spacecraft engineers. We were all airplane engineers, all of us who built the LM the first time around. We became spacecraft engineers in our act of building. In 1963, anyone who worked just a few months in the space program was considered an expert. Many of us went back to school to catch up on the latest space technology. Everybody shared what knowledge he had. Aerospace has been called the leading edge of technology. During those LM days, you knew you were on the front lines."

Milt's descent-stage supervisor, Bob Ekenstierna, was a sheet-metal worker who collected and repaired ancient metal armor. LM had to be assembled with almost eighteenth-century technology. Every part was made almost entirely by hand. You couldn't just stamp out a fitting from aluminum or titanium without creating stress lines within, so, to make a certain fitting, a worker would often start with a block of metal and mill it out by hand, just grind away until he got the desired shape. This by itself was an historical anomaly—they simply don't build machines that way—and it was no mere accident of history that an ancient armorer wound up in charge of such an operation.

For decades, now, physicists and musicians have been trying to understand just what it was that made the great Italian violins so great. To hear a Stradivarius or a Guarnerius is to put all of today's violins forever in the shade. We can apply all the modern technology available to us, yet we will never approach their sound. It has in fact been said that the quality of modern violins decreases proportionally with the amount of technology applied to their construction. How does one make a Stradivarius? One doesn't. Not today, at least, because it's a lost art: the offspring of a rare and beautiful marriage between state-of-the-art technology (for a given point in history) and a mystical element of human craft. The machine that Milt Radimer came to know so affectionately as that "Dumb Thing" was the product of such a marriage (the same can be said of very early airplanes, the first electron microscopes, and some classic automobiles). And because it was in its day the ultimate in human technology, LM could not be mass produced. How does one go about building the ultimate in human technology? *By hand*, that's how.

Bob Ekenstierna brought the skills and patience of a knight's armorer to the LM descent stage. Curiously, he gave only fleeting notice to the historic significance of what he was building. "Every airplane we built had never been built before. So, when LM came along—hey, it was quite a feat to do, to be able to go to the moon. There's no question about it. But it was no greater than building each airplane. Each airplane never flew before. As far as I'm concerned, I could be building anything, even a cigar box. You give it your best. LM was just another job, I thought. I was happy to think they thought I was good enough to build it, to take care of that section.

". . . You give it your best."

"—give it your best." That's what made "Eky" 's job so important. He gave his section of the ship the same care, the same attention, and the same mystical element of human craft—"something extra"—that his predecessors must have given to each link in a knight's chain mail. This analogy did not escape Grumman executives. They borrowed suits of armor from him and displayed them in corporate offices and in every large building. A promotional booklet equated knight's armor with modern technology: "Chain mail became obsolete in the 15th century, when arrows launched from crossbows began to penetrate the links. Our craftsmen understand the need for up-dating ideas; and meet the challenge such changes present . . ."

"There were designers," Eky says. "We got the blueprints and we built what they told us to build. There were many things that they wanted us to do, and it really wasn't possible to do it the first try. And Engineering came down and we talked over what we could do and so forth, and drawings were changed, and everybody worked together. It wasn't one person's thought, you know. All you had to do was reach for the phone and you had an engineer down on the floor before you put the phone down. That ship had to get out. We had to build it and we had to build it in a certain time, before the Russians built one. And there were lots of opinions on how each part should be made. People thought this or that should be done a little bit different or a little bit better, but that was all thrashed out. You were looking for the best opinion regardless of whether it came from a riveter or an engineer. It wasn't a production run. They just wanted the best. It had to be.

"It had to—

"I'll tell you, a lot of those men—most of them—drilled holes by hand that you couldn't do better by machine. They made a set of corner posts in Plant 5, and then a subcontractor was going to make them out west. As the story goes, they had a little problem reading the drawings, and we sent men out to California to show them how to read the drawings. That's how complicated some of the parts were. These men were all darned good mechanics and were strong, conscientious people. You want a fellow who's going to go out there and if you want a hole of a certain size drilled in a certain place, he's gonna drill that hole for you. If he's gonna go out there and be nervous about doing it wrong, and if he's gonna get all taken up by the fact that it's a moon ship, you don't want that man. 'Cause that's when things get messed up. There were people who came around and would have liked to work on the LM, but I told them that it wasn't possible at the time. The truth was that I couldn't use them. You know, that's what I mean. You had to be strong in mind to work on the job. It's funny, you had to be good and you had to know you were good. That's about the size of it."

11. WHITE SANDS

"**B**oy, I could tell you stories about the LM propellants," Eky says. "I'm sure glad *I* never had to handle them. Nasty stuff! You could dip a stick into the oxidizer and snap it on the ground into the snow and the snow would catch fire. They were only allowed to have a very small amount of the propellant on Long Island because the moisture in the air could set it ablaze."

"I don't know why the propellant was as toxic as it was," recalls Lynn Radcliffe, "but one thing was certain: Keeping it anywhere near Bethpage or Calverton was out of the question—too close to civilization.

"Now, there was a Senator Clinton P. Anderson from New Mexico who headed the Senate Sub-Committee on Space. He knew we were going to have to test the LM engines, once they were built, and this meant that several tons of propellants had to be stored somewhere. Well, Anderson was the big gun who really pushed hard from Washington to get the necessary funds, and to get this thing organized. Now, if a project calls for wide-open spaces and you want to make the desert green, as all New Mexico senators do—green with money, that is—you put a program down there.

"They put me down there, too, perhaps because I'd been in the flight-test department right from the start of my tenure at Grumman, which was June 9, 1942. My job during World War II had been to conduct in-flight tests on torpedo bombers, and I stayed in the flight-test business right through the development of the jet age. Finally, I moved out of the test business and into the people business, into the administration end of things, the people problems and so on. My background as a tester who was also experienced in working with people probably set the stage for my adventures in New Mexico, where I was sent to organize the first of Grumman's three major bases away from Long Island. The other two, of course, were in Houston and Florida."

Dead as an old bone.

Boulders strewn clear to the horizon.

Sheets of shifting sand.

Lynn Radcliffe guessed that the moon or Mars would look something like this, except for the bright-blue sky, and rattle-snakes. How in God's name was he ever going to coax Long Islanders away from their beaches and woodlands and all the conveniences of nearby Manhattan here to the foothills of New Mexico's San Andres Mountains? And if he *could* get them to volunteer, where would he house them? North American Rockwell had already built their test site for the Service Module rocket engine. It stood less than a mile from the proposed Grumman test facility. Unfortunately, Rockwell had come to the desert more than a year ahead of Grumman, and the nearest town was a little place called Las Cruces, which was eighteen miles away in the Rio Grande Valley, and Rockwell had snatched up all the housing. Lynn had also been beaten by the NASA crowd and by people from the missile range on the other side of the San Andres. Rockets, it seemed, were a growth industry in New Mexico.

It had been that way for a long time.

Lynn had heard stories about White Sand's early, chaotic development, during which many of the standing rules of rocketry had been laid down. There was the time ground control lost power seconds after a lift-off—a lost missile, looking for home, *anywhere in New Mexico or its neighboring states*—all because someone wanted to fix a broken Coca-Cola machine and had pulled the circuit breaker at the worst possible moment.

Rule: *Ground control must operate on its own, self-contained circuitry.*

A rocket was being prepared to carry scientific equipment into the ionosphere when a Jeep pulled up in front of the ground-control blockhouse and soldiers began hammering a long stake into the ground.

"What are you doing?" asked one of the scientists.

"Oh, that. That's the aiming point for some tests with the Honest John rocket."

"Aiming point? What do you mean, *aiming point?* This is our established station, assigned by range."

"Don't worry. We never hit the aiming point anyway."

Rule: *Procedures for assigning targets should be tightened up a little.*

Rockwell and NASA and just about everybody else had bought up all the housing in Las Cruces, and now there was no place to put the Long Islanders.

Rules: *There weren't any.*

Right. Okay. So who is running this town? Lynn wondered.

The mayor was a "dirt farmer" who did his mayoring on afternoons, and although Lynn found the Chamber of Commerce eager to help, nobody had any clout. He met with two bank presidents, and they would have liked to help, but . . . but . . .

"I understand," Lynn said. "Now, who do I see to make something happen around here?"

"I'll tell you who runs the town," one of the bank presidents said. "You've got to see Orville Priestly."

Orville Priestly was the owner, publisher, and editor of the Las Cruces *Sun News*, and that's where the power was. He was a bear and everybody was afraid of him. "I made my little pitch," Lynn remembers. "I simply said, 'We want to live in your town and become part of it, but we need your help to get housing rentals.' Priestly listened, and he said at last, 'Well, bless your heart.' And I was in. He wrote fiery articles; he made phone calls; he summoned the president of the Builders' Association and gave him orders just like he owned the construction business. Five different builders came with me to Bethpage, showing our workers what kinds of homes they could build for them and at what prices, and no money changed hands. It was all done on a handshake and in the Southwest a handshake is better than a signed contract.

"It was a strange place, White Sands. At first we couldn't get people to move from green and steamy Long Island into the desert, and when we finally convinced them, they wouldn't come back. The desert was so alien. And the sunrises! I started to love it, even though I'm a boating type, and in New Mexico the tide was always too far out. And Las Cruces was a bunch of nice people, genuinely friendly and down to earth. The only time they'd turn surly was if you didn't treat them fairly. Then I suppose they would go to the other extreme and—boy, you're out. But the townfolk were just marvelous to us. And finally we were the townfolk. I even ended up sitting on some board of directors, discussing how we were going to bring new business into the place."

By late 1963, the configuration of Gumman's rocket site was finalized, and NASA put the Army Corp of Engineers under contract to build it. The Army hired contractors from Las Cruces to put up the main assembly building and block houses. They ran tunnels out to an engine-firing stand, then laid in the electricity and plumbing.

Ascent- and descent-stage engines and a system of smaller, attitude-control rockets would have to be tested under a simulated space environment. This meant altitude chambers had to be built—giant vacuums powered by superheated steam and requiring enough electricity to keep a city the size of Cleveland alight for two days. Lynn was thankful to God that development of the steam system was NASA's job. The vacuum chambers would certainly be as difficult to build as the engines they were designed to test. The system seemed to delight in blowing itself up, or imploding, or both.

As base manager of the White Sands facility, Lynn would direct the men who tested the rocket engines while rarely touching the machines himself. His main purpose was to deal with people, especially that peculiar NASA species: "Before NASA came around, Grumman was kind of an annex to the Navy. We had all grown up together. Then, all of a sudden, here we were with a relatively new operation. I got scared when I learned that NASA people were just as insecure about space as we were. They were ninety-day wonders, and we weren't even that. But one thing they knew: They were going to organize it and they were going to do it by discipline. I began training my 'Grummies' in discipline—oh, it was like kicking a dead horse sometimes (no get up and go), trying to get men to accept NASA's new rules. My biggest problems were the old-timers at Grumman—and I was one of them. I think the only smart thing I did was to understand early on that we were the contractor, NASA was the customer, and we were going to have to play by NASA's book."

But the old-timers—

No snotnose kid from Florida is gonna tell me how to make a spacecraft. I've been making airplanes all my life and what's the difference, you know?

"They would go off on their own track. They wouldn't go very far, though, before a NASA quality-control man nailed them. I'd get notified that one of my people wasn't going by the book, and I'd have to lecture him on discipline and put something out in writing. But little by little everybody got shaped up, and I got fewer and fewer complaints as 1964 drew near."

Rocket engineer John Dickenson went to White Sands in the autumn of 1963, bringing with him a crew of newly hired engineers from the Atlas missile program who knew how to handle live propellants. They were definitely needed. There were tanks with internal pressures close to six thousand pounds per square inch. If a pinhole developed in a tank's skin and you were foolish enough to wave your hand in front of it, the stream of high-pressure gas would slice off your fingers. If you stood in front of it, it would puncture your thorax and blow you up like a balloon. Already there had been one very poor advertisement for working on the space program. A technician was filling out a report, and he apparently clicked his pen on a fuel tank, finding a weak point in the metal. Searchers eventually located his pen, and a nub of bone embedded in a fence post.

Almost as soon as John arrived in New Mexico, a chemist in charge of handling rocket fuels gave him a demonstration. He set a one-quart mason jar on a plate of inch-thick tank armor, poured in a half quart of "safety solvent," put a hose leading to a supply of fuel oxidizer in place, added a blasting cap, and then retreated to a safe distance of about two hundred yards. John got to keep the armor plate as a reminder. In its center, a hole matching exactly the dimensions of the mason jar's bottom had been punched out. He began to wonder what kind of man would be willing to fly in a machine filled with that stuff. Astronaut Wally Schirra summed it up with a nervous jest: "It's going to be like sitting on top of fifty million parts, each of which was built by the lowest bidder. You wonder what in the hell you are doing there!"

Message: In this program, you are responsible for the lives of America's greatest heroes, and for the history of the world, and, perhaps more important (at least on a personal basis), for your own life. One little slip-up and you could be dead not only before you knew what hit you but indeed before you knew that you'd been hit by anything.

Rule: *Discipline, my boy. Discipline.*

There was plenty of that in NASA. Perhaps too much. You couldn't move a box off a truck without having to call out a seemingly endless series of steps that had to be signed off by the mechanic who did the work, then verified by an inspector:

Bring hook over to box. (check) (check)

Attach hook to top of box. (check) (check)
Lift box six inches. (check) (check)
Move box to point B. (check) (check)
Lower box six inches. (check) (check)
Demate hook from box. (check) (check)
Return hook to point A. (check) (check)

Extreme paper-consciousness, they called it. An engineer had
to write up a sheet describing step by step what he wanted to
have done for every operation, "down to the most minor detail,"
John recalls. "It took quite a while to get everybody indoctrinated
to follow these directions precisely. The reason for all this detail
was, if you had an accident, you could go back and verify what
conditions had been just prior to the accident. You knew what
positions valves and hooks and levers had been in, who had done
what, and who had signed off on it. That became the basis of
the whole LM program."

"Paper everywhere," says quality-control inspector Harry Walther. "Stacks and stacks of books. We began to say, 'When the
paperwork equals the weight of the vehicle, we'll know it's finished.'" This was meant to be a joke, but several years hence,
when the first LM was ready for shipping to Florida's Kennedy
Space Center, a freight car full of paper would have to be sent
ahead of it.

"We *needed* all that paper," explains Grumman's quality-
control program manager, Joe Kingfield. "NASA did get a little
carried away, though. Slight overkill. Sometimes you wondered
if they wanted to know the name of the guy who dug the ore out
of the hill before they melted it down into aluminum. That's how
far back the traceability seemed to go."

Hypergolics.
That's a polite way of describing two substances that hate the
looks of each other. Rocket fuel (stored in one set of LM tanks)
and rocket-fuel oxidizer (stored in another set of LM tanks) could
be brought together even in the vacuum of space to produce
powerful explosions. Looking ahead, the major difficulty was

going to be getting the two substances out of the appropriate tanks and into the rocket-thrust chamber while you were floating around at zero-gravity or flying upside down or sideways over the moon. This problem was similar to the one Wernher von Barun had solved for igniting a booster rocket after it had spent a number of hours in space with weightless fuel sloshing around in its tanks, except that in LM, the situation was complicated by the fact that you wanted to be able to throttle your descent-stage engine up and down very precisely.

The solution came easily enough, through analogy, when, at one of Grumman's famous Friday-night get-togethers at a bar called the Astro, on Long Island, some forgotten genius pressed his thumb over the lip of a beer bottle, shook vigorously for about three seconds, and then sprayed the bottle's contents into some-one else's face. The prank was intended to impress a secretary, but its true impact was on the rocket experts from New Mexico.

Aha!

Why not do the same thing with LM? Shoot the fuel and oxidizer tanks up with carbon dioxide or some other gas, build up pressure inside, and force the liquids out into the explosion chamber.

That's essentially how it was done, except that the gas they used—shot in from a separate tank—was supercooled liquid helium, not carbon dioxide. Helium was preferred because it was a chemically inert (noble) gas. It did not combine with other elements to form compounds, as did carbon and oxygen.

"It was something that had never been done before," recalls rocket expert Manning Dandrige. "The idea was resisted by Max Faget, a leading spacecraft designer at the Space Task Group who hated the smell of anything having to do with cryogenics. We had a good deal of difficulty getting the helium-pressure system in, but it was bound to save us eight or nine hundred pounds in pistons and pumps at the top of the rocket stack, which is where weight really counted, because it was going to cost something like twenty thousand dollars to lift each pound from the top of that stack to the moon.

"Von Braun was very interested in our helium system. He was interested in anything that could save weight, and he asked, 'Gee, can I use this on any of the other stages?' And we spent a lot of time on that question. Von Braun . . . there was something funny about him. You know, he always traveled with his assistants. Two of them were Ernst Stühlinger and Eberhard Rees, and history seems to have neglected these men, who in many ways were the real brains of the outfit. But when you were in a room with von Braun and Stühlinger and Rees, the only person you saw was von Braun, and the only thing you'd remember was what von Braun said. I had a number of meetings with all of them. I know I spoke with them, but I've never been able to point to a piece of the rocket and say, 'Gee, that was Ernst's doing.' "

While Manning Dandridge and his associates tried to convince Max Faget that helium was the way to go, Tom Kelly studied the moon from Bethpage. He knew everything that could be known about the lunar environment—which was next to nothing. What little he did know was, from time to time, disquieting. He knew, just for a start, that the temperature was −240°F in the shade and +240°F in the sun. LM's fuel and oxidizer would freeze near 30°F and boil near 100°F.

Rule: *From the moment you load the propellants onto the ship at the launchpad until you fly up from the moon to rendezvous with the Command Module, you must maintain temperatures between the freezing and boiling points of the propellants.*

Tom Kelly: "I guess we weren't more than a few months into the program when we realized that what we wanted to do thermally with the LM was to just isolate it from its surroundings. We wanted to make it like a big Thermos bottle. It tended to lose heat if you didn't have it well insulated, causing the propellants to freeze."

The outside of LM became a patchwork of alternating bright, reflective surfaces and dark, heat-absorbing areas. Du Pont invented a thin plastic film called "mylar." Coated with aluminum, the tan-colored film turned gold. The layer of aluminum was so thin that you could put it up to a light and see right through it, but its reflective, metallic surface provided protection against the sun's rays without the weight of metal. The way to make this insulation most effective was to build it up in successive layers and then make sure that the layers didn't touch each other, because to touch was to produce a path of conduction, through which heat would be lost. Where mylar was used—all around the descent stage—it was crinkled up, then flattened out. The wrinkles themselves prevented the pieces from sticking together. This would eventually become one of LM's most prominent features: its covering of gold foil, looking as if it had been wrapped hastily around the ship, perhaps as an afterthought.

There was nothing hasty or sloppy about it. When the actual construction began Grumman would organize a separate factory where blankets of insulating material could be taped together on a full-scale LM mannequin. The insulation would then be delivered to the final assembly area on the mannequin, just like a new suit of clothes.

Assuming that the insulating jacket did its job and got you down to the moon's surface with still-liquid, still usable propellants, there remained other fuel worries. The ascent engine, after tearing itself loose from the spent descent stage, was either on or off. There was no throttle. "You could turn it on or off any number of times," says John Dickenson. "And of course there was no ignition problem. All you had to do was mix the hypergolics and they lit, but one of the things we had to learn was how long the engine would burn with the amount of propellant you had on board. You knew very precisely how much fuel and oxidizer you put in, yet there were several things that could vary. For example, what if one tank got hot and the other got cold? The densities of fuel and oxidizer could change relative to each other. What effect would that have? So what we did was to run a whole series of tests. We took one tank and ran the propellant through pipes in a box that had cakes of ice floating in it, and we ran propellant in the other tank, through water that was heated up nearly to boiling. This told us what would happen if when you landed on the moon one tank ended up on the sun side of the ship and the other ended up in the shade and the insulation wasn't quite right and your propellants ended up right on the hairy edge of boiling and freezing. It turned out not to be as great a problem as we had originally feared. But there were other possibilities. Plenty of others. You're pumping helium gas into the tanks. Are you in fact making ginger ale out of the propellants? Are you dissolving helium in them so that when you burn them they'll be contaminated with little bubbles of inert gas that are going to cut down on thrust? So we put propellants in tanks and pressurized them with helium for about a week to see what effect it would have on the thrust, and it turned out to have none at all.

"You know, the testing could have gone on forever. There were so many parameters that could vary. But what had to be decided was, What are the most important ones? What will have the most effect?"

Yes, and how do you predict which ones will get you in the end? You don't, because you can't see them. They're hiding down there, in the circuitry, in oxygen tanks, in an overlooked comma that should have gone into the Bit Error Comparator, in innumerable flaws of design and logic that would squeak through to the moon undetected. The LM builders were exploring so many new problems that unpleasant surprises had become a statistical certainty.

They could draw some comfort from the "fact" that they'd dredged up every possibility and subjected it to their engineer's intuition, to the scrutiny of computer simulation, even to physical tests.

But none of these tools could provide a guarantee against questions unasked—and the nightmares that lurked beneath them, waiting to hatch out.

12. JUDGMENT

Because astronauts were trained engineers and test pilots, they became an important "subsystem" on the Lunar Module. In this capacity, they were very much in evidence at Grumman headquarters in Bethpage. LM project officer William F. Rector advised astronauts to participate in mockup reviews and design decisions. "You'd better be part of it," he urged, "because you're going to fly it."

One time, all hell broke loose over an "eight ball"—an artificial-horizon instrument used for altitude reference.

And Boy! How hell broke loose.

Arnold Whitaker remembers: "Grumman had proposed putting an eight ball in the LM, assuming that the astronauts would want it. The first thing NASA did was to say there's no operational requirement for it and to take it out. Then the astronauts came along and said, 'That's ridiculous. We must have it.' So we put it back in. By this time, we're late. Dr. Shea had a program review and said, 'What's holding you up?' and we said, 'This is one of the things . . .' and he said, 'Take it out. I'll accept the responsibility for it.' The astronauts found out and said, 'We won't fly the vehicle until you put it in,' and NASA put it in, this time with a kit (for easy removal later)."

By mid-November 1963, the second full-size wooden LM mock-up (with *two* eight balls, one for each pilot) was nearing completion. Even so, it was plagued by incessant mutations.

Even allometric growth.

"Did you know," said Cornell geologist Thomas Gold, "that

static electricity might bring moon dust swarming right up the sides of the ship?"

"Nothing you say will surprise me anymore," Tom Kelly answered, as he toyed with a desk model of the still-evolving LM. "You must have fascinating nightmares."

"Two or three at the moment. Look, Tom, I'm afraid you're going to have to spread the ship's legs farther apart and enlarge the foot pads even more—out to at least a full yard."

"Whatever for?"

"I think many of my colleagues have overestimated the load-bearing strength of the lunar surface. That dust can run pretty deep, believe me. And dust is a terribly good insulator against the sun's rays. What if there's sheets of billion-year-old ice here and there, just below the surface? And what if you came down on it?"

Tom knew better than to dismiss Dr. Gold's ice hypothesis outright. The old man had been right about too many other spooky things. For all we did know about the moon, thought Tom, there could be elephants up there, so why not ice?

"I thought we'd gotten rid of the ice worry, Doc."

"Oh, in theory maybe."

"And in practice?"

"Not really. I've heard of stony meteorites that had water in them—carbonaceous chondrites, they're called. Some people think they're moon rocks, possibly blown free by lunar volcanoes. There's one that fell in France near the turn of the century . . . one in Kentucky . . . another in New Zealand. I mean, there's ice all over the place. About fifty years ago something made sonic booms over England or Scotland or someplace like that, and the next morning there were blocks of ice as big as sheep in some farmer's pasture."

Tom Kelly wasn't listening. He was thinking about hills on the moon. Nobody knew how steep they would be. He could see the ship coming down on the side of a hill that was a giant dome of hidden ice, a frictionless surface, down which the ship slid, gaining deadly momentum, then reaching a solid curb . . .

Mutation . . .

The legs jutted out wide, too wide now to be accommodated within the confines of a *Saturn* rocket. Retractable legs therefore had to replace the simpler, lighter, fixed-leg gear. To find the most suitable folding linkages, designers put the legs through a series of geometric changes. Their complexity multiplied, and the ship's weight went up with their multiplication.

"We let our imagination run away from us," Tom Kelly would one day say with a groan. "We had conflicting advice from the lunar scientists. They were telling us all kinds of strange things. If only we were allowed some knowledge of the moon's surface. The landing gear in particular would have been smaller and simpler. We really didn't need anything much more elaborate than helicopter skids."

But nobody knew. Truly nobody. And large legs, wired up with sensors and microcircuits, became an automatic consequence of human minds forced to adapt (or preadapt) LM quickly to changing views of an unknown environment. LM's legs more than compensated for conditions on the moon's surface—no ice, no deep dust, no frictionless slopes. That these things did not and could not have existed seems obvious today, as do most "facts" when viewed with twenty-twenty hindsight.

"Fact," Tom Kelly announced to the RCA representatives. "We can't have the astronauts wasting precious time replacing burned-out fuses and equipment. I'm telling you, in-flight maintenance will degrade reliability instead of improving it, especially if you intend to store your spares in the cabin and expose them to all that humidity and the possibility of being sat on."

"You are probably right. And we have accepted the fact. But does Grumman have a better idea?"

Tom looked the electronics expert straight in the eye. "We do," he said. "It's called redundancy."

"What are you suggesting? Spare parts? It sounds the same to me."

"It is. But instead of having the astronauts fumbling around looking for spare parts, and then physically screwing them in and out, we *could* wire the spares right into the ship. Let the astronauts rely on warning systems to detect burnouts. Then all they have to do is flip a switch and activate the backup, or the backup to the backup, and all the electronics in the cabin could be hermetically sealed to protect against moisture and contaminants."

The idea was brilliant, and so simple. But, as Joe Gavin, the slender Bostonian who managed Grumman's LM program, would later admit, "It was the simple things, the things we took for granted, that produced the most problems."

Tom Kelly: "We had a number of hermetically sealed relays and switches and cockpit instruments. It turned out that we had more troubles with the hermetics, probably, than if we'd left the components alone. When our workers pulled the air out of the hermetic casing and sealed it off, they were sealing it off with solder, and the vacuum very often sucked little scraps of solder directly into the system. We'd been putting vacuum-sealed cases in airplanes for years, and they worked fine in airplanes, perhaps because gravity and g-forces tended to keep the solder balls out of trouble. But in a spacecraft in zero-gravity, the balls can migrate anyplace and jam switches or cause a false activation. So we had to invent a test that would vibrate the sealed electronics—a crude way of simulating zero-gravity—and we monitored the electrical contacts to see if vagrant bits of solder were causing trouble.

"Fine. The equipment checked out, and we stamped it off as being free of contaminants and approved it for use. And then one day some old Grummie started pulling stamped and sealed components off the shelves and putting them to his ear and shaking them and—*golly*, guess what? After we'd developed all that expensive vibration equipment . . . well, some hermetically sealed instrument panels had glass faces, and an inspector did something that nobody had thought of. He took a unit out of the stockpile and held it so that the glass was facing down, and then he shook it. Dust and dirt and solder balls fell down over the glass plate. We had a heck of a time getting our instruments to pass *that* kind of test."

✱   ✱   ✱

"Leaks! We couldn't pass a simple *leak test*," recalls Joe Gavin. "As soon as they began assembling tanks and tank plumbing at White Sands, we learned that they were detecting leaks in the propulsion system. But they were such *small* leaks. They were using spectrometers to detect little molecules of escaping gas, so what was the big deal?

"You know, we'd dealt with aircraft fuel systems for decades, and we thought we understood the problems of leaks, but a leaky joint in a LM is different from one in a jet. Seals made out of gold or some other noncorrosive metal were going to have to be developed before we could build the ship."

Nitrogen tetroxide was a very good propellant, but it had one very bad quality: It "knew" how to find a leak—even an exceptionally small one—and once it found one, it would squeeze through, enlarging the hole as it did so, and allowing more and more corrosive liquid to seep out behind it.

The ship could actually eat itself in space.

Howard Sherman, a preliminary-design engineer in charge of crew systems, remembers other worries.

"We called it 'edible structure'—boards made out of organic deposits. If the astronauts ever got stranded and had to stay alive, they could eat part of the vehicle. So we made this mash that looked like dog food, and you could mold it into boards. But to make it structurally sound, we had to really compress it, and it became too heavy, and we figured they'd probably run out of oxygen and suffocate before they ever had to eat the stuff anyway, so we finally said no to the idea. Then we started hearing from people around the country who were interested. Especially the military."

"But it tasted awful," says Mike Solan. "We couldn't even sell it to the Marines. We did have a few secretaries, though, from time to time, who were named Miss Edible Structure."

"There was concern about micrometeoroids," Howard Sherman says. "There was talk about patches that you could slap onto a meteoroid hole. They were about the size of half dollar. We figured, if the hole wasn't small enough to be covered up with a half-dollar-size patch, you'd be dead before you could reach for the patches. In the end, I don't think the astronauts carried patches up with them. There were a lot of design considerations like that. Things that never actually went into the ship. For example, the lift-off engine—the lunar-ascent engine—though we were going to put some back-up systems in it, it itself had no back-up. Now, what happens if the electrical circuitry fails in spite of all the back-ups and you can't get off the moon? We talked about putting a manual valve on the ascent engine so you could go back there and pull it just like a motorboat engine. Remember, the way we ignite that thing is by hypergolic fluids' coming together. So if we pull the valve, the fluids could flow. But that idea was thrown out because the name of the game was, If we're gonna do this thing, let's make it reliable enough that *it's gonna work.*

"All right. It's reliable. But what if the ladder got smacked off, or the front hatch got bent a little bit out of frame during landing and you couldn't get the door open? So we put guide rails out the top of the ship and down the side in case you had to climb out the docking hatch to get down to the ground. It's not the most convenient thing in the world, but you traveled a long way to get there, and it would be a sad day if you couldn't get out and have a look around."

"Look here. Look here," NASA said. "You've got to stop this. Stop making all these changes and get on with it."

Arnold Whitaker: "We had a problem. People kept coming up with new what-ifs, and from these would come design changes, delaying our attempts to get on with the manufacturing process. NASA came to Bethpage one day and said, 'You've got to freeze this design. You've got to stop the changes.' And I got the job of finding out why everything was changing, and I did a study of the previous six months of LM evolution and tabulated the changes, indexed them, and traced each one back to its source."

It turned out that eighty percent of the changes had been

dictated by NASA, not Grumman. And the details! NASA had one of Arnold's assistants running an in-depth study, which required the assistant to fly back and forth between Bethpage and Houston, to help them decide whether a four-inch cover plate should have three screws or four screws. They were engineering the ship down to minutiae, which was at best a questionable tactic, especially since no rigid specifications for the *Saturn* launch vehicle existed as yet.

"All set to go, Arnold?" asked Dr. Shea.

"You've got to be kidding."

"Okay, let's hear the worst."

Arnold began leafing through volumes of tables and drawings. "Look at this. All the vehicles are interacting with each other. You change something here, and it triggers a ripple effect that resounds through the entire system—a downstream perturbation of changes. Things keep mutating, and it's well beyond our ability to control. We're just building a small portion of this thing, the landing vehicle."

"What's your suggestion?" asked Shea, as his eyes followed the changes from one series of drawings to the next.

"I think you really need to do one final detailed systems study and freeze the whole vehicle configuration."

"Very well, then, we'll do that."

"Huh? Just like that?"

"Just like that. I guess we'll be back to you in about six weeks."

"That simple?"

"Definitely not. I'd appreciate it if, in the meantime, you told your people that I want *no more mutations*."

Dr. Shea might just as well have been protesting the tides. LM was evolving rapidly into the most elaborate assemblage of tanks and pipes and computers that ever belonged to mankind. What the descent stage alone would contain, when they abandoned it on the moon, might well qualify as anthology of our civilization. Taken together, either by a future human species that would go to the stars or by an alien species that would come from the other direction, they would tell much about man's daring and genius, and even his fallibility. In a far more benign environment than the Earth, they would last almost forever. They would still be there, telling their story, long after the pyramids had turned to lime.

13. HOUSTON

Engineer John Coursen had just been accepted aboard the LM program. It made him prouder than he'd ever been in his life, and, as if to add spice to John's dreams, the man who now focused American eyes on the moon arrived at Houston Airport while he sat on a bench waiting for his flight to Bethpage.

The reception line is formed—and there is Mrs. Kennedy, the First Lady, stepping from the plane.

Two years ago I said that—er—I introduced myself in Paris by saying that I was the man who had accompanied Mrs. Kennedy to Paris. I'm getting that—somewhat that same sensation as I travel around Texas. Nobody wonders what Lyndon and I wear. . . .

People broke and ran out to the president's plane. John Coursen joined them. Mrs. Kennedy came down the steps and they gave her roses. The president reached over wooden barriers and began shaking hands. John was impressed, though he didn't think of himself as being a very impressionable man. One can only wonder what his impression would have been if he'd known how strange (even downright creepy) the president's behavior was becoming.

Weeks earlier, Kennedy had asked the White House photographer, Robert Knudsen, to film a script he'd written: The president's chest opened up in a slow motion spray of blood and bone. He went down, groping for the bullet hole, grimacing as Jackie stepped daintily over his dying body. A red tide surged from his mouth, and he choked. And choked. And choked.

On the afternoon John Coursen saw him, the president confided to friends, as he traveled through Texas, "Thank God I wasn't killed today."

But tomorrow was November 22, 1963.

Tomorrow was another day.

14. SIZING IT UP

Dear Arnold Whitaker,
Following our meeting of two months ago, we have attempted here in Houston to finalize a specification for vehicle configuration, but remain unable to arrive at an agreement. If I may be frank: you people at Grumman identified the problem. We're going to contract you to do the study.

Yours faithfully,
Joseph Shea

Dear Mr. Shea,
Many thanks for your letter of January 20. My LM Program Manager, Joseph Gavin, has advised me that I am to freeze the configuration of the Apollo vehicles. I must point out that Grumman may not be capable of conducting this study,

which I am now responsible for coordinating. As you proba-
bly know, all of our staff will be working round the clock
merely to complete the job we already have, that is, building
LM. Nor do we have NASA's experience and visibility over
the whole launch vehicle. I respectfully request that you
reconsider.

Sincerely,
Arnold Whitaker

Dear Arnold Whitaker,
Do it.

Yours faithfully,
Joseph Shea

Dear Mr. Shea,
Thank you very much for your letter of the fifth. I have laid
out the following plan to carry out the study, taking into
account the kind of experience that will be needed to carry
out a systems analysis of the entire vehicle from launch to
splash down. We need experts on first and second stage
boosters . . . on the Command and Service Modules . . . on
parachute systems . . . we clearly do not have all these
talents within the Grumman organization. If we are to han-
dle this study, NASA will have to supply these talents, be-
cause it is NASA that has the booster rocket experts, and
people in the various organizations with experience in many
facets of Apollo that we do not have here in the LM portion
of the project.

Sincerely,
Arnold Whitaker

There, that ought to hold him, thought Arnold. Once NASA
understands that we don't have the right people, they won't make
us do the study.

But they did.

NASA wrote the configuration-freeze study into Grumman's

contract, and Arnold spent the better part of 1964 touring America, talking to engineers about each element of *Apollo*, and frequently sending them to Bethpage for further interviews. In the process, he triggered at least one major mutation. The weight of the vehicles had to be redistributed. Fuel would be taken out of the Service Module and added to the Lunar Module.

Arnold could not know at the time that this mutation would one day be exapted to save the lives of *Apollo 13* astronauts Fred Haise, Jack Swigert, and James Lovell.

15. MOCK-UPS AND MOCK-OUTS

The first aluminum LM mock-up was ready in October 1964. Top NASA personnel, rocket experts from around the country, and astronauts were invited to climb on, in, out, and around it. Attention focused on equipment layout in the cockpit, lighting provisions, location of displays and controls, general mobility within the cabin, and (of course!) more mutations. When astronaut Roger Chaffee complained that squeezing through a round hatch with a square backpack was "simply not on," the forward hatch was squared off.

Wernher von Braun came down the ladder, smiling and laughing and hooting. "You've got to go up there," he told Jesco von Puttkamer. "Go in there. It's great!"

Even greater was the "zero-g LM." They built its cockpit right into the belly of a jet that could simulate weightlessness by flying parabolas. At the top of a parabola, the plane and its occupants would experience several moments of zero-gravity, much like a stone thrown into the air, which, at the end of its climb, would hang motionless and weightless before it started to fall. During those moments of zero-gravity, astronauts could test the restraint system—safety belts—that had replaced LM's seats. The plane could also fly inverted parabolas, thus simulating the five-gravities that might be experienced during deceleration and descent from lunar orbit. The astronauts had to be able to operate the ship's controls with swift precision, and the restraint system had to be strong enough to keep them standing. If it wasn't, they could fall to the floor, at five times their normal Earth weight, and five times as fast, with spine-breaking force.

These tests were completed, and LM took final form, even as the first *Gemini* capsules were being prepared for flight, even as crowds gathered beneath New York's Unisphere, whose three giant rings represented John Glenn's three orbits, even as cosmonauts Komarov, Yegorov, and Feoktistov* left the earth in *Voskhod* 1 and Khrushchev congratulated them via radio telephone and promised them many triumphs when they returned. (There were indeed many triumphs, but none from Khrushchev, for he was deposed overnight and declared an "unperson," and the official greeters were Kosygin and Brezhnev.)

And *Pravda* exulted, "Sorry *Apollo*! Now such prophecies that the Americans will never catch up can bring forth only an ironic smile. The gap is not closing, but increasing." Perhaps it was. Out in the New Mexico desert, as Lynn Radcliffe was trying to activate the test facility, trying to establish discipline, the first rig arrived. It was an ascent-stage engine with things on it—just things: ropes of tubing and a couple of tanks and valves (lots of valves). To look at it, you'd think it was the most ungainly thing in the world. And thanks to Nikita Krushchev, there was nothing else in the world that looked quite like it.

---

*Soon, Konstatin Feoktistov would become the chief designer of the *Salyut* Space Station. He was sent along as a *Voskhod* passenger so he could see and feel space firsthand. The Russians wanted him to know what it was like out there (chaos in a teapot), since he was going to be designing manned spacecraft. It was good thinking on the Russians' part. The American equivalent would have been to send Wernher von Braun or Tom Kelly on a *Gemini* mission.

16. THE LONG ISLANDERS

George Skurla: "It wasn't too long after Grumman got into the program. It became apparent that the big final payoff of all this would be the actual stacking of LM on top of this 365-foot-high launch vehicle, preparing it and making sure it was ready to go before committing to launch. And the word went out that they would have to find someone to be a leader of that pack, at the Kennedy Space Center."

As a child, George Skurla was fascinated by airplanes and dirigibles. He built models of almost anything that flew, grew up to study aeronautical engineering, and earned a private pilot's license. He signed on as an apprentice engineer at Grumman straight out of the University of Michigan. By the time Grumman won the LM contract, the boy who loved to build models had become assistant director of flight test, and the job of finding the people needed to perform the final assembly, test, and checkout of the LM fell directly into George's hands.

Then 1964 came round, and George was asked to pick someone from flight test who would head the Kennedy Space Center operation, someone who would first prepare the facility to receive and service the ascent and descent stages, direct their mating, testing, and stacking, and then commit the total Lunar Module for launch. In the course of choosing potential candidates, George thought, Gee, maybe, just maybe, I'd be interested in that job myself.

"Hey, would you . . . would you have any objections if I threw my name in for consideration?" he asked his supervisor.

"What do you want to do that for?"

"Well, I'm not sure. I've spent years working in the flight test and structural analysis of airplanes, and here's a whole new world. Here's NASA coming along, and spaceflight."

"I know, and you'll hate it, believe me. I've heard of the kinds of things that go on at the Cape. Sixteen-hour workdays, seven-day weeks: They *eat* people down there."

George submitted his name anyway, in addition to several others. He told Joe Gavin and Bob Mullaney, "I'd like to be considered for that job."

"Yeah," they said. "We'd like you to take the assignment."

"Well, now I had reason to pause, because first of all I was kind of settled into Long Island. I had a wife and four young children. I'd made improvements on my home, and Florida was a place that—frankly, I didn't know whether Cape Kennedy was north or south of Fort Lauderdale, or Jacksonville. I didn't really know where the Cape was."

"Marie?"

"Yes?"

"You know, I have a pretty good job here. I'm assistant director of flight test. I like living in Huntington. Do you really think I ought to take this job?"

"Well, George, why don't you go down and look the place over?"

The Kennedy Space Center was hot and sticky and flat. And where were the four seasons? George wondered. It didn't snow here, and the leaves never changed colors in autumn, and spring didn't blossom. The restaurants all seemed to have names like Sneaky Pete's Hideaway and the Mousetrap Steak House, and instead of Broadway shows there were the Redstone Cowgirls doing their triple-X ball games. Everything was scrubby and swampy. But out there, on Merritt Island, they were testing a giant crawler that would one day ferry the *Saturn* rocket to the launchpad. (In 1977, the crawler's shape would be borrowed for a movie called *Star Wars*.) And over there, three miles away from the crawler, the steel frame of the Vehicle Assembly Building was rising from the marshland.

George went home and returned with his wife. They looked at schools and homes, and the more they looked, the more George began to feel that he could never be happy in Florida.

"Well, what do you think?" he asked Marie, as they followed Route A1A to the airport. "You know, really, this isn't what you want to do. You don't want to live down here, do you?"

"I like it."

The blood drained out of George's face. "You *like* this environment?"

"Yes. It's a whole new world. What have we got to lose? I've always loved the sun and sand, and the boys wouldn't need snowsuits anymore."

"Well, you know, if we come down here, it's going to be *total* involvement for me. We won't have much time together. It will be an assignment lasting three to five years. Can you take being away from home that long?"

"Well, I'm game, and home will be where we're all together. Honey, we're going to the moon and I want to be here. Cape Kennedy will become the focal point of the world. Please say yes. I know you can do that job."

That night, George stood in his back yard, adding things up: Marie wants to go. She's willing to go. The boys are still young enough not to miss friends or their school. Marie can have her mother and family visit her in Florida, so she won't be lonely. He walked once around the yard, looking at the lawn chairs, at the brick wall he'd built with his own hands, at the moon.

"Can I leave all this? Oh, my. Can I tear myself away from this and be happy?"

A disembodied voice answered, "Look. If you don't go"—he heard her close the screen door—"you may regret that you never were part of this." She reached out, "I think this is going to be a great program"—and took his hand—"the greatest in our lifetime, and I think this is an opportunity you should accept. *Let's go for it.*"

"So I became one of the first members of the Grumman Kennedy Space Center team, which eventually grew to sixteen hundred people and all their families. Grumman was the last major contractor coming on the scene: We were the *big unknown*. I was going down there with the responsibility of handling the final vehicle that was going to do the job of actually taking these guys down to the surface of the moon and getting them back up. And, of course, if anything failed in the process, if they were marooned on the moon, you can imagine the repercussions that would be heard around town and the embarrassment to this country in the eyes of the world. And my head would have been knocked off real fast."

Whenever Colonel Rocco Petrone called George to his office, there was cause for headaches.

What is it *this* time? George asked himself as he tried to analyze the expression on the colonel's face. He remembered how proud he had been to say "I'm from Grumman," and how quickly Rocco had smacked him down for it. (*I don't care where you come from. You're working on our NASA team. You work on the Apollo Kennedy Space Center team. You may be from Grumman, and that guy may be Rockwell, and that guy, over there, may be IBM or Boeing or Chrysler, but first and foremost you're working on the KSC launch team here. And remember that.*) Company pride, and the intercorporate competition that so often went along with it, were *verboten* under Rocco Petrone, the former football star who now directed the whole Kennedy Space Center launch operation. He was determined to orchestrate corporate loyalties right into the NASA organization, into one partnership, into one complicated stack of launch vehicles and payload . . . and if you didn't like it, he'd see to it that you were out of a job, *real fast.*

"Well, Rocco, what is it?"

"What the hell is the matter with your people?"

Oh, them, thought George. My angels with dirty faces. Like it or not, he supposed people from Long Island came from another world as opposed to the guys from Saint Louis or Houston or even Los Angeles. Grummies were coming down here in black pants and black leather jackets. They were talented engineers and technicians, but they didn't quite fit into the Florida scene, which was palm trees and sandals and nice sport shirts and beige polyester pants, and all the other contractor people looked like that. And—

"Your people!"

"I'm listening. What about them?"

"They . . . one of your guys wants to start a Hell's Angels motorcycle club. Another one was standing in the shadow of Launch Complex 37 at lunchtime the other day and he . . . he . . . GOLF BALLS. He was hitting *golf balls* around! Another guy was flying a—one of those gasoline-powered model airplanes on a string. If that had broken loose and flown into the side of a rocket on the pad—"

"Oh, God . . ."

" 'Oh, God' is right! What the hell is wrong with people from Long Island? We caught a guy on the walkway going across the main aisle of the Vehicle Assembly Building, five hundred feet up; he was up there making paper airplanes and sailing them over the rail down into this thing we're trying to build, this thing that's supposed to be the world's biggest hangar."

"One of my guys?"

"One of your Grumman guys."

"All right, Colonel. Say no more. I'll call a meeting."

The air was sticky and close that evening, perfect weather for laying down the law.

"Why do you have to act like Long Islanders?" George asked, in a tone appropriate to a classroom of disruptive schoolboys.

No answer.

"Okay. Environment must be to blame."

Silence.

Great, George thought. They were supposed to laugh at that one.

"Now, I've got my hands full with a bunch of guys that aren't really sensitized to the fact that when you're around a launch vehicle in this world of Kennedy Space Center and man going to the moon, you can't act like you were brought up on Long Island. That's for openers. Now, I'm going to tell you a few things you're not going to like. From now on, nobody goes on vacation unless I approve it. Don't make any weekend plans either—until further notice. We're down here to get a job done. We're in a very critical situation. The guys up north are designing and build- ing this thing. They're working overtime, and we'd better have the ground-support equipment ready when the LMs start coming."

Silence.

"I hear your guys want to form a softball team."

Silence.

"Absolutely no softball."

Someone hissed "Shit" under his breath. George snapped his head in the direction whence it came. There was a shuffling of feet, with some embarrassment.

"You don't understand what's going on," George said to no one in particular. "I can't afford to have a key engineer, techni- cian, or test-program writer play softball and break an arm. Not in this pressure cooker, I can't. Someday they'll be launching moon rockets every two months; that's going to mean three stacks of vehicles in flow at one time and thousands of cables and black boxes, because the LMs have to be checked out. This is where the world is coming to, guys. You won't see newspapermen run- ning around Bethpage looking for this and that. They're down here, at Kennedy, because this is where we launch."

The men thought George's ban on softball a bit strange, but he was only beginning. Soon, he demanded that all quality- control inspectors were to have their eyes examined. Quality- control men were notorious ballbusters, and along came "Outrageous George," busting the ballbusters' balls.

"Hey, George! You're a very funny guy. Too bad you're not going to last at the Cape."

People stopped joking when some of the quality-control guys

started turning up color blind. All the ship's wires were color coded—all fourteen miles of them.

Then George began breaking up the inspector teams. He wouldn't let John, as an inspector, get familiar with Jack, as a technician. He knew that if John and Jack got friendly with each other, then sooner or later lunchtime would come along, and Jack would say, "Come on, John, let's go to lunch."

And John would say, "Well, I just want to take another look at these wires."

"You looked at them ten times already. It's okay."

George kept rotating the inspectors, making doubly sure they never became too friendly with the technicians whose work they were supposed to be checking.

17. THE LIGHT STUFF

Up north, on Long Island, had begun the war against weight, nudged along by a $25,000 bonus from NASA for each pound that could be pruned from the spacecraft. Thus began the Scrape and SWIP (Super Weight Improvement Program) effort. Within months, LM would lose 1,770 pounds. This effort made the lander more difficult to fabricate, more fragile, and more vulnerable to damage. Structural components began to evolve in strange ways. Shapes became more complex, requiring careful machining and a sculptor's skills to remove any excess metal—an almost unbelievably time-consuming process, even after workers had been found who were crazy enough to make these odd-looking parts. Add to this an ever-growing concern for keeping everything clean, and a squeeze between manufacturing requirements and schedule pressures. "At a program-management meeting," recalls Arnold Whitaker, "George Titterton [the Grumman senior VP] wanted to know why we were behind schedule putting the vehicle together, why the shop was having so much trouble getting parts where they were needed, and one of the shop foremen came in with a light cardboard box. He said, 'I'll show you why everything's late.' And he dumped out a whole box of machined parts. Very complex fittings, too thin to be even reasonably heavy sheet metal. But it wasn't any sheet metal; it was complex machined fittings. And he said, 'Man, we never built parts like this before in any quantity like this, and every fitting on LM looks like this.'"

Nothing was ever built to be so strong and yet so light. LM's ladder could be used only at one sixth Earth gravity. If someone tried to climb it on Earth, it would fall apart. Bolts were shaved down to remove as much weight as possible. Ball joints were hollowed out. Molecule-deep layers of metal were milled off with acid. Weight was that crucial. A few extra pounds could cost seconds of fuel (seconds; that's how fuel is measured in space) and might make the difference between a few seconds to spare and an aborted landing. Ironically, forty-pound guidance instruments and display panels could be replaced today by *Apollo* spinoffs weighing mere ounces, such as advanced microcircuitry and liquid-crystal displays. But, lacking these tools, George Titterton took a terrible risk and asked, "Why in the hell don't you astronauts go on a diet?" With the ill fortune that often follows the brave, he became the only man in history to be booed out of a SWIP meeting by eight astronauts.

And Scrape and SWIP went on.

And on.

And on.

Eky: "The outer aluminum skin of the ship was so light . . . the skins were so thin when we first started to use them that you had to handle them with a piece of corrogated cardboard. I could literally see the outline of my hand on the other side of the metal. Ugh! Seeing through metal. We had cardboard faced on both sides of the metal to keep it stiff. You handled the skin that way or it would buckle. You'd get it up there and put clamps on it and take the cardboard away. And there was a covering on the metal so you didn't scratch it. It wasn't like building an airplane, believe me. That was something that was never done before.

"In the tests, before they flew anything, they learned that the skins weren't enough. They couldn't take the g-forces during launch. And we had to take the skins off a couple of the units and put heavier skins on. We had to have special tools in order to drill the rivets out, so we didn't make the holes larger, because if the hole was larger, it wouldn't be like the drawing. And they wanted everything perfect. They didn't want any repairs on anything. We had this big roundtable meeting with NASA. They were all worried about switching the skins, and they haggled back and forth for a few hours, and finally someone asked me what percent of the rivet holes would be ruined. I said, 'Well, I guess about . . . only five percent.' And they asked, 'Well, can we hold you to that?' and I said, 'Yes, you can. I'd say you can.' And they said, 'That's good enough. Five percent. We can live with that.' So they ended the meeting and everybody got up to leave and they all sighed and shook hands, and then somebody from NASA turned around and said, 'Oh, Eky. By the way. How much is five percent?' And I said, 'About two thousand rivets.' And they sat down and started all over again."

One two-thousandth of an inch—roughly the thickness of two sheets of newspaper—that's what was going to hold all the air inside LM. One hard kick and you could put your foot right through the wall of the ship and into space. The astronauts would have to be isolated from the skins with fiberglass shields and plastic covers and false floors. And Tom Kelly would worry, when men were on the moon, especially when it came time to plan overnight missions, when the astronauts would come in from a full-day excursion and take off their helmets and gloves and backpacks and settle into their hammocks for a few hours sleep. They'd be relying, then, for a long time, on the structural integrity of the skins, and this troubled Tom. It troubled him very much, because he knew that the cabin had scores of angular bends in it—very complicated geometry—and if there was a weak rivet or weld, or a crack somewhere . . .

Cleanliness obsessed the LM people. In Bethpage, parts were assembled in a place called the Clean Room: a very large, stark white room lit by fluorescent lights and populated by men wearing white suits, white booties, white gloves, and white face masks. The floors were spotless and—you guessed it—white. In the center of the room stood LM. It wasn't white. It was black and silver, and it drooped red tags and ribbons of gold foil. The workers moved around it in almost total silence, like priests gathered in ceremony around a central altar. No foreman shouted instructions. The men knew what to do, and they were doing it. According to Milt Radimer, "It was a different atmosphere. Very quiet. They went into this white thing and just became silent."

Says Joe Kingfield, a former quality-control manager for Grumman, "A thumbprint, a dropped washer, dirt, a water-glycol spill not properly cleaned, might have jeopardized the mission and the safety of the crew. Thousands of parts were scrupulously cleaned, inspected for contamination, and then bagged in plastic until assembly."

In Plant 5, the final assembly area for LM, the spacecraft was hoisted upward, rotated, and inspected for foreign objects. "One time we heard this clunk-clunk sound," Joe said. "It sounded like a pair of sneakers in a clothes dryer. We thought someone hadn't properly installed and secured an expensive piece of equipment. We later found that a technician had left a Simpson meter in one of the moon-rock boxes."

To prevent a recurrence, Joe began to think about assigning cabin monitors to each ship. He was aware—too aware—that if a discarded tool drifting in space made contact with the wrong wire and let loose a spark, in an environment where, to save the weight of extra tanks and to avoid the complexity of mixing nitrogen and oxygen and other gases in the "right" proportions, NASA had opted to provide a pure-oxygen atmosphere—in such an environment one little spark could turn the whole cabin into a furnace. No, that's no good, Joe thought. We have to make sure the ship is spotless. So, he asked his program manger, "How about us having a cabin monitor?"

"What's a cabin monitor?" the manager said.

"I'd like to have somebody sitting by the door of the cabin after we start to pack the LM full of equipment, and I want him to record everything that goes in and everything that comes out. If a worker needs four screws in there, that's all he takes in is four, not six or a whole bagful—"

"What's the matter with you? Are you diabolical or something? Haven't we got enough bloody damned bureaucracy around here? Go tell that to NASA. They *love* bureaucracy, and I'll bet even they say no to the idea."

He did.

They did.

MEMO

To Grumman Contracts Department:
Mr. Kingfield's request for a change [the introduction of cabin monitors] has been denied. We hope that you have enough faith in your people to know that they understand the seriousness of the project, and that they will take all necessary precautions. We are, after all, dealing with professionals. And the system you propose will be prohibitively expensive. It is therefore our unanimous opinion that it should be declined.

NASA Contracting Office

Okay, thought Joe Kingfield. That's fine. But don't say I didn't tell you so.

And so, predictably . . .

An astronaut was running electrical tests in the cabin, and hit a glitch in the system. He lowered an overhead panel to see what was short-circuiting the wires and a pair of pliers slid out of the ceiling and hit him on the head.

A week later, each worker was checked as he entered and left the LM. Every tool, every piece of equipment that went in was recorded on a list, and when the worker exited, every item was either checked off the list as having been brought out with him or accounted for as being installed. And still . . . "I can remember looking for a twenty-four-foot extension cord," says Joe. "It went into the spacecraft and never came out. You know, it never came out, and we knew damn well that it wasn't in there, because we searched and searched and it just wasn't in there." To this day, nobody knows what happened to that extension cord. It didn't go to the moon, of course.

Well, of course it didn't go to the moon.

(But we can't account for it in the books, Joe.)

"When anything went wrong," recalls one former supervisor, "no one thought about placing the blame. The big concern was fixing the problem. Mistakes were admitted. Everyone knew that a mistake that went unadmitted or unnoticed might have meant a one-way ticket for those astronauts. That was foremost in everybody's mind."

(But we can't account for it in the books.)

Well, of course it didn't go to the moon.

"I understand they had men working on small parts," Eky says. "They might originally have been watchmakers or what have you, because of the technique of their work, and they had to raise the work high, so they didn't look over it, because dandruff from their eyebrows might fall on the parts. If that got into space and was burning on a wire and smoking, or if something was floating around there, Mission Control wanted to know what it was, or at least what it was not. Over at Plant 5, they'd rather have a man work in the cockpit—after everything had been cleaned—who didn't take a bath every day, because they didn't want dry skin flaking off and floating around.

"We built a clean ship; that's for sure. Everybody was his own inspector. After we finished the descent stage, the whole thing was mounted on a tumbler and sort of turned upside down and given a good shaking out. That would get rid of shavings from rivets and rivet heads, things you couldn't possibly get out with a vacuum cleaner. You'd also listen for loose parts. But one time a riveter's tool, a bucking bar, fell out. It fell out right through the hull of the ship, and, oh, hell, they called me down and this one NASA inspector wanted my riveter fired immediately. Well, I checked over the inspector's reports, and according to the forms he'd signed, the ship had been inspected inside and out for loose fittings and cleared for tumbling—by *him*. I said, 'Hey, look. You said this thing was clean and you put your name to it and I'm telling you that you messed up on your job. How do you miss something as big as a bucking bar?' It was as much his fault as it was the riveter's, and I damned well kept my riveter.

"That one NASA inspector acted like a tin god. He kept busting everybody's ass. Like when Chet Senig would ship the ascent stage over to me. It was shipped in open air on the back of a truck, which is why it didn't go through a final, thorough cleaning until it got over to my building. And fresh off the truck this NASA clown would climb inside and if he found any dust or pieces of rivets or a smudge in it, he'd write me up. And he did it every time. And he had to be real nasty about it. He'd come over to me before he wrote me up and say, 'I'm being nice to you. I'm being fair and I'm letting you know in advance that I'm writing you up, so you can prepare for it.'

"And one day this other NASA inspector found the bastard's identity badge lying in a hallway and he gave it to me.

"Heh! Heh! Heh!

"He must not have liked the guy either. So I started paging the 'tin god,' who happened to be at a meeting with the big brass. Some other guy kept answering the phone. He warned me that the inspector was getting madder and madder and wanted to know who this foreman thought he was to be calling him. Somebody at the meeting suggested that maybe he should go down and find out. So here he comes, mad as hell, and I told him, 'I'm going to be nice to you. I'm being fair and I'm letting you know in advance that I'm writing you up.' 'Oh, yeah,' he said. 'You've got nothing on me.' And I said, 'Okay, where is your badge? Do you know where your badge is?' And this guy started looking through his pockets, and I decided to turn up the heat a little more: 'Well, you're going to lunch today, aren't you? How do you expect to get back in past the guards?' And he said, 'Give me back my badge!' And I wouldn't.

"I told him, 'I'm going to write you up and say I found this in the ascent stage.' He said, 'You didn't find that in there!' And I asked him how much he'd pay me to say I found it in a cathouse in Hicksville.

"I let him sort of simmer on that for a minute; then I gave him his badge. And that's one sour fellow who never wrote me up again."

Joe Kingfield: "You have to have a back like a crocodile to be in my business. In quality control you get nothing but bad news. And I'm one pain in the ass in the company. I mean, my job is to walk around poking my nose into everybody else's business and then to tell them how they've done it all wrong."

NASA quality-control inspector Mel Friedman: "Grumman had its own quality-control department. The government was paying Grumman, and LM was Grumman's responsibility. The only thing NASA quality control did was to assure the government that Grumman was doing its job. In other words, if I picked up a problem that Grumman had overlooked, it meant that people like Joe Kingfield weren't doing their jobs.

"From my end, I wasn't supposed to accept anything that did not meet the criteria one hundred percent. If, during a test, a piece of equipment was supposed to give a reading of ten volts, plus or minus one volt, that was it: nine to eleven volts. Nothing else. I was surprised to learn that this rule was being disregarded almost all the time in the early days of the program. If it didn't come right up to specification, NASA would let it pass if our constraints were going to delay the program in any way. Of course, redundancy helped a lot, and the earliest LMs were not manned, but my supervisor in NASA seemed determined to meet Kennedy's deadline, and in my opinion a lot of risks were taken because of that, even on the manned vehicles.

"We stopped shipments in the middle of the night. We stopped tests in the middle of the night. And we got calls from Houston: 'No more. No more. No more stopping.' It troubles me to this day, that the kind of quality control we were fighting for early in the program was not demanded by NASA until later in the program, until *after* the first men landed on the moon. You think it would have been the other way around."

Grumman quality-control inspector Harry Walther: "The job was never complete until it had that final NASA stamp on it. After our Grumman inspectors went over the vehicle, we had to turn it over to the NASA inspectors. And NASA double-checked everything. By and large, NASA people didn't want to hear common sense. All they wanted to hear was the way it read on paper. If it wasn't written on the blueprint or on the specification sheet, then either the specification sheet had to be changed or the whole job stopped. NASA had the final say; believe me. That was one program where the government really put the screws down. They said this is the way it's going to be. And in a lot of cases, they turned out to be completely right."

"But we had this one NASA inspector—absolutely miserable," recalls Al Beauregard, a supervisor on the *Eagle* (also known as LM-5). "He drove me crazy. He drove poor Bob Ekenstierna crazy. He drove *everybody* crazy. He'd write Eky up on the ascent stages every time one came over from the plant—and the ascent stage wasn't even Eky's part of the ship! He got me so riled once I stared calling him 'Baby,' and the name stuck."

"Nobody likes us," says Herman Clark, a quality-control inspector for LM-5. "I saw that thing when it was nothing but a big hulking piece of metal. I looked at every darned hole, every joint. The quality-control inspector is a sort of nitpicker. We're

the ballbreakers, in plain English. We're the most unwanted people. The quality-control guy is a guy that not many people like,
because it's his job to criticize another man. I was the only black
man in my area—the inspection part—and I directed a number
of white people [a pretty rare situation, in those days], and I got
damned good cooperation from these guys. My outlook is, I don't
have to win your heart, but I will win your respect. I think the
LM guys respected me. We had over there a pretty good relationship going. The people who worked on that project, on the LM,
took pride in it. The guys were not there to fight a racial problem.
If you've got a problem, take it out of here."

"We had a problem," Eky recalls. "NASA was worried about
what would happen to the LM if the bell-shaped cowl around
the descent-stage engine glanced off a rock on the way down. By
that point in the mission, that close to the surface, it didn't really
matter if the bell broke—or even the descent engine. Its purpose
had been served by then. But if the bell contacted a big rock and
pulled the whole ship over on its side, you've got big trouble. So
NASA wanted to test this possibility in a field by dropping an
engine several feet onto a simulated lunar terrain, with the bell
taking the whole mass of the LM against a hard surface so they
could see if the bell would remain rigid and tip the ship over, or
if it would poke up into the ascent-stage engine and prevent
takeoff. It was estimated that the test would coast about half a
million dollars. But near the end of 1965, we began to feel the
budget cuts. So NASA never got the money to make this test.

"Now, when you're building the descent stage, you put the
engine mounts on top because the thrust of the engine is from
the bottom. So, when you wanted to take the engine out, you
lifted the whole descent stage and very carefully pulled the engine
out through the bottom. One night when they were doing this,
the wrong switch got flipped into reverse and the descent-stage
hoist let go and dropped the whole thing on top of the engine.
The quality-control guys were down there and a minute later
phones were ringing all over the place. They called just about
everybody and his grandfather, and when I got there somebody

was looking at the engine and crying: The poor bell was squashed up like an accordion. But it didn't poke through where the ascent stage would be. And I'm looking over the damage and some NASA inspector is pacing back and forth saying 'Shit' over and over, and finally he turned to me and said, 'Well, what are you going to do about it?' And I said, 'Well, I think you wanted to do your test, and now you know what would happen if you hit a rock, and you got it done for only a fraction of the cost!' "

And everybody was happy again.

19. CONFERENCE

George Skurla continued to build his team.

He'd brought with him hundreds of people from Long Island and hired hundreds more from Florida. The Gemini program would soon be phasing down, and already George had "stolen" a few people from McDonnell Aircraft Corporation, with the justi-fication that he wanted to maximize their experience on the Mer-cury and Gemini programs for Apollo. NASA liked his nerve, and told him so. Then he stole one of NASA's key test managers.*

From on high, someone in the NASA hierarchy began to question loudly and at length whether anyone from Long Island, George Skurla in particular, should be handling the LM program. Hearing this, Joe Gavin flew to Cape Kennedy and called a pri-vate meeting with Skurla and the director of launch operations.

"Just one question," said Joe Gavin to Colonel Petrone. "I know people have been wondering if George Skurla can hack it

---

*Wiley Williams, a Mercury and Gemini test director who became a LM test director and is now one of NASA's higher management people at the Kennedy Space Center.

down here, and I know that in some circles his job is thought to be in jeopardy. So, what do *you* think? Do you think that the job is getting done? Are you satisfied with Skurla's leadership here? Yes or no? Don't be bashful."

Rocco wasn't bashful, George thought. *None* of the NASA people were bashful. They were arrogant, they were smart, they were young, they were aggressive, and they were ruthless. When they found a man they didn't like, that was it. They would just say, "We want that guy off the program," and Grumman management had no alternative but to please the customer. George had seen four base managers fired from other companies. There were two changeouts in the Rockwell team. IBM changed out, and Chrysler, too. There was no such thing as job security in the space program. "Superchief" Rocco Petrone was a burly man—sleeves rolled up, muscles bulging, always perspiring—and he really believed in harassment. Rocco had been beating Grumman up on a number of "contractual agreements" that were simply beyond George's control, and George truly had no idea what Rocco was going to say. To his relief, the colonel answered, with apparent pride, "Joe, I'd have gotten to you a lot sooner than this, and George would have been out of here quicker than boiled asparagus if he couldn't hack it. I'm satisfied with George, now. And I support him."

"Thank you, Colonel. That's all I wanted to know."

In the years leading up to the *Eagle*'s landing, George would learn more working with Rocco Petrone than he had learned in the previous twenty years working in Bethpage. Under the leadership of a man who loved to bust heads, George learned a great deal about management, about doing it right, doing it on schedule, and being meticulous. And, as they stepped out of the conference room and onto the spaceport that day, George spoke fondly, fully aware of the echo from the past: "Rocco, I think this is the beginning of a beautiful friendship."

20. DISEASES FROM SPACE

EXERPT FROM MICROFILM N63-13597
DECLASSIFIED CODE 1
NASA CONTRACT NO. NAS 7-100
PREPARED BY GREGG MAMIKUNIAN AND MICHAEL H. BRIGGS

VARIOUS CLASSES OF MICROSTRUCTURES IN THE 5 TO 30 MICRON* SIZE RANGE HAVE RECENTLY BEEN STUDIED IN SAMPLES OF CARBONACEOUS METEORITES BY CLAUS AND NAGY, WHO HAVE NAMED THE OBJECTS "ORGANIZED ELEMENTS." ON THE BASIS OF DETAILED MORPHOLOGICAL STUDIES AND STAINING REACTIONS WITH BIOLOGICAL DYES, CLAUS AND NAGY HAVE SUGGESTED THAT THE "ORGANIZED ELEMENTS" ARE MICROFOSSILS OF AN EXTRATERRESTRAIL LIFEFORM, INDIGENOUS TO THE METEORITE PARENT BODY.

"There can be no doubt," said Nobel Laureate Harold Clayton Urey, "that if the substances and structures present in carbonaceous meteorites were found in terrestrial objects, they would be regarded indisputably as biological."

"One of the most fascinating results of all the planned exploration of the solar system," Urey wrote in a letter to *Science,*

would be the proof that life may exist somewhere else than on the earth. It is an old suggestion that the carbonaceous

---

*1000 microns=1 millimeter=1/25 inch.

meteorites have been coming from the moon. If the moon escaped from the earth (or was captured by the earth in a process that may have been very complicated and violent), it is not at all impossible that it could have been temporarily contaminated with terrestrial water. If indeed the surface of the moon carries a residue of the ancient oceans of the earth at about the time that life was evolving, the Apollo Program should bring back fascinating samples which will teach us much in regard to the early history of the solar system, and in particular with regard to the origin of life. The possibility that water has been present on the moon, has been pointed out recently by Thomas Gold. However, if the residue of indigenous biological activity in meteorites is indeed real, and if the meteorites do not come from the moon, other more complicated and possibly more interesting histories for these objects must be devised.

A new hazard considered with increasing seriousness in 1965 was the possibility of contaminating the moon with earthly bacteria or virus particles, things against which lunar organisms, if such existed, might have no natural defenses. On the heels of this thought came another: What if it worked the other way around? What if we brought pathogenic organisms back to earth?

The isolation and identification (from carbonaceous meteorites) of complex ring-shaped carbon compounds, nucleic-acid bases, fatty acids, alcohols, sugars, droplets of protein, and precursors to chlorophyll added spice to the danger of such dreams. Detailed studies showed these substances to be similar to but quite distinct from organic molecules found in living tissues. They came from out there, somewhere, which was something one had to stop and think about for a moment.

University of California chemist Harold Urey and Victoria University geologist Michael Briggs speculated that the meteorites had originated as deposits splashed off the moon's surface. It was a perfectly good thought, but the timing was disastrously wrong. Four years later, the first rocks returned from the moon would contain no hint of organic deposits. Urey's position as a Nobel Laureate would protect him from undue ridicule, but ivory towers were lined with teeth, and they had to bite *somebody*. They'd call Briggs a science novelist, a literary slut, an ass; and they'd eventually laugh him clear out of the academic world. Some of his former colleagues are still laughing, which betrays their ignorance of the fact that Briggs found refuge at NASA's Jet Propulsion Laboratory, where everybody knows that pieces of the moon and Mars and other bodies *have* been splashed off into space (presumably by asteroid impacts), and that from time to time these pieces *have* fallen to Earth. Planets, as they whirl around their suns, can and sometimes do exchange pieces of rock (and perhaps life) with each other, as if they were passing bits of gossip over a backyard fence.

The *Viking* and *Voyager* probes ultimately vindicated Urey and Briggs, by showing us moons with stains that were the chemical basis of life. The only thing wrong with their idea, it seems, was that they were looking at the wrong moon.

And then there were the "organized elements." Nobody knew what they were—and still, nobody knows. Some astronomers dreamed that these microstructures were viruses and bacteria landing on Earth from interstellar space, stored deep-frozen in carbonaceous meteorites and responsible for everything from flu epidemics to the origin and evolution of life. These dreams were viewed by the U.S. Public Health Service as the stuff of nightmares. Backed by the National Academy of Sciences, the PHS petitioned NASA: "The introduction into the Earth's biosphere of destructive alien organisms could be a disaster of enormous significance to mankind. We can conceive of no more tragically ironic consequence of our search for extraterrestrial life." The point made, Congress hastily granted funds for the construction of a special quarantine facility in Houston. The Lunar Sample Receiving Laboratory, built hurriedly and almost as an afterthought, became one of the most elaborately safeguarded biological facilities in the world.

On March 18, 1965, Brezhnev permitted the launch of one more remodeled *Vostok*, this time called *Voskhod 2*, before turning the Soviet space effort over to *Soyuz* and Korolev's own version of LM. On fire and rolling thunder, Aleksey Leonov and Pavel Belyayev were lifted 150 miles into space. Passing through a secondary cabin—an airlock—Leonov stepped outside the spherical *Voskhod* and became the first man to "walk," or rather "swim," in space. Inside, Belyayev heard Moscow's first radio announcements of the flight and watched his companion drift past the window, gleaming and vague in brilliant sunshine, framed in the absolute black of space. Leonov pushed off from the hull, and Belyayev felt a perceptible jolt in the opposite direction. A thin tether connected him to *Voskhod 2*, his backpack providing for his every need— *self-contained life support* . . . the Russians were testing their moon suit.

Leonov had become a spaceship in his own right, and when he tried to reenter the airlock, he discovered to his horror that he might stay that way. The ballooning effect of pressurized oxygen had stiffened the suit's joints. He could not bend his waist far enough to get his legs into the chamber, and Belyayev's breathing became hard and irregular as he considered the possibility of reentering the atmosphere with the airlock door open and his friend dangling outside.

Leonov resorted to a desperate tactic, venting air out of his suit, reducing its internal pressure by nearly half and increasing mobility of the joints—and virtually assuring that, within minutes, his blood would begin to boil. He scrambled feet first through the hatch, pulled the door closed behind him, then pressurized the airlock to its life-saving maximum.

Later, the ship's computer failed, and Belyayev tried to bring the *Voskhod* manually through the atmosphere, down to the broad, flat plains of Kazakhstan. The two cosmonauts eventually found themselves in a powerless and heatless spacecraft, half buried in snow. Belyayev opened the ship's air vents, popped open the escape hatch, and stepped out onto a landscape that was entirely wrong: mountains and tall birches, dark and deep and cold. And no search planes.

Still . . . their arrival had not gone unseen. Wolves had heard the sonic booms, had watched the parachute bloom behind the meteor, had heard the retrofire kick on an instant before touchdown. And now, the scent of a campfire and the murmur of voices were unmistakable signs of food. For a time, the fire kept the wolves at bay, but their hunger was overmastering. They pressed closer . . . closer . . . ever closer, until at last Belyayev and Leonov abandoned the fire and retreated to the safety of their capsule—which turned out not to provide a great deal of safety, for the escape hatch had bent and would not close all the way, and the two men would not live very long in their space suits without the warmth of an electrical heating system (no such luck) or a campfire (outside, with the wolves). And there they sat: two thousand miles off target in the frozen Urals, taking turns staying awake and holding the broken hatch closed while wolves prowled on the other side and waited for the cosmonauts to grow cold and tired, waited for the hatch to open a little bit, waited for the opportunity to claw their way in and bite the hands of the hatch holder. In a day, helicopters would locate the ship's beacon, but until then, Belyayev and Leonov were trapped between teeth and ice.

Three days later, John Young and Gus Grissom rode the first manned *Gemini* capsule into the far sky. They used translation thrusters to change the ship's orbit, demonstrating that one could fly easily from one path to another. This was the secret to rendezvous, docking, and eventual lunar landings.

On the ground, Lynn Radcliffe's White Sands team had been working fifteen- and sixteen-hour days, seven days a week, since Christmas. Even so, they were more than two months behind schedule.

It's just inhuman, what we are doing, Lynn thought. Everybody is falling over with fatigue, trying to achieve this visible, possibly realizable goal of an ascent stage firing on April 15.

And yet, as the date approached, damn if it didn't look as though they were going to make it.

Lynn got on the line to Bethpage: "Joe? Joe Gavin! If we do this, we've got to say thank you to this gang down here. You're up there. You don't know what's going on. We're *living* at this facility. If we make it, I'd like to reward them with a day off on the company—a two-day weekend, which will seem like two months' vacation after what we've been through."

"You got it," Joe said. And it became their secret.

On the morning of April 15, 1965, Lynn watched from a blockhouse crowded to twice its permissible capacity as an engine no larger than a basketball burped 3,600 pounds of lifting power into a flame deflector. They fed it enough fuel for a five-second burn. Five seconds, that was all. If the engine was going to tear itself apart, Lynn wanted to have enough unmelted pieces left to reveal what had gone wrong. And when Lynn looked up at the TV monitor and saw through the clearing smoke that the engine was still out there, in one piece, on the test stand, he jumped up and started hooting and clapping backs and shaking hands. It got contagious: They heard the growing commotion over a speaker phone in Bethpage. "Oh, the commotion," Lynn remembers. "You'd think we were going to the moon.

"Yeah. We felt like we were the spearpoint to the moon.

"That night, we had a party at a place called the Hitching Post, a local gin mill halfway between Las Cruces and the test site. I had gotten seven hundred dollars out of Grumman for this party, and the gal who ran the place, Betty Chandler, put out all this Mexican food as her part of the celebration. She was gonna let us know when we'd spent the seven hundred dollars on drinks.

Now, Betty was a typical Western gal. Looked something like Dale Evans, replete with boots and buckskin, and she was just a great gal. She knew most of the people, always had her ear to the ground, and seemed to know more about my operation than I did.

"Anyway, we all got pretty high pretty fast that night, 'cause when you're that tired, it doesn't take much. We were just very worn out emotionally, and I remember practically going to sleep at the party at about eight o'clock, and fearing that I would go to sleep at the wheel in the six or seven miles from the Hitching Post to my house. So I left—and my people were feeling no pain. Betty announced that they'd run out of the seven hundred dollars, and from that point on it was gonna be pay as you go. Well, Al Seward, my guy in charge of quality control, was feeling no more pain than anybody else, and he said, 'No way on this night are Grummies gonna pay for their drinks. They're on me.' And you know, off they went and spent another six hundred dollars.

"I called Bethpage and they slapped my wrists and came up with the extra dough, but Betty and I decided it was time that Al Seward learned a lesson. I don't know if Al knows this, but I'm afraid I was the guy behind it. Betty and I and maybe one or two others were in on it, and I kept saying, 'Gee, Al, I'm sorry. I tried to get the money from the company. And you gotta admit, you said the drinks were on you.'

"Now, every operation has to have an artist. There's always someone who can do caricatures; it's like a national law. This guy's name was John Paul Jones, and he did a life-size caricature of Al—Perfect!—with his mouth open, which it usually was in those days. I think it was called the 'Last of the Big Mouth Spenders,' and you'll find it hanging in Al's office today.

"So we let Al sweat for three or four days, and Betty was needling him and he was getting downright unpleasant about this thing. She said, 'Lynn, you better break it to him or he's gonna kill me.' He just didn't have the money at that time, I guess. Finally I summoned as many people as we could fit in my office.

Then I called Al in and made a little announcement: 'Al, you've been had,' and we presented him with his framed caricature."

While Al Seward roasted, the robot probe *Mariner 4* raced toward an encounter with Mars. It would soon reveal the red wilderness to be a cratered wasteland: dead, probably, like the moon, and for similar reasons. Nobody on Earth had anticipated craters on Mars: not the scientists, not the science-fiction writers. Not even Isaac Asimov.

In June, Ed White performed the first American space walk. Three months later, Pete Conrad and Gordon Cooper logged a record-breaking eight days in space. Then, in December, Frank Borman and Jim Lovell in *Gemini 7*, and Wally Schirra and Tom Stafford in *Gemini 6*, performed the first space rendezvous, and from there Borman and Lovell went on to nearly double Conrad and Cooper's world record.

Only ten years earlier, space had belonged to the science-fiction writers. Now broadcasts from orbit were commonplace, if not downright boring.

No science-fiction writer would have believed, near the end of 1965, that men would one day go to the moon and then abandon it. Yet the fall of Apollo was already within sight. The success of the Gemini and *Saturn 1* programs had, in the eyes of many Americans, outshone the Soviet space effort, and led them to believe that the space race had been won. With such complacency about, Congress turned its attention to President Johnson's "Great Society" and to the mushrooming conflict in Southeast Asia. Both were consuming more tax dollars than anticipated, and the slack had to be taken up somewhere. For fiscal 1967, NASA had submitted a budget request of $5.58 billion. The president sliced off $560 million, and Congress axed an additional $44 million.

An uneasy murmur ran through NASA.

22. WITH ZOND TO THE MOON

As 1966 began, Russia's *Luna 9* soft-landed on the moon. The little robot transmitted the first pictures from the lunar surface. In March, *Gemini 8* performed the first docking in space. Two weeks later, the Soviet Union announced that *Luna 10* was in orbit around the moon—another space first. On May 30, the United States hurled *Surveyor 1* at the moon. It followed a von Braun trajectory: straight at its target. Four days into flight, *Surveyor 1* fired its braking rockets and slowed from 1,025 to 398 miles per hour. It reached the crater Flamstead, in the Ocean of Storms, at a mere 5 feet per second.

Engineer: "What happens if *Surveyor* sinks completely in the lunar dust?"

Surveyor scientist Sheldon Shallon: "Well, we would have learned something right there."

The three-foot pads touched safely down within nineteen milliseconds of each other. Alone under an airless sky, the craft looked upon a dead land: powdery, pounded, and dry. Distant mountains revealed no hints of jagged peaks. Their features had been softened by some kind of erosion: a three-billion-year downpour of tiny meteorites. But the rain had not produced the anticipated covering of deep dust. *Surveyor 1* did not, as many had feared she would, sink into the surface and vanish.

Dust there was, but only a few inches of it, and the particles adhered to one another, not to the spacecraft. After years of doubt and waiting, *Surveyor 1* proved that men could land safely on the moon and walk around, at least if they landed in a very light craft a few feet away from *Surveyor 1* and did not walk very far.

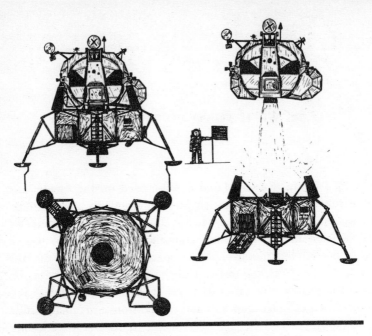

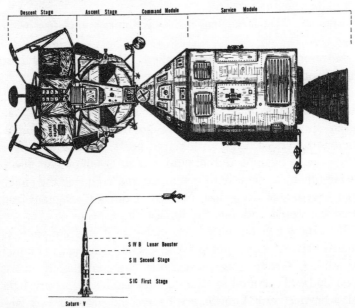

Descent Stage   Ascent Stage   Command Module   Service Module

S IV B Lunar Booster

S II Second Stage

S IC First Stage

Saturn V

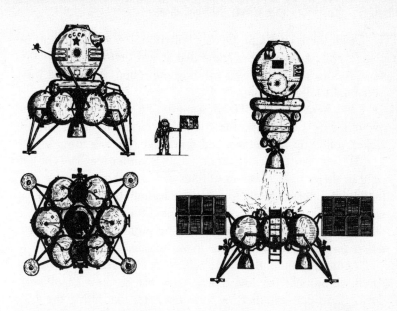

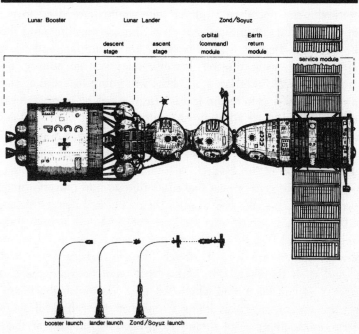

Lunar Booster · Lunar Lander · Zond/Soyuz

descent stage · ascent stage · orbital (command) module · Earth return module

service module

booster launch · lander launch · Zond/Soyuz launch

Mission profiles of *Apollo* and *Zond* vehicles

Down there on Earth, George Titterton, the vice-president in charge of LM operations, knew that it was getting close to the wire. A Russian satellite was orbiting the moon. A manned mission might follow any day.

Every hour counted. Titterton moved his desk from his executive office right down into the assembly area. He hung up his suit jacket, rolled up his sleeves, and said, "We're going to make it."

"He was our General Patton," Milt Radimer recalls. "He got right in there, right in the front lines with everybody else. He was that much interested. We had this one badmouth NASA inspector who said Titterton was pushing. But Titterton was always a pusher. He pushed the airplanes and he pushed the LM. But he didn't push it to a point where it was unsafe.

"About that time, they were setting up the area in Florida for when we brought the LM down. They had to do a lot of work down there that couldn't be done up here, like fitting the LM inside the rocket. I knew Titterton wanted me to go down and coordinate the operation, and my kids would have liked to go, but my wife didn't want any part of it. She was teaching, and she liked her job. Besides, I liked working for Grumman, and I just didn't want to leave the job, because once you go outside, it's hard to get back in. I knew my boss was going to ask me, and he's my friend. I didn't want to hurt his feelings by turning down his offer. So I started hiding out with the night crew. I don't know if it was a good thing that I didn't go, but I was very happy when I got transferred to another project. They gave me the whole forward section of the F-14."

Eky: "It was getting near that time, time to start moving things down to the Cape. We had to mate the ascent and descent stages, had to see how everything fit. You see, LM was a pretty-big-sized unit, and how things fit together depended an awful lot on temperature. Aluminum will stretch like the dickens if you heat it. And then there's all the wiring that went between the two stages. Did you know that when that unit was up on the moon, and the ascent stage was going to take off, they had all those wires—fourteen miles of them—running from the ascent stage into the descent stage, and it had to be disconnected before you took off or you didn't take off? That's all there was to it. You couldn't use wire couplings that just pulled out when you gave a good, hard yank. Do you want to trust a wire coupling to hold through a *Saturn V* lift-off and all that g-force and vibration? Uh-uh! Try flying a ship with a few loose wires. So, it was all solid connections, which is why we put a guillotine inside the descent stage: to cut all the wires. Everything had to be timed just right. The explosive bolts had to trigger the guillotine and the blade had to cut some pretty thick cables, and at the same time, the ascent-stage rocket engine, which was never run before, had to start.* We had a lot to think about. And the ascent engine, it was built perfectly. The irony was that it was only built to last a few minutes. But that's all it was needed for, wasn't it? That's all there was to it."

No, that was not all. There were the nightmares, and the ascent engine, indeed the whole ascent stage, provided plenty of them. Other than his wife, Joe Kingfield had told no one as yet of the images that came back to haunt him night after night:

One of the squibs didn't fire. The guillotine stuck . . .

get us out of here

. . . and the ascent stage lifted off, still connected to the descent stage by miles of wire . . . stretching . . . dragging the descent stage over the moon . . .

Get us out!

Then the ascent stage began to fall—

GET US OUT!

Years later, Joe would be unable to watch a lift-off from the moon.

---

*Lynn Radcliffe explains: "The Teflon seals and other materials in the engine were good for only forty days after exposure to live propellants, so if you test-fired it or let live propellants get anywhere near the seals, you had to do your mission within forty days or throw the engine away. *No test firings*, which means we had to make it right, make it reliable, so that when it was first fired in the vicinity of the moon, it would work. Now you know why we were chewing our nails when it came time for the actual landing. My God . . ."

*　　　*　　　*

Milt Radimer: "You know, all the astronauts I met, Armstrong and all of them, were different from the rest of us. They believed in everything. They always believed they were going to do it. There was never any hesitation in their minds about whether the ship was going to work. And, truthfully, we tried to make them feel that way when we saw them. We didn't mention our inner fears about the LM tipping over in moon dust or not being able to take off. We took them through the shop, showed them what we were doing, and told them, 'Hey, this is it. This is the best job we can do.' "

And far off in the Soviet Union, Dr. Korolev was giving his best to *Soyuz*, and to its more advanced offspring: *Zond* and the Russian LM.

The LM was a hollowed-out steel ball surrounded by tanks and legs. Its cabin was essentially a *Zond* Command Module, looking like a diving bell, with skin a half-inch thick. There was an ascent and descent stage, just as in the American LM, but the pilots did not stand like trolley motormen, looking down through triangular windows. Instead, they reclined in couches and peered out through a periscope in the cabin wall. Once on the surface, they would deploy solar panels from the descent stage, whereas the American LM had to draw its power from very costly, very heavy, and sometimes unreliable batteries. The descent stage had two engines, and the ascent-stage engine poked down between them, providing a triple-redundancy safety factor that *Apollo* did not have.

As for the lunar-mode issue, Soviet engineers had reached the same conclusion as John Houbolt and Tom Kelly. They opted for Lunar Orbit Rendezvous. However, the Russian LM and the *Zond*/*Soyuz* lunar orbiter were monstrously heavy. They could never be sent to the moon on a single rocket, so an Earth Orbit Rendezvous/Lunar Orbit Rendezvous combination was needed. First, the booster rocket that would break the ship out of Earth orbit and nudge it toward the moon was to be launched. When tests showed that it was in the right orbit and functioning properly, a second rocket would ferry the LM into orbit and place it on a parallel course alongside the booster. Then, once the LM checked out, three cosmonauts would follow in the *Zond/Soyuz*, chasing two radar blips round the world at five miles per second, catching the pieces of their moon ship.

And then the push into deep space.

23. SABOTEURS

Batteries were a black art. They had to be reliable, and nobody knew exactly how they worked. When you got a set of batteries that worked as effectively as you thought they should, they were like gold. After you loaded them onto a truck, they had to be provided with air conditioning, insulated against vibration, and protected against all sorts of other possibilities—even sabotage.

"Doc" Tripp, who was then working on America's first space telescope, recalls, "Those batteries were shepherded around, I swear, just as though it was a Brink's truck full of gold. I was aware that we were competing very strongly with the Russians, and one way to beat us, of course, was to sabotage our effort here. I don't know how many saboteurs there were on the program. I never met one, as far as I know, but apparently there were. And one of the places I remember where we got really involved with protection and security was with the batteries."

The truck carrying them had an emblem on it: concentric rings, like a target, which was exactly what American farmers liked to use it for. When the first shipment arrived in Bethpage, the sides of the truck were full of bullet holes.

Rule: *Don't send the truck out with a target on it. Make the truck as inconspicuous as possible. Make it look old. Paint it up with dirt and grease.*

Sure enough, Grumman never found bullet holes on a dirty old truck.

24. TEMPERATURES RISING

The first vehicle Harry Walther worked on was LM-3. It was little more than a frame and skin when he began, and it looked to him like the inside of a garbage can. He shook his head and said, "It will never happen, never happen."

Harry was one of those guys from QC. You know the kind: the ones with the backs like crocodiles who were always bitching about little ribbons of metal shavings and flecks of dust that got left inside the vehicle. Harry would check your every rivet against the blueprint. Always he was checking the blueprint.

As the Bethpage team's twelve-hour days stretched into fourteen-hour days, and seven-day weeks, tensions soared. *Nobody* had more than a millimeter fuse—

Don't touch those pliers, Jack. Those pliers are mine. Touch those pliers and I kill you.

People were yelling, throwing things at each other. Seeing this, Harry tried to valve off some of the pressure by forming a bowling league. He named it the Lunar League, and "come hell or high water or Russian LMs," he made sure that his people closed shop every Friday night and drove out to Woodbury Lanes, where LM-3 quality control played against the propulsion team, and propulsion against electronics, and the ascent stage against the descent stage. And, believe it or not, it relieved a great deal of pressure, which was a good thing for LM-3, because she was going to be the first to fly a manned mission, though none of her builders knew, at this time, if she would fly at all.

25. THE WORLD'S GREATEST PORSCHE LOVER

Almost everybody at the White Sands test site, and in Las Cruces, and Bethpage, and half a dozen other places, including Florida and Houston, knew that Lynn Radcliffe's Porsche was about to turn a quarter of a million miles. Lynn did not know that everybody knew, or that anybody cared.

But they did care.

You see, a quarter of a million miles is the average distance from the earth to the moon. Lynn knew this, and, of course, so did anybody else connected with the space program.

For months, the odometer had crept up from 238,000 miles to 240 . . . 242 . . . and now the big morning had come, bringing with it an excuse to throw a surprise party.

Lynn planned to go out at lunchtime and run off the last three miles, so that when the car rolled up to the gate, it would just be turning 250,000.

And, as you already know, everybody knew.

He returned to find knots of people jamming the path to his office. Then the flashbulbs went off. NASA had sent one of its official photographers to cover the event. There was a banquet and a giant banner offering congratulations, and a cake topped with a trophy and a metal caricature of Lynn standing by his Porsche, "all of this formulated by NASA," Lynn recalls. "There was much hand shaking and congratulating. The NASA photographer went outside and took pictures of the car. You would have thought I'd just gotten to the moon."

"You have," they said. "Two hundred fifty thousand miles!"

"Well," Lynn replied. "My problem now is getting back."

LM-1 and LM-2 were mounted on test stands at Bethpage. Near them was a place called the Acceptance and Checkout Equipment Room, or ACE Station. This place was connected to the LMs by a maze of wires and computers. Inside the vehicles, astronauts and consulting pilots ran their tests. They pulled levers and flipped switches to make sure that a given action would initiate the right electronic signal and send it to the right part of the ship to fire the right engine with the right amount of thrust. A few astronauts—one was Fred Haise—were practically living in the ACE Room, inching their way through something called OCP (Operational Checkout Procedure), which would eventually clear the LMs for flight.

To Dr. Shea's annoyance, the work was proceeding slowly. None of the LMs was anywhere near completion. He had hoped for LM-1 to be received in Florida by early 1967 and for an unmanned test flight only a few months later. Now the whole moon landing might be held up for lack of a lander.

By Christmas, the work was nearly finished at White Sands. Now, amid rumors that the facility would soon be closed down, von Braun, Rees, and von Puttkamer thought it was time to go out to New Mexico and take a tour, while they still had a chance.

Lynn Radcliffe got the impression, as he guided the Germans through the buildings, that they were looking down their noses at his operation. These men had designed and built booster rockets as tall as office buildings. What must they think of an attitude-control rocket that could be carried in the palm of your hand?

They were polite enough, Lynn thought, especially when they were standing under a fully fueled descent stage in the altitude chamber and Lynn noticed a little puff of white vapor. A little puff of white vapor: that's the polite way of putting it. Fuel oxidizer, when it leaks, forms a red cloud. It will burn your skin. It will destroy your eyes. It will eat your lungs. The fuel itself, when it leaks, is ten times worse. One molecule of fuel inhaled with two million parts of air will kill you, *very quickly*. And when *that* stuff leaks, it forms a white cloud.

Lynn looked up and saw fuel steaming from the bottom of the rig, and Ron Hughes, his chief test conductor, was giving a lecture about the descent stage. Lynn tried subtly, with hand signals, to stop Ron, but Ron's adrenaline was flowing. Von Braun was standing right next to him: THE Wernher von Braun. From behind von Braun's back, Lynn mouthed the words, "Ron, get out of here, *now!*"

Ron returned a puzzled glance. He hadn't read the words on Lynn's lips.

Lynn said, "Everybody out of here, *now*. We got a fuel leak," then pushed von Braun bodily through the door.

He spent the remainder of the week cringing with embarrassment. Leaks were a common problem, but Lynn knew of only one time and place that could have been worse.

And then came confirmation of a rumor: The White Sands test facility would be shut down in September of 1967.

Lynn wrote to Joe Gavin:

I am rebelling today against the possibility of closing this site. Because of the schedule, we should get to the moon. Kennedy said we will do this in the decade of the 60s. Very well, then, we're going to do it for John. But all that we have done here to date, and all that we will have done by September of 1967, will be to prove that the LM's propulsion systems (and associated interfaces) can work. We will not have shown that they will work, first time, every time. We have proven only the concept—and we cannot truly know that the ship will work without an awful lot of plain old dog work—that is, reliability testing. We need more engineers assigned down here, not fewer. We must keep right on going. As we find out new things that need to be checked, we want

*to have a team here that can do it. They say we are in a
race with the decade. This is dangerous. If we do not change
our attitude about schedule and start worrying more about
quality, we're going to lose some astronauts.*

*Yours truly,
Lynn Radcliffe*

P.S. Best wishes for the New Year.

26. FIRESPILL

Nineteen sixty-six passed. Not to be outdone by *Luna 10*,
America inserted its own satellite in lunar orbit and gave it one
of the most unimaginative names of the decade: *Lunar Orbiter 1*.

During the first week of the new year, the first Apollo commander, Gus Grissom, spoke with news reporters about the danger of his dreams: "We're in a risky business, and we hope if
anything happens to us, it will not delay the program. The conquest of space is worth the risk of life. . . . Our God-given curiosity
will force us to go there ourselves because in the final analysis
only man can fully evaluate the moon in terms understandable
to other men."

A few weeks later, on January 27, 1967, Grissom found himself
encased in the *Apollo 1* Command Module, which was itself encased in a Clean Room and service structure and connected to
an umbilical tower. Below him was the *Saturn 1-B* rocket. Beside
him were Edward White and Roger Chaffee. By 1.00 P.M. they
had begun the "plugs out" test. One by one, all external electrical
and environmental in-feeds would be pulled to determine
whether or not the spacecraft could function on internal power

alone after the umbilical tower lines dropped out and lift-off commenced. If all went well, *Apollo 1* would fly in February.

A thousand men were at work in Cape Kennedy's Launch Complex 34. Twenty-eight of them were located in the service structure. Three others, mechanical technicians James Gleaves and L. D. Reese and pad leader Donald Babbitt, were working inside the Clean Room. In *Apollo 1*, all traces of sea-level atmosphere had been purged from the three astronauts' space suits and from the cabin. Pure oxygen was substituted—a standard operating procedure. Communications problems stretched the test out to sunset. Somewhere in, or on, or around the ship was an unattended live microphone that could not be tracked down and turned off. At 6:30, Grissom sighed. He might have been thinking about the lemon he'd hung outside the spacecraft. A minute later, his voice played out from the Clean Room address system: "Hey! Fire! We've got a fire in the cockpit—Ah—Owwohwoo—"

"Get 'em out of there!" Babbitt cried.

He spun for the squawk box, his first instinct being to notify the blockhouse, to get help—not that anybody down there could be of practical assistance. *He* was in the Clean Room. It was his game now. All his.

The squawk box! Got to let them know . . .

He never reached the squawk box. From behind him came an awful concussion. He impacted against a wall and when he looked back . . .

"Get 'em out of there—"

Babbitt's face flashed out pallid white. From the spacecraft leapt sheets of actual flame.

God no! No, God! No!

He turned and ran. Gleaves followed. Then Reese.

For one terrible moment, they were all three running in the realm of dreams. In seconds they recovered and rushed back into the Clean Room, gulping noxious air, scrambling for fire extinguishers, gas masks, anything.

"Get them out—"

They clawed at the ship's hatches.

On the ground, Rocco Petrone watched a television monitor whose transmitting camera was fixed on the window of *Apollo 1*. His monitor showed a bright, searing glare inside the capsule. Behind the window, white-clad arms flailed and pounded, slowed, then fell away. "The hatch!" he called.

Blow the fucking hatch! Why don't they blow the—

He realized with horror that the hatch would not blow. Could not blow. The Apollo contract had specified a shirtsleeve environment, because astronauts in bulky gloves and helmets might not be able to operate sextants and other delicate navigational tools. If an accidental detonation of explosive bolts, such as the one that sank Grissom's *Liberty Bell* 7 in 1961, happened in space with a "naked" crew . . . So the Space Task Group designers had rejected an explosive-operated hatch in favor of a manually operated one.

It was 6:32. Babbitt, Gleaves, and Reese, joined now by two other technicians, fought the flames. Babbitt tore violently at the booster cap, feeling his fingers burn. He did not care. At last the cap gave way, and they peeled through to the outer and inner seals. It was 6:37 P.M. By now, two physicians were on their way from the blockhouse. It didn't matter. Twelve hundred miles away in Houston, flight director Christopher Kraft had been monitoring biomedical data coming cross-country from Ed White. He'd seen the rise in Ed's pulse rate, a rise that continued for fourteen seconds, then stopped abruptly.

The first man to enter the spacecraft could not see the astronauts through the smoke, but it was easy enough to feel the way they died. Too easy. Grissom and White were a heap of steaming flesh wrapped in aluminum and molten nylon. Their space suits were intertwined below the hatch. Behind them, still holding open the communication lines, lay Roger Chaffee.

George Skurla was working in his office at the Operation and Checkout Building, not far from Launch Complex 34. Two hours passed. No one walking by his door in the post-catastrophe haze had thought to step in.

A few minutes past eight o'clock, he closed his paperwork, picked up the phone, and decided to tell Marie that he was coming home. But he couldn't reach her. All the lines seemed to be out.

Stepping into the hallway, he saw a circle of people with heads hanging low. One of them had tears in his eyes.

"What gives? What's up?" he asked.

"They had a fire out on the pad."

"What! You're kidding! How about—how did the crew make out?"

"They're gone."

George heard the tapes later—the screaming—"Ah—Owwo-howoo—"

"Fire! I smell fire!"

"Fire in the cockpit!—Ah—AAH—"

"We've got a bad fire . . . We're burning up! Get us out of here . . . get us out . . . get us out . . ."

Test conductors had been sitting at consoles when the first cries came over the headsets. Three of them, including the test director, had fainted.

It was all upside down. Death in orbit was believable, and you planned strategies to avoid it. That's why you did plug-out tests and prelaunch simulations. Astronauts couldn't die in a Clean Room two hundred feet above the ground. (Could they?) No. Not in a Clean Room. Clean Rooms were safe. How could you die in a Clean Room? How could you die in an unfueled rocket? How could you die in a simulation?

Somehow, the questions had gone unasked.

They could draw some comfort from the "fact" that they'd dredged up every possibility and subjected it to their engineer's intuition, to the scrutiny of computer simulation, even to physical tests. But none of these tools could provide a guarantee against questions unasked—and the nightmares that lurked beneath them, waiting to hatch out.

waiting to hatch out.

waiting to hatch out.
waiting to—

If you'd been riding east on the Long Island Expressway, you might have noticed an MG sportscar pulled over on the shoulder of the road. Inside, Milt Radimer listened to the passing traffic, the tears running free. A year earlier, he had come to know and admire Roger Chaffee:

"He told me how since he was a kid he was always interested in exploration and getting to the moon. That's what he said his purpose in life was, and he wanted to meet the people who were building the vehicle for him. I said, 'You're kidding. We have a couple thousand of them here at Plant 2. We're building the whole descent stage out there, and all of the components—a lot of components and parts and everything.' He said, 'I want to meet them all.' And he was sincere about it. And we took him through the plant. We showed him the descent stage first. I introduced him to Bob Ekenstierna, who was a supervisor, and Eky explained everything to him. This fellow was listening to everything, taking it all in. He was looking at every rivet, every part of the descent stage. And everyone in the department lined up and he wanted to shake their hands. And he did. He told each one of them, 'You know, your job is so important to me, and to an awful lot of other people. There's no gas station on the way, no place where I can pull over, like you can in a car.' He told one man, 'If this line fails'—and the man is bending the line on a machine—'you know, I have no way of getting this fixed. When you're making this, you gotta make it the best you can.'

"Roger actually changed everybody's mode of thinking. It wasn't just a piece of metal anymore. It was Roger Chaffee. He just impressed the hell out of everybody. Even the secretaries flipped over him—especially the secretaries. Then I looked over Roger's shoulder and there's a bunch of fellows over there building a fixture. Now, everybody forgets them. Nobody ever thinks of the tool-and-die people. It's there; the tool is there. We build it, and there's the unit. The tool is forgotten. It never goes anywhere—not into space, at least. It doesn't mean a thing, but without it you don't do anything. And it's got to be exact, and these fellows do precision work. And I said to Roger, 'Would you like to meet the follows who build the tools that build the space-craft?' So, he said, 'Sure. I'd love to.' He was just that way. He talked with everybody. It seemed like he had forever."

27. AFTERMATH

An editorial cartoon in the Los Angeles *Times* showed the specter of death holding a *Mercury* capsule in one hand, a *Gemini* in the other. In the background, a pall of smoke hovered over *Apollo 1*. Death said, "I thought you knew. I've been aboard on every flight."

"Unbelievable," Senator Walter Mondale said. He had, from the start, regarded the American space effort with utter contempt, arguing that money spent by NASA would be better spent here on Earth. His contempt was now fueled by an inch-thick stack of photos. One of them showed a wrench embedded in the wiring of *Apollo 1*. Others showed the innards of Command Module number 014, which had been dismantled for a comparison with *Apollo 1*—what was left of it. Wires were tangled and nicked. You could see the exposed copper, everywhere, like an awful night-mare waiting to come true.

"Unbelievable," he said again. "Absolutely unbelievable."

Joseph Shea, whose gift of overview had been vital to the inception of Apollo, was now driving the Command Module pro-gram apparently with such force that meeting schedules had taken priority above quality control.

Armed with such phrases as "criminal negligence" and "skele-tons in NASA's closet," Senator Mondale began his headlong charge with the ever popular cry "Whitewash." But whitewash was the furthest thing from the minds of NASA and Rockwell managers, as Mondale could have easily guessed from the fact that he now possessed incriminating photographs that had begun circulating within twenty hours of the firespill.

"Stop the witch hunt and get on with Apollo," astronaut Frank Borman called out, amid an accelerating chain reaction of accusations and firings. "We at NASA are trying to tell you that we are confident in our management. We are confident in our training, and in our engineering and in ourselves. I think the question is really, Are you confident in us?"

The question was really, How did men allow delivery dates to become more important than perfection? Every Command Module builder knew that it was imperative—*imperative*—that spacecraft were to arrive in Florida like shotgun shells: no repairs necessary, and ready for loading. No one in the Rockwell hierarchy had challenged Joseph Shea. No one had told him, "No way! We're not stampeding to get ships out simply to make a schedule. *So you just wait. You just wait right—*"

—there, right there—

Dr. Shea was up north, in Bethpage. He was addressing the LM team. He knew that he would soon (very soon) be leaving the space program, especially if Senator Mondale had any voice in the matter. "Hey, look," he began. "We had a problem. These things happen. But we're going to go forward. Nobody feels worse than I do." And Joseph Shea, who had planned on joining Grissom, White, and Chaffee for the test, lit a match, and then, seeming to forget it, continued talking. Nobody remembers what he said. Nobody heard. They saw before them a broken man, truly broken, holding a lighted matchstick.

They watched it burn.

In Florida, one of the quality-control inspectors for *Apollo 1* drove his car in front of a train, killing himself and his entire family.

*   *   *

In Washington, President Johnson knew now that there would be no moon landing by the end of his term—not by an American spaceship, at least. And there was the escalating "police action" in Vietnam, and an unpopular tax increase to finance it, and the birth cries of public resistance—and those *Beatles*. Yeah, yeah, those *Beatles*. Suddenly, everybody was beginning to look like them . . . and sound like them.

In New Mexico, Lynn Radcliffe received word that the White Sands test facility would be kept open—indefinitely. But Tom Kelly wanted him back on Long Island by July, to help put the spacecraft through tests before delivering it to the Cape.

In Bethpage, "As above, so below" became the phrase of the day. What happened to the Command Module could also happen to the Lunar Module. Tom Kelly initiated a review of flammable materials in LM. Joseph Shea's new replacement, George Low, sent materials experts to assist. They learned, just for a start, that nylon cloth would have to be replaced by some inorganic fiber that could not ignite or produce toxic fumes. The people at Corning Glass had just what was needed: something called Beta fiber. One of its most important uses would be as "booties," or firebreaks around circuit breakers.

The forward hatch was the next concern. It would be redesigned to guarantee a crew exit, during ground tests, in no more than ten seconds.

And LM would fall another four months behind schedule, in addition to the schedule delays that had become a worry even before *Apollo 1*.

Meanwhile, *Soyuz 1* took the sky.

28. THE FALLING STAR

On April 22, the Soviet press announced that *Soyuz 1* would fly within forty-eight hours. *Soyuz 2* would follow a day later. The mission was heralded as "the most spectacular space venture in history: an attempted in-flight hookup between two ships and a transfer of crews." It was to be a dress rehearsal for the Earth Orbit Rendezvous phase of lunar landings.

Colonel Vladimar Komarov was the sole occupant of the three-man *Soyuz 1*. Having commanded *Voskhod 1*, he was the first cosmonaut to fly twice in space. At age forty, he was also the oldest.

Toward the end of his first full day in orbit, it became clear that one of the solar panels had failed, and a problem with the attitude-control rockets had left the entire thirty-five-foot length of *Soyuz 1* tumbling slowly end over end, like a baton thrown round the world.

Instructions were radioed up, but, "I can't stop the spin," Komarov said. "I'm doing what you say. It still isn't working."

The *Soyuz 2* launch was scrubbed.

"It still isn't working! Stabilizing fuel almost used up—"

The ship windmilled along its orbit at thirty revolutions per minute. There was gravity inside, a centrifugal force that caused pens and other objects to fall toward the ceiling.

"Stabilizing fuel now exhausted. Please, give me a countdown to reentry. Get me out of here . . . get me out . . ."

"Will do, *Soyuz 1*. Will try to bring you back on the seventeenth orbit."

But Komarov was unable to align the *Soyuz* for the braking

maneuver, and the ship went around the Earth again, then dove into the atmosphere over central Russia, glowing cherry red against a solid wall of air—at twice the reentry speed for which it was designed. In his couch, Komarov's weight soared to 1,700 pounds, and he feared for a moment that he might become a carbonaceous meteor in the Nizmennost skies. And then the g-forces abated, and he was falling . . . falling . . . falling . . .

"*The parachute is wrong!*"

From ten miles up.

"Parachute . . . para . . . para . . ."

It was all curled and torn behind him. Through the window he glimpsed forests and wheat fields coming up fast. The wheat fields . . . they looked so close . . . so close that he could almost reach out and t—

At an American listening post in Turkey, a National Security Agency employee heard the *Soyuz* signals drop off at more than five hundred miles per hour. A Russian voice came on: "It's all over."

"Was he still spinning during reentry?" another asked.

"Was he able to jettison the Service and Orbital Modules correctly?"

"There's a crater."

A half dozen other Russian voices interrupted, all of them intent on the failure and its possible causes. They were in shock, and from shock they spoke. The American put down his headset. "Callous bastards," he whispered, then went outside and got a beer, and looked at the sky.

Now the Soviets, too, would have to step back and reevaluate, but few could draw much pleasure from a "rebalanced" space race. Indeed, NASA administrator James Webb took the occasion to ask, "Could the lives already lost have been spared if we had known each other's hopes, aspirations, and plans? Or could they have been saved if full cooperation had been the order of the day?"

29. PARALYSIS AND RECOVERY

They built a full-size LM simulator, completely fitted and rigged with control consoles and astronaut restraints. They pumped it full of oxygen. Then they started fires, and filmed the deadly flare-ups, and studied the films. They built firebreaks and fireproofing into the simulator, and tried again to burn it up.

LM program manager Joe Gavin: "We had to campaign all the electrical systems in the cabin. We devised ways of coating the back of the switch panels and covering wires. And we ran tests where we deliberately overloaded the systems to see if we could start a fire. We ran thousands of tests on materials to see how they burned, and we learned that some things that did not burn in a normal atmosphere flared right up in a pure-oxygen environment, including flesh. I guess, initially, not enough attention was given to the fact that an oxygen atmosphere was different from the air we are presently breathing, and, of course, the fire at the Cape was a terribly dramatic indicator. That led to a redesign of both the Command Module and the Lunar Module, which set the program back at least a year. I would also say that our final success might have owed more to that tragedy than most people realize. We weren't just looking for fire hazards. We went back and looked at every single system."

"Ever heard of overkill?" Doc Tripp asks. "We had a lot of unexplained things, which normally you would let go, on the chance that it was all right. But in *this* program, if anything came up that we didn't understand fully, or if it didn't work exactly the way we thought it should work, it was immediately subject to an investigation—"

Gavin's Law: *There's no such thing as a random failure.*

"—a detailed investigation. Schedules were affected, of course, every time we ran into one of these unknowns."

Questions unasked . . . waiting to hatch out.

waiting to—

"We had cracks in the metal, due to—we weren't sure what they were due to. I remember we got into bigger and bigger microscopes, until finally we were scanning the ship's skins with electron beams. And the more we magnified the cracks, the more questions we came up with, many of which couldn't be answered because we were looking at things people had never seen before. Under an electron microscope, a little crack became a—it was like flying over the Grand Canyon in an airplane: You could look in the bottom of the canyon and see giant aluminum boulders. There got to be a point where I asked, 'Where do we stop with this scientific approach of trying to explain everything down to microscopic detail and get on with the program?' because we had tools that were being used essentially for the first time; and we really didn't know how to interpret what we were seeing with the tools."

Tom Kelly: "*Apollo 1* really caused us to go back almost to the beginning and reexamine every fine detail. Incidentally, that is the time period in which the common sense of Bob Gilruth and Max Faget really came to the rescue. Some of the NASA and Grumman people got so afraid of mistakes that they were unwilling to move froward, but Gilruth and Faget agreed: 'Yes, we have to be as safe as we know how to be, but we can't be so terrified of doing anything that we fail to move the program to a conclusion.' "

The caution system and warning lights in LM-1 were, if you will pardon the understatement, very complex, which made it easy to trigger a false warning. If you did everything in the prescribed sequence, no warning lights came on. However, if a situation demanded that some of your steps be executed out of sequence, the whole board could light up, even though all your equipment was operating perfectly.

At a design-review meeting, one of the ACE room operators, frustrated nearly to tears, explained, "It's all wrong. We get warnings as soon as we turn the ship on. We're going to have to change all the wires."

Dr. Gilruth broke in. "Look. Do you own an automobile?"

"Yes."

"When you first turn the key, before you start the engine, don't you see warning lights that really don't mean anything?"

"Yes."

"They tell you the generator isn't charging because the engine isn't running, but you *know* the engine isn't running, so you don't worry about it. You go ahead and start the engine and the light goes out, right? Well, it's the same problem here. If you do these steps out of sequence, you're going to get a false warning light, and as long as you know about it in advance, you should be able to say, 'Okay, I know and understand that, and I'm not worried about it.' And then you wait for the light to go out."

Saved the day, thought Tom Kelly—saved us a whole lot of days, I reckon. This is how it has to be. We have to have confidence that our men can make the ship work. That *we* can make it work. The old rider's cliché holds true: When you're cantering toward a fence, you have to believe you can jump it, because the horse can tell, being an empathic creature itself, just what you're feeling, and if you're afraid, it will decide there's something to be afraid of. You've got to throw your heart over the fence, and the horse will follow it.

30. TOMMY OUTRAGE

He was the first man in history to fly into his own bullets and shoot himself down. That was in 1954, during the F-11–F1 days. The test called for firing a complete load of twenty-millimeter bullets in two bursts at low altitude and supersonic speed. In thick air, near sea level, the only way Tommy Attridge could get his plane up to supersonic speed was to put it in a slight dive: a dangerous maneuver. "But, what the hell?" one of his supervisors said. "Test pilots certainly get paid enough for it."

Tommy accelerated at seven eighths of a gravity during the dive. Descending on the Atlantic from eighteen thousand feet, he fired a five-second burst, followed by a five-second cooling period, and another five-second burst. Then he pulled up and leveled off at eight thousand feet, but air friction had slowed and scattered bullets, putting a stream of them in his way. One went into his windshield. One went in the engine, one in the nose, one in the left air duct. He winged north over Long Island's Peconic Bay, thinking himself very lucky to be still taking in air and flying a plane that seemed to be operating—at reduced power but operating nevertheless . . . until he put the flaps down. That's when *the bitch* took the bullet that was lodged in the air duct, where it had lain in wait like a blood clot on a lung, and sucked it back into the turbine—into her heart—where it could do the most harm. Suddenly the turbine sounded like a Hoover vacuum cleaner picking up rocks, and the plane just died in the sky and Tommy guided the corpse as gently as he could into the scrub oak of South Peconic. A wing tore off. So did the horizontal stabilizer and the nose cone and the whole right side of the fuselage. Tommy broke a leg and four vertebrae. To his right was open air, and trees that looked like mowed grass—and smoke.

The search team found him two hundred feet away. "Why did you walk away from it?" they asked.

"Because I had four thousand pounds of fuel burning about eight feet behind me, and that motivates you quite a bit."

Thirteen years passed, and Tommy was about to fly a new reconnaissance plane in California when Grumman president Lew Evans called and ordered, "Forget it. You've just been assigned to the LM program."

Whahell? he thought.

He called his friend Howard Wright, who shared Tom Kelly's office and was the grand designer of LM's electrical systems. "What's this all about, Howard?"

"Well, it appears that as we approach flying the LM, the engineers are starting to get cold feet. I think the fire at the Cape has got them spooked."

Tommy leaned forward. "Go on."

"All right. What we need is some people with flight experience, and your name was one of the heavies that was brought up as a vehicle director for the LM program."

"That's neat," Tommy said. "Now, what does a vehicle director do?"

"Well, you'll have to get the details from Lew Evans on Monday, when you get here. The short of it is that our people are having second guesses about what they've designed, and we need someone to step in who has faced, if you will, life-and-death decisions. We want you to tell us if the ship is safe. Can it do the job? Or do we have to redesign and delay to make it better?"

"But you've got astronauts out there. Astronauts are test pilots, aren't they? Didn't Neil Armstrong come out of the X-15 program?"

"Yes, but—"

"But the astronauts!" Tommy recalls today. "When I got to Bethpage, we sat and talked all night about achieving the mission and getting back from it. That's the bottom line in any test flight. But the astronauts had a problem. They wanted to be aloof from the engineering details."

"You're crazy," Tommy protested. "That's part of any test pilot's job. You're supposed to be engineers."

Jim McDivitt, Rusty Schweickart, Alan Bean, and Pete Conrad stood together. "We're not test pilots anymore, stop calling us that. We're astronauts."

Tommy could not believe what he was hearing. These men knew what their job required, but as far as they were concerned, it was up to everybody else to do their work. It was a 180-degree turnaround from the way they had operated in the past. And they got their way, most of them. At a flight-readiness review meeting, Frank Borman announced, "I don't think you guys realize your responsibility."

"What's your problem, Frank?" Tommy asked.

Frank smiled. "Oh, we don't have a problem. We don't *have* to get involved in the details. That's somebody else's problem. And, damn it, Grumman had better make sure the ship works."

Tommy Attridge: "It was as simple as that. Frank rewrote the whole scenario so that he didn't get involved with LM at all. He just went around the moon one Christmas Eve and sang Christmas carols to us and, you know, became a hero. That was Frank's way of really not taking big risks.

"There were exceptions to the Borman mold, of course. Fred Haise was one. Ed Mitchell was another. But some of the astronauts were more harm than good. In checking out LM-3, Jim McDivitt and Rusty Schweickart went in and did everything to perfection. Everything fit perfectly. Everything worked. Then Pete Conrad and Alan Bean climbed in and destroyed the vehicle that had already gone through the same tests with two other astronauts. They dented the floor. They ripped a piece of equipment out of the bulkhead. They demonstrated their ability to burn out a TV camera on the moon, which they would manage to do when they flew *Apollo 12*."

And so Tommy went to work on the question, "Must we build

it better?" And he learned very quickly that when you're dealing with Lunar Modules, better is the enemy of best.

"We have the best radar in the world today," the man from RCA explained. "But tomorrow I can make it better because just yesterday they invented this new transistor, and if I put the new transistor in here and couple it with this new diode and add this integrated circuit—you know, we didn't have integrated circuits when General Electric built your present system . . ." He trailed off, noticing Tommy's frown.

"Go on."

"Now that we have integrated circuits, we can build it better. So, what do you say?"

"Sure. Why not? We can keep putting a better one in every day. Let's see if we can't stretch this thing out till 1990."

After Tommy had (quite diplomatically) thrown him out of his office, the RCA man went on to the next-highest authority.

"They were scared to death," Tommy concludes. "I don't remember the name of the guy—and I'm glad I don't—who refused to let General Electric's rendezvous radar into space, but he did refuse. He swore on a stack of Bibles that it was no longer any good."

No longer any good—in spite of the fact that it had been tested in a vacuum, with no problems at all. But the new radar was better. Even if it did have a tendency to get confused by its own signal and to lock up on itself. Even if it was, as a result, absolutely useless. Even if attempts to correct the problem were to cause such delays that *Apollo 8*, planned as an Earth-orbital mission with men flying in LM-3, would have to fly without a LM.

The fuel tanks that would go into LM-3's descent stage were being pumped up to three times the pressure they would have to hold in space. If they passed this test, then surely they would hold up during the actual mission. From an adjoining room, protected by explosion blankets, Tommy Attridge watched. The first leak showed up almost two days into the test. The test stopped.

"Look," Tommy said. "The chances are that only one little valve has to be tightened."

"We'll have to depressurize the tanks," the test director said firmly.

"You can't. To do that will take thirty-six hours, then about thirty-six hours to bring them back up to pressure. *Three days*, man, just to come back to where we are now. I can't afford it. Just give me the wrench and I'll go in there and tighten it up."

"Don't joke. It's silly and it's dangerous."

"It is not."

"Is too. You can't do that."

"Who the hell says I can't? I'm gonna walk in there. It's my life. Don't tell me. I'm gonna walk in there and I'm gonna give it a little turn with the wrench and see whether or not the leak goes away."

"You think so," the test director said, still looking at the dials. The pressure dropped almost imperceptibly, like the minute hand on a clock. "I'm calling Tom Kelly."

Within minutes, the word had gone all the way up to Lew Evans, who immediately called a meeting.

"What the hell is this all about?" Tom Kelly said. "You're an idiot, Attridge."

"What do you mean?"

"You're gonna go into the room with the pressurized tanks and try to tighten up a fitting?"

"Certainly."

"Just suppose it blows?"

"So, you wipe me out."

A wry grin came over Tom Kelly's face, as he considered and rejected a dozen comebacks.

An engineer named E. Z. Gray said gently, "Guys, suppose the tank had ten pounds per square inch instead of one hundred?"

"There wouldn't be a problem," Lew Evans answered.

"Suppose it had fifty? That would be okay, right?"

"Yes."

"Suppose it had ninety?"

"Well . . . oh, shit. Go ahead and do it."

Tommy Attridge: "All it needed was a one-eighth turn of the wrench. Doing it the other way would have been a long, arduous procedure. And then, if we'd gone thirty-six hours back down to normal pressure and thirty-six hours back up, only to learn that we hadn't tightened the connection quite enough, then another three days—this was just typical of what went on. Everything was ultra, ultra conservative; and, well, there are times when we've got to take certain risks, or we never get off the ground. I mean, the exploration of space is by its very nature a very dangerous game."

31. HEROES

Heroism, or recognition for heroic deeds, is an elusive thing. Perhaps, it is at bottom a matter of who has the best press agent. President James Monroe was not the architect of the 1823 Monroe Doctrine (it was framed by John Quincy Adams). Charles Darwin did not originate the "theory of evolution" (several others, including the Greeks, had beaten him to it). Albert Einstein was not the first man to sense and describe relativity (actually, he got the idea, in part, from H. G. Wells's 1901 science fiction novel, *The First Men in the Moon*). The Wright brothers were not the first to fly in a powered aircraft (a New Zealander, a Russian, a Frenchman, and a Briton had gone before them). And Grissom, White, and Chaffee were not the first, nor the last, to die for Apollo.

In a "space-simulation experiment" after the firespill in spacecraft number 012, two men in a similar oxygen-filled chamber were drawing blood samples from rabbits when a spark ballooned into a roaring hellfire. Ironically, the tragedy occurred during memorial services for the *Apollo 1* crew, on January 30, 1967.

Elsewhere, a spring-loaded LM leg unfolded prematurely, and a technician fell to the floor with his head caved in.* Other times, Apollo killed subtly.

Tom Kelly: "There were three of us running the LM assembly and test operation. I was in charge, and I had two assistants: Howard Wright and Lynn Radcliffe. Throughout the month of June 1967, we were trying to make sense of this whole mess— and it *was* a mess at that point. We were leaning very heavily on some of our engineers and test conductors and test directors. I mean, we were really pushing them. We were giving them deadlines and we wouldn't take any excuses and, you know. . . . Well, one day one of the fellows we were leaning on very hard collapsed right on the job."

"What the hell are we doing here?" Lynn Radcliffe said. "We don't know anything about these people. We don't know what their physical condition is. We don't know what personal pressures they are under. And still we're pushing them and pushing them, and sometimes they break."

"You're right," Tom Kelly conceded. "Absolutely right."

"Yes. And we haven't given them any leadership training. We've got people who've been suddenly elevated from being an engineer to being in charge of these complex tests with thirty or forty men working under them, and we haven't given them any training. We haven't given them any help. All we are doing is beating on them, watching them grow prematurely old before our very eyes from week to week. What the hell is the matter with us?"

Lynn fell silent and they sat together over cups of coffee without talking. A chill of gooseflesh passed over Tom. Then Lynn said, "We'll have to fix it soon. You know that, don't you?"

"Yeah." Tom drained his cup. "Soon."

More than five hundred people were assembling and testing the Lunar Modules. Lynn, Tom, and Howard Wright geared up

---

*February 1967.

the Grumman medical department for a massive physical checkup and threw psychological counseling into the bargain.

"You wouldn't believe the problems that some of these men had hanging over their heads at home," Tom Kelly says. "There were drinking problems, families deteriorating, depression bordering on suicide. We hadn't known anything about this. We were just cracking the whip over their backs, right? So, thanks to Lynn and the medical department, we ran these five or six hundred people through a very thorough program. It took about two months, and we were able to identify the ones with really serious problems—the ones who just shouldn't be in a high-pressure environment—and ease them into lighter work away from the LM. We were also able to give assurance to other people. A few were afraid, for example, that they had medical problems, but they simply didn't have time to go to a doctor because of the hours we were demanding.

"Another thing we did was institute a special course in management training. It was a two-week program for those people who had been elevated into supervisory positions without any real preparation. We had thrown them in to sink or swim, and some of them were already drowning. We wanted everybody to succeed, so we rented a Holiday Inn and conference rooms and got them off to management school and rest for two weeks.

"The biggest thing that came out of all this was not exactly what we accomplished by these medical and education programs but the fact that suddenly the people working for us realized that somebody cared about them, that we weren't just beating them over the head relentlessly. The result was a terrific *esprit de corps*. The whole operation, over the course of a few months, really started to click. And we were able to put these vehicles together and test them in a much shorter period. I remember one night, some of the red tape got knotted up, and it turned out that we wouldn't be able to pay one of the crews for the overtime they'd have to put in that night. They were in the middle of a very critical test, too: one of the kind where you had to run straight through the night or stop in the middle and start the whole thing over again. We were going to lose about a shift and a half worth of work. So we told them, 'Look, we screwed up on the paperwork and it looks like we're gonna have to stop because we might not be able to pay you. Something to do with government regulations.' And they said, 'Hey! No way! We're not stopping. We don't care if it's for no pay. We're going to finish this thing up and that will be that, okay?' "

"I'm talking about dedication," says George Skurla.

"Apollo left a lot of human wreckage in its wake. A lot of human wreckage. Cocoa Beach had the highest divorce rate in the country. The guys were so fascinated, especially the younger ones—so totally committed—it was an intoxicating thing. I lived and breathed it. Every night, before I went to bed, I'd call the checkout room: 'What's the latest status?' Then I'd go to sleep, wake up at five A.M., call the checkout room right away: 'What's going on? What happened while I was sleeping?' Eat. Jump in the car. And that went on and on. After a while, you start to look like something out of *Night of the Living Dead*. Joe Gavin looked like the walking dead. I looked like the walking dead. Circles under our eyes. Concern. And Larry Moran was on a hospital bed saying, 'I gotta go. I gotta go. I gotta make the schedule up.' He died. John Coursen, who headed the ground-support equipment, was in here one Saturday—the last day his son was home before they were shipping him to Vietnam.

"Talk about dedication. Talk about being emotionally involved. We were. *We were.* I know personally. I fell down. They put me in bed for two weeks. I didn't know what I was doing. It took me a month to get squared away, and I was completely exhausted, burned out. That job down there, it was nerve-racking. Just put yourself in a job like that, with that kind of responsibility."

Some men—Jesco von Puttkamer was one—thrived on the responsibility and the long hours.

"I used to dream about the future and about what could be, and I have spent my life trying to make it all true. And science fiction has brought me along. It was long hours during Apollo, and, for me, it's been long hours ever since. But it's not work. It's a hobby. How often can you have that in life? Who is so fortunate that he can turn a hobby into a job? It's fun. I'm having a *hell* of a good time. But I'm living it twenty-four hours a day, so I don't have children. I have a wife and no children, and she of course comes only *after* space. You know, space is number one, and that is an unfortunate thing if you have a family. In von Braun's case it was even worse. He had children—two daughters and a son—but his family didn't see much of him because of his involvement in space. He also lived space twenty-four hours a day, and Saturdays, and Sundays, and holidays—even when he went on vacation."

As you read this, two of those "eight balls" that once brought frustration into Arnold Whitaker's life are orbiting the moon inside the *Apollo 11* ascent stage. They were assembled by a woman named Myrtice Holland, whom Grumman had "borrowed" from Martin Marietta in 1966:

"At first, women weren't permitted to work overtime. It was a New York State law. But NASA-certified solderers were scarce, and I was one of the few, and the law had to be changed. If it wasn't, Grumman wouldn't have been able to hire women into the LM program. They weren't too keen on hiring us anyway, in the beginning. They told us they hadn't had women assembling vehicles since World War II—with the single exception of Peggy Hewitt. But I think it was the wisest decision they ever made: to hire us girls back in here, because we're very good at what we do. We tend to have very small hands—very good for intricate wiring—and you find that a lot of men's hands are very big and awkward, as far as getting into small places is concerned. And we have a lot more patience than men do for this kind of work. That's my feeling, in most cases. Men get frustrated with little wires; for me, it's a relaxation. I guess women are just born with that attitude because to raise children you need patience and a predisposition for tedious work.

"So they hired me and one other NASA-certified girl. And

the hours did get long, but I enjoyed that, because I had it easy at home. I had my mother living with me, and she would take care of the house. My daughter was in her teens and her grandmother was there with her. Plus the money was good.

"The only pressure that I really felt was the fright of making a mistake. There were no serious consequences for a mistake, except for your own bad feelings. Everything was tracked so closely that if a piece of equipment failed somewhere down the line, you knew it was your mistake, because your badge number was used to stamp off every piece of work you did. If you blew it, you knew you blew it, and you never made that mistake again. You knew that it had to be right. You double-checked yourself over and over. When you picked up a wire, you looked at the wire number; you made sure it was in good condition and that it was the right wire before you put it in that panel. Even though, when you routed wires to a meter, there was always redundant wiring to take up the signal, even though the equipment would be tested afterward, you still watched closely. And then you had a NASA inspector who inspected every solder connection you made. They didn't do just a little check with the eye; they did it with a ten-power magnifying glass.

"I built the panels and then they went into test, and if there was any type of problem with a component failure, well, then, I and a few others went down to rework them. And all of this was done with gloves on, which took some getting used to. Imagine tying your shoes with gloves on. Then imagine picking a thin wire out of a bunch of similar wires and routing it to the right place."

Myrtice Holland left a very strong impression on George Skurla's assistant at the Cape, Bill Voorhest. One year, as he toured the buildings where LM's electronic equipment was being wired together, a Christmas party was in progress. He came across Myrtice, working alone on a job that simply *had* to go out—out to the moon. If you tour Plant 44 today and you find her and you tell her that her badge number, 086624, is circling the moon, you will bring tears to her eyes.

"I don't think I have ever worked on, nor will I ever be as lucky to work on, a program such as the Lunar Module," says Bill Voorhest. "I've been with Grumman for forty-two years. I've worked on every major program. I never worked on a program that was so all-encompassing, that required total, *total* concentration constantly for such a long period of time. You would work on an airplane program and you'd have maybe ten months of day and night work, whereas the LM—that thing went into years of exhausting days. I saw marriages crack up. I saw people have heart attacks and die right on the shop floor. I saw people become ill because they were absolutely dedicated. Imagine not having Sunday dinner with your family once in two years. Imagine what must have driven one of my electronics managers, a man named Dick McGlauglin. I used to worry about him. He'd never go home. He was so wrapped up in this machine that he just couldn't let go. I threw him out once. I said, 'You gotta go home.' I went away and an hour later he was back again."

Another of George Skurla's assistants, Bob Watkins, recalls, "Sometimes the pressure got funny. Very often, we had to have a part, and we had to have it *now*. One Friday night, Tom Carmody, who ran our purchasing department, called a vendor in Chicago, and the vendor told him that there was no way he was going to work over the weekend. He was closing the plant down and that was the end of it. Then another fellow walked into the room, and Tom said, 'Ah! Here comes George Skurla, our base manager. I'm going to put him on the phone and he'll tell you how important it is.' And to do him credit, he presented himself so convincingly as George Skurla—'*Where the hell is your national pride, fella?*'—he got the Chicago factory to stay open straight through the weekend.

"I came into work the next morning, only to be greeted by this story. And, wouldn't you know it, the man who ran the factory was so impressed by 'George' that he wanted to fly to the Cape so he could personally hand the part to him. I told the story to George, and he was a little upset about people using his name falsely, but he did recognize that the need was legitimate. So we brought him up to speed on what the part was, and what he had said to the owner of the company. The guy came in the following day and George greeted him profusely and bought him a cup of coffee and pounded him on the back, telling him how he'd just saved the whole space program."

"Stay away from LM," Al Beauregard's friends warned him. "The LM program is real bad news. Long hours. Picky NASA people. Stay in flight test. You'll be a lot happier."

No, thanks, Beauregard thought. No LMs for me. No way. Not me. I'll sit that one out, thank you very much.

Then the phone rang. "Hello, Beauregard. You're on LM as of tomorrow. You're now spacecraft director of LM-5, and your new bosses are E. Z. Gray and Ross Fleisig."

"But . . . but . . . but . . ."

"It had a dramatic effect on our personal lives," says Joe King-field. "It took an awful long time for wives to realize that they had lost their husbands until we got onto the moon. It was hard, too, on the kids. One day I woke up knowing that there were things that you would be doing normally with your children while they were growing up. And I was missing those things.

"I missed my kids' growing up."

32. THE LITTLE BOY WHO TALKED TO SPACEMEN

Jack Swigert and Ronald Evans had spent the night at George Titterton's son's home, which is why his daughter-in-law, Myleen, received an afternoon phone call from a somewhat annoyed first-grade teacher.

"I had to discipline George during show-and-tell today," the teacher said.

"What for?"

"He stood up and told the class he had breakfast with two astronauts this morning."

"And?"

"I told him to sit down, and he was very insistent. I think you'll have to do something with him. He could be having . . . you know, problems."

The teacher began to elaborate. Myleen listened for a while, until the word "hallucination" crept into the monologue. Then she interrupted. "Oh, no. You've got it all wrong. George *did* have breakfast with two astronauts. And so did I."

The phone got very quiet.

33. MOVING TOWARD OPERATIONS

Artie Falbush and John Logalbo were busy inventing new ways of brazing and repairing fuel lines. Now, content with their methods, Artie flew to White Sands to try his luck on a test vehicle fully loaded with fuel and oxidizer. He wanted to know if they could change components, reconnect pipes, and seal leaks should an emergency arise one or two days before a launch. The repair technique was called "induction brazing." Microwaves were passed through solid-gold rings, which melted and formed a seal. They chose gold because it did not corrode, and LM's fuel oxidizer was one of the most corrosive substances on Earth.

The thought of a man shooting microwaves through a rig full of live propellants made Lynn Radcliffe's replacement understandably nervous. He sent a safety officer down to accompany Artie.

"No sweat," Artie said. "I'm just gonna run a radio-frequency current through here, heat the ring up, and melt the gold. If the rig doesn't blow within the next fifteen seconds, we're home free."

"I'll tell you what," the safety man said. "I'm gonna stay here. I'm gonna stand right next to you. Because if this thing blows, I don't want to be around here tomorrow to answer any questions."

There were no questions to answer.

It worked beautifully.

"Let me tell you something," says George Skurla. "Those two guys were truly supercraftsmen. When they made a connection or sealed a joint, it was as good as gold—literally. Artie and John developed these techniques using something called 'double-O rings,' and there would come a time when I'd be sending them all around the country to fix leaks and change pipes. And those guys knew me, because I used to be right with them. We had a wonderful relationship, the three of us . . ."

"I'm gonna kill the next person who sticks his nose in here!" Artie snapped.

"Hold your tongue and get to work," John said.

"Get to work? How? We've got so much interference here. I'm trying to get something done and all these people are butting in, and they don't know what they're doing. They don't know the first thing about these new techniques, *but everybody has to be a big shot.* I tell you, John, I'm gonna kill the next son of a bitch who walks in here."

George Skurla walked through the door and said, "Hi!" For a moment he was puzzled by the tension on their faces. Especially Artie. He looked as if he . . . really wanted to kill somebody.

"Hi," John said, but Artie turned his back to George and began agitatedly clamping two pipes together.

"How's it going?" George asked.

"Well, you want this LM built," John began. "How are we going to build it when everybody is in our way? NASA is the biggest offender. We've got quality-control man named Baby who'll be going out of here in a box if I see his face again—"

"Baby! I'll kill Baby!" A stainless-steel pipe shot across the floor.

"Artie!" John shouted. "Go take a walk. Get out of here."

"Son of a bitch!"

"Artie, you shut up!"

Artie left, muttering George's name, and a string of words (nice words).

John saw a flash of anger in George's eyes. "What did he say?"

"For you to get outta here. Get outta here. Get lost."

Being the boss, George had a number of possible responses, one of which included firing. But he did as he was told and got lost, then passed the word. From then on, everybody, including Baby, kept his distance and let Artie and John conduct their experiments with relative impunity.

Meanwhile, the Cape geared up for the flight of *Apollo 4.*

The highest point in the state of Florida is 525 feet. It is called the VAB, which stands for Vehicle Assembly Building. In terms of volume, it is to this day the world's largest man-made structure. (Except, perhaps, for the volume of rock and earth and human bone contained in the Great Wall of China, which, incidentally, is the last man-made structure that can be seen by unaided eyes heading into deep space. For those who enjoy trivia, the last visible structure built by any living *thing* is Australia's Great Barrier Reef.)

In June of 1967, the first, second, and third stages of the world's first *Saturn V* were being stacked inside the VAB. A maze or towers and catwalks surrounded them. A technician named Kupzyk was there, awaiting delivery of the first LM. From atop the service towers, trucks on the floor looked to him like toys in a five-and-dime store. It gave him a queasy feeling. The first time he walked to the rocket, he inched across spread-eagled and white-knuckled. Thirty feet out into the breeze, he felt the catwalk bounce up and down. Kupzyk tightened his grip, and began a very short prayer: "Oh, God! Let me get out of this alive." And then the laughter erupted behind him. It was a trick they liked to play on all the Cape Kennedy rookies: jiggle the catwalk and watch them die of fright. But what happened next was no trick. The VAB enclosed such a large volume of air that it actually arranged its own weather. Clouds had formed two hundred feet above Kupzyk's head, and presently, as the sun blazed outside, Kupzyk was caught in a brief, gentle shower. He found it both confusing and refreshing.

LM-1 would be here soon. Oh, yes, soon. It would go directly to the LM checkout area, where Peggy Hewitt had been testing test equipment for more than a year and honing her team's methods down to a fine art on a phony LM. If LM-1 passed Peggy's tests (and, oh, what a big if), it would be pushed up into a hollow cone built by McDonnell-Douglas—right underneath the Command and Service Modules. This assembly would then be hoisted up and stacked on top of the third stage.

Next came the job of moving the giant stack of vehicles from the VAB to the launchpad, a job that qualifies as one of the most fascinating engineering feats of the entire space program. The solution was almost childishly simple, as are most solutions once we have been shown. The whole stack was mounted on a box-shaped platform with four arms on top. The arms grasped a metal ring that girdled the *Saturn*'s first stage. This ring was a strong point on the rocket—necessary, though expensive in terms of weight and fuel. The box, or platform, was not built permanently into the floor of the VAB; it was, instead, supported on four jacks. When the time came to ferry the rocket to the pad, one of the crawlers George Skurla had seen during his first visit to the Cape would drive under the platform, lift both platform and rocket upon its back, then drive out to the pad, three miles away, at one half mile per hour. On the crawler, the weight of each tread plate alone was two tons, so the roadbed consisted of coarse rock, spread evenly. About one mile from the pad, the road inclined five degrees uphill. To prevent the rocket from leaning over and toppling, the crawler was designed to level itself automatically on the treads. After depositing the platform on jacks at the pad, the crawler would be driven away, and the Saturn Launch Umbilical Tower (or SLUT, which out of sheer force of etiquette, was short-

ened to LUT by the time *Apollo 11* flew) was made ready to feed
fuel and electricity into the vehicles. Meanwhile, the crawler
made a return trip with the mobile service structure, a tangle of
steel and tubes and Clean Rooms and rocket-encircling office-
workshops.

On June 27, 1967, three months after its originally scheduled
launch date, LM-1 was shipped to Florida on a plane so un-
flightworthy in appearance that they called it "Guppy." Indeed,
it did look like a pregnant fish.

NASA's Kennedy Space Center inspectors were the first people inside LM-1. Shortly, the word came out, and the word was
bad, and it went directly to Colonel Petrone's office. "What the
hell are they doing up there, George? What are your people trying
to pawn off on us? Two hundred *discrepancies!* That ship's a piece
of junk."

"Yeah," Tom Kelly recalls. "When we sent the first LM down
to the Cape, they wrote a lot of chits against it that had not been
written up here. In other words, we thought we were shipping it
clear of any problems, and when it got down there, it was full of
problems. But a lot of these problems seemed to be subjective
things—various interpretations of the ship against whatever specifications were in the book. In any case, we didn't want that happening more than once, so we decided we'd do things differently
with LM-2. Before we shipped it to the Cape, we'd bring the
Kennedy Space Center inspection crew to Bethpage to examine
the vehicle with Joe Kingfield and our resident NASA inspection
crew. We'd get them in the tent with us and make sure they were
absolutely satisfied before we handed the next LM over."

". . . *a piece of junk.*"

There were leaks. Leaks! Enough of them to hold LM-1 up
for at least another two months. "Oh, God!" George said. "How
will we have the LM ready in time for *Apollo 4?*"

"We won't," Rocco Petrone answered. "She'll have to fly with
a LM mock-up instead."

George phoned Tom Kelly. "Hey! You guys had better get

your fannies down here. We've got a problem. Grumman is holding up the parade. I can't inherit all the errors of omission and
commission from Bethpage. Our time lines are so tight that we
don't have time to fix the LM. When that thing came down here,
ascent and descent stages were supposed to fit together and not
have problems. Now we've got helium leaks."

"How bad is it?" Tom Kelly asked.

"It's going to need a hell of a lot of work. *Apollo 4* is going
up without us, and our reputation is *smudged*. Now it's a question
of—of, you know, is the ship gonna work or not?"

"Of course it will work."

"I know it will. Just send me some engineers, and Falbush
and Logalbo—fast. And the next time you send me a ship, I want
it delivered in a cellophane bag with a red ribbon around it. And
I don't want to do a goddamn thing to it except put the ascent
and descent stages together, put it up against Peggy Hewitt's
ground-support checkout equipment, check it out, stack it in the
VAB, take it to the pad, load it with fuel and helium and oxygen,
and let it go."

". . . *a piece of junk*."

Colonel Petrone pounded his desk. "LM-1! You guys up there
are building junk. Garbage!" He looked up and saw a cold glint
of pain and anger in George's eyes.

"Time out, Rocco."

"Huh?"

"I said time out." George leaned forward and began banging
his index finger against the colonel's chest. "You can't talk that
way! We've got a problem and we'll fix the problem. You can't
say just because we have a leak of one little sugar cube a day of
helium that the whole ship is junk. That's the kind of leak we're
talking about—the volume of a sugar cube. It isn't a bottlefull a
day. They're counting lousy molecules with those sniffers. But if
you want an airtight ship, you'll get an airtight ship. In the meantime, I want you to stop calling our LM garbage!"

*   *   *

During the next sixty-five days, Artie Falbush and John Logalbo plugged leaks. Every time a hole was located and closed, a new one seemed to turn up elsewhere. Finally, however, LM-1 became one hundred percent leakproof, and Artie and John went home to Bethpage.

Then during a test, the descent engine's main fuel line burst wide open.

It was back to Florida for Artie and John. The jacket of gold foil had to be peeled open. Fuel-tank covers were pulled down, and the engine was pushed to one side. Then the fuel line was dragged out. It would have to go back to Long Island for repairs. It was over six feet long—a bundle of pipes embedded in a heat exchanger that was supposed to pull warmth from the hypergolics to gasify the liquid helium, which would in turn pressurize the hypergolics. In other words, with the line ruptured, the ship had died (and you can probably guess what Rocco Petrone had to say about that).

While Artie and John packed the heat exchanger in a pine box, a Grumman Gulfstream jet was fueled for the trip to Long Island. Nothing, this day, was meant to work as planned. There seemed to be a lot of bad luck floating around the eastern United States, most of it aimed at men and their machines. About thirty seconds after the Gulfstream left the airport, the first storm warnings began to filter in. The plane was one hundred miles south of Washington when the pilot said, "I think you guys better come up front."

"What is it?" John asked.

"We're not going to make it to New York. The whole state's socked in."

Artie looked twenty miles ahead, and what he saw frightened him. "What's all this lightning going on here?"

"Tornadoes," the pilot said.

"What?"

"I've radioed all the airports. We might make Washington, but I dare not go any farther."

"Absolutely you dare not," Artie said. "Let's get downstairs. Let's get out of here . . . get us out of here . . . get—"

—us out . . . get us out—
The words echoed in Rocco Petrone's brain as he stood in the drizzle of Launch Complex 37. He searched the *Saturn 1-B* for hints of corrosion. Soon, this rocket, *Apollo 5*, would fly outside the earth, carrying with her LM-1. Less than a year earlier, she had occupied Launch Complex 34. They'd called her *Apollo 1* then, and Gus Grissom had been her commander.

Betty Grissom closed the newspaper and did some quick mental calculations. According to the article, Congress was trying to get more money for the widow of a chief justice who was living on five thousand dollars a year. Betty and the kids were living on only thirty-six hundred dollars a year. But it's not all *that* bad, she thought. I do get medical privileges until I remarry, and the boys are covered up to age twenty-three if they're in school. Then again, it's not all that good. Gus was only a captain when he was selected, and captain's pay was not very high. He was lieutenant colonel at the time of the accident, and my pension is based on that. Bad news: Military astronauts get less pay than civilian astronauts.

"No, it's not all that good," she muttered.

"Okay. How bad is it?" astronaut Pete Conrad asked. He'd been sent to speak with her about a letter her attorney had drafted.

"I really hate to think how we'd be getting along if we didn't have that publication money. We're surviving now only because of our prorated share of the money from *Life* magazine. And I've watched my share shrink as the number of astronauts grows, and now these greedy people want me and the other girls to stop drawing from the proceeds. Well, damn it, Pete, we signed a contract—years ago."*

---

*There was one lump sum to be divided by the total number of astronauts. As the number of astronauts grew, each one's share decreased proportionally.

"You know, Betty, if your husband was just in the Air Force, you would have been given one year to get out of your house if you were in base housing."

"This situation is different. The astronauts themselves signed an agreement to share publication proceeds with all other families, including the—the"—she found the word ugly, and difficult to say—"*widows*."

"Betty, there were only seven astronauts when you signed that pact. By the time we land on the moon, there will be seventy. The original seven are getting old. They'll be retiring in a couple of years. The newer ones won't want to share the money with the widows. They won't even know who Gus Grissom was."

"If they don't know who Gus Grissom was, then they'd better find out. And now, you can leave. Get out of my house. Get out."

"Let us in. We got to talk to you."

"Get out of here. Go away before I call the police."

"We're from NASA. We had to land in Virginia because of the storm. We've got to rent a car and get to New York—"

"Spacemen, eh? Well, why don't you fix your flying saucer and get out of here?"

"We didn't come in a flying saucer. We came in one of those little NASA jets."

The man in the car-rental office peered out at Artie Falbush and John Logalbo. They looked creepy, sort of like Long Islanders. And what the hell were they carrying? A pine box? A coffin?

"What've you got in there? A body?"

"Look, mister. We *have* to rent a car," Artie said with a groan. "I'm not getting any drier standing out here in the rain talking to you. You do rent cars, don't you?"

"Do you realize what time it is? It's one in the morning."

George Skurla could have told the man that if he insisted on tickling Artie's temper, he was taking a terrible risk. And the government would probably back Artie up one hundred percent if he kicked the door in and then proceeded to scare the living daylights out of the old man while John searched for and stole the keys to a station wagon—all in the service of God and country.

"What are we going to do with this thing here?" Artie's voice had risen high and squeaky. "Mister, we got a quarter-of-a-million-dollar piece of pancake. What are we going to do?"

John Logalbo: "So the old man rented us a car. We made him call Grumman and NASA, and he was glad just to get rid of us, I guess. We drove all night through storms, and then, when we arrived, a bunch of guys were ready to grab this heat exchanger, and Artie said, 'Wait a minute. You ain't touching nothing here. I don't care who you are. This has got to be molded right the way it is. We have to cast new parts in the same exact shape, because if I take this back to the pad and it don't fit inside the ship, I'm outta luck.'

"And I said, 'You don't know how difficult it was to take this massive piece of equipment, with an engine here, right next to it, and just maneuver it up and out of the ship. And the same way it came out it has to go back in.'

"It was almost funny. After riding twenty-six hours, we still had another argument, with how to take this piece of equipment and patch it up. Artie wouldn't let them touch it. He told them he'd break their arms if they tried."

Artie Falbush: "Finally, Paul Dent, my project manager, took it over and supervised the changes exactly the way we told him to. And the next morning they rolled out Grumman's Gulfstream jet and we got some sleep on the way down to Florida and then put the heat exchanger in the ship. And then one day, the ship flew.

"It flew good."

34. COSMOS

At about the same time that Artie and John were wrestling with their leaky heat exchanger, a new presidential campaign was getting started; a squirrel broke into the LM Clean Room and had to be shot; Jesco von Puttkamer's favorite TV program, *Star Trek*, was pushed by Rowan and Martin's *Laugh-In* into the Friday slot from ten to eleven P.M. (where it died); and Russia's *Cosmos 186* was being prepared for orbit.

Cosmos was an unmanned version of *Soyuz*. On October 27, 1967, it punched through to space, settling into low Earth orbit. Three days later, *Cosmos 188* was launched with such accuracy that the two machines were initially only eighteen miles apart. For a time, they bounced radio waves off each other; then *Cosmos 186* fired its thrusters and began closing the distance. A half hour later, *Cosmos 186* and *188* had successfully completed the world's first automatic rendezvous and docking. They undocked after only a few hours, then headed for soft landings in central Russia.

The Tass News Agency announced that automatic rendezvous and docking would be a valuable technique for constructing space stations and interplanetary probes. Indeed, it would, in the years to come, be used to deliver modules to the *Salyut* and *Mir* space stations — even food and mail.

35. APOLLO DAWN

The sky was beginning to brighten in the east, and out there, where breezes stirred, the Atlantic sparkled like a field of polished beads, brass bright against Bible black.

Two golden eyes broke the water's surface near Merritt Island, twin periscopes gazing in opposite directions.

A jolt sent row after row of ripples radiating from the shore. At the same instant, a dazzling diamond—brighter than the sun—materialized amid expanding billows of red and yellow. The eyes disappeared, sought shelter on the marsh floor. Under the water, the noise was unbearable, and the little creature suffered permanent damage to its hearing.

There was as yet no sound in the air above. Shock waves are transmitted more rapidly through soil and water, so the nearest humans saw the *Saturn V* ignite, and felt the thrust of 7.5 million pounds beneath their feet, six seconds before they actually heard it. And when they did hear it, it arrived as a long, rapid-fire series of concussions so fierce that even the steady, controlled narrative of Walter Cronkite came apart: "The—it—the building is shaking. . . . B-boy, it's terrific. The building's shaking. The big glass window is shaking as we're holding it with our hands. *Look at that rocket go!*"

The *Saturn V* cast distinct shadows that foreshortened as it ascended. In minutes, it would be flying in vacuum and silence, but now, as the shock waves died to a tolerable roar, some were asking not whether *Apollo 4* would or could rise (undeniably it had) but whether Florida had sunk.

Inside, computers talked to computers. There were no humans aboard, merely a Command Module, the Service Module that sustained it, and a mock-up of LM wired for a variety of tests. After two orbits at an altitude of 115 miles, with weightless propellants beading up and sloshing around in its tanks, a few pounds of hydrogen gas were vented out the back of the third stage, thrusting the ship forward and pushing liquid hydrogen and oxygen to the bottoms of the tanks—just as von Braun had said it would, back in 1960. It was the first restart of a cryogenic stage in orbital flight.

One thousand and sixty miles out in space, the Command Module/Service Module assembly was ordered to separate from the third stage, and the Service Module fired its hypergolics, adding another 620 miles of altitude. For five hours, ground crews monitored the effects of deep space on the cabin environment. There were none, to everybody's relief.

Pointing the ship's nose toward Earth, the Service Module engine fired again in what had all the appearances of being a suicide dive. Remaining fuel reserves were burned off full force, and *Apollo 4* accelerated to a speed of seven miles per second, the same speed future *Apollos* would be coming home at—home from the moon. At an altitude of two hundred miles, the umbilical arm that delivered air and power from the Service Module, around the heat shield and to the Command Module, or capsule, was pulled free. The Service Module was jettisoned. Then, using its own thrusters, the capsule oriented its blunt end (its heat shield) toward Earth. At an altitude of seventy-five miles, it penetrated the atmosphere-reentry zone. The Service Module, not built for passage into this zone, continued on for about ten seconds, then exploded into a violent and beautiful meteor shower twenty miles above the Pacific. Two hours later, spacecraft 017 was brought aboard the USS *Bennington*.

The first flight of a Command Module, the first flight of even a simulated LM, the first flight of a *Saturn* V rocket with upward of a million parts that could have failed, had gone off with barely a hitch.

On Thursday, November 9, 1967, the door to the moon lay open.

36. GHOSTS IN THE MACHINE

Saturn 1-B 204.

Mission title: *Apollo 5.*

Primary mission objective: to boost LM-1 into low Earth orbit.

Crew: none.

No crew? Well, of course, no crew. That was a clearly under-stood though unspoken law: No men were to fly in *Saturn 1-B 204*. Ever. This is not to say that NASA was acknowledging a belief in ghosts or spirits or anything else supernatural, but the space organization did believe that there was something basically wrong about sending a crew up in a rocket with so many bad memories attached to it.

And there was something else, probably nothing more than a trick of the imagination. Still, if you touched the vehicle—those memories—a touch would bring them out

—get us out—

bubbling up out of the subconscious.

No, there were no ghosts in *Saturn 1-B 204*, nothing quite so dramatic, nothing more than a . . . a lingering resonance, an echo. Not the kind of echo you'd read about in some as yet unwritten Stephen King novel.

(I don't know why, but it seems that all the bad things that ever happened at the Overlook Hotel, there's little pieces of those things still layin around like fingernail clippins.)

But an echo nonetheless. It was, perhaps, merely the footfalls of ordinary human memory, painful events that should never be too intimately embraced, which may explain why more than a century passed between Lincoln's assassination and the next performance at Ford's Theatre, why Kennedy's limousine was crushed into a cube of iron and buried, why you would probably never buy a car that a child had choked in and a woman had killed herself in (especially if its name was Christine).

Nope. No spirits in *Saturn 1-B 204*.

Nope. No astronauts either.

No, it's not as if scientists actually believe in the motility of consciousness, not as if we seriously consider the idea that the emotions people experience can live after them, like odors absorbed onto barroom walls. No, scientists don't *really* believe in these things, not really. Then again, on a one-to-one basis, very rarely and in secret, some will admit to the possibility of a whole new science yet to be explored, and they dare not risk their reputations and their careers to explore it. There is an internationally known geologist who had a near-death experience during surgery, stepped outside his body, and saw things that were impossible for him to see from the operating table, things that were happening simultaneously in different parts of the hospital, things that *had* happened, and things that had not happened but would.

We know of an astronomer who was troubled by dreams of a little girl suffering in his room. He learned later than an eight-year-old had died of cancer where he slept.

We know of a paleontologist who can pick up a rock and tell you where that rock has been. Suddenly the desert we are standing is no longer a desert but a forest that grew here one hundred million years ago. He holds the rock—a timegate—and looks ahead (through the trees?). "Come," he says. "Follow me. I'll show you where the lake was, where the stream deposited the amber, and . . .oh, Charlie, there's something else near the stream. A Tyrannosaur died there." We walk. We dig. We find the lake and the amber. The expedition that arrives after us finds the Tyrannosaur.

We know of a geneticist who, like the paleontologist, explores nature through . . . through what? supernature? "When I was really working with chromosomes, I wasn't outside the microscope. I was right down there with them and everything got big.

I saw things nobody else did. I was even able to see the internal parts of the chromosomes—actually everything was there. It surprised me because I actually felt as if I were right there and these were my friends." And this approach to discovery, laughable as it may seem, led Barbara McClintock to a Nobel Prize.

We know of a rocket that had no crew.

"I think it is a little strange that a machine, which is pure hardware, pure technology, can touch something in you," says Jesco von Puttkamer. "I think it proves, somehow, my feeling that if you take substance, like aluminum and sand and steel, and apply your consciousness and your effort to it, you turn it into something of a higher grade. It is still inanimate matter, but it is more viable in a philosophical sense. It has a—a little soul, all by itself. And it talks to you! It says something beautiful to you. Especially when the machine, or pieces of the machine, come back from space. It is not just a hunk of what used to be sand and aluminum bars anymore.

"It is an entity.

"How can a pure machine turn into something that has meaning? That's what I call the soul of the machine. And the *Saturn* and the LM definitely had very strong emanations. Some people tell me, when they touch a piece of the LM or a rocket or a shuttle that has returned from space, that for them it's almost like getting an electric shock. Maybe it's their imagination. Who knows what it is? But they feel like . . . *pop!* And that's it: They are getting a little electric shock in their spirit. There is something strange about spaceships, which I shouldn't be talking about, as I am here, and I don't understand it, but I feel it definitely."

He is not the first man to feel it. Atop *Saturn 1-B 204*, in the Clean Room, during the winter of 1968, George Skurla and Bill Voorhest closed the hatch on LM-1. This was the last operation before Colonel Petrone ordered everyone away from the launch tower and sealed the aerodynamic shell that surrounded the LM. This was the last time anyone would touch LM-1, and, knowing this . . . *pop!* Something swept over George and Bill. Something overmastering. Something like . . . *a shock in their spirit?* They put a sheet of mylar between their lips and the hatch (Rule: *Keep it meticulously clean*) and kissed it "good luck."

Someone behind them got the giggles. Then someone else. Bill did not care. Neither did George. There was nothing funny about what they had done. If anything, it was an act of . . . love? hope? A protective measure against . . . against what?

They would do it for the next LM as well (that would be LM-3). They would do it for LM-4, LM-5, LM-6, and LM-7 (especially LM-7), never once daring to have a launch without kissing the ship good-bye and good luck.

It became a religious ritual.

January 22, 1968:

"Thirty-eight degrees and cloudy at eight thirty. Time for a report of late developments. The vehicle designed to ferry U.S. astronauts to and from the moon late next year is orbiting the earth for the first time tonight. Now, from the news room, we switch you to our on-the-spot reporter at the Kennedy Space Center". . .

"It was a very interesting launch from the standpoint of, well, we had an exceptionally clear sky. There were no clouds, and you could see the rocket as high as eighty miles up. This was amazing. We saw the first stage drop off and burn up, and the ignition of the second stage very clearly when it was up about forty miles. We could see all these things. But this clarity of sky and lack of clouds deadened the noise. Clouds usually deflect some of the noise back to the ground and make the rocket sound a lot more raspy than it really is. And today we had none of that. And, as the rocket lifted up on this bright teardrop of flame, it simply passed us by, and it seemed an awful long time before we got this sound, which was being dissipated in the atmosphere and not directed at us by any cloud cover. The sound wasn't what you'd expect from so mighty a rocket."

"I felt like I was part of Christopher Columbus' crew," Bill Voorhest recalls. "Nowhere can a little guy raised in Hicksville

[Long Island] ever come to achieve a little bit of history such as we people who had the privilege of working in that program. Watching that thing go up, praying every inch of the way that everything would work out fine, and the way the acoustics of the rocket just enveloped your whole body, you just—you almost became part of the machine. Tears were streaming down my cheeks. That's what happens to your body at a launch. You're just tingling with emotion. And there's something else there. Some part of the people who touched her is in there, in the machine. It's all combined somehow: man and machine. And seeing this huge, *huge* mass just take off so gradually, to just go up there. "It's like . . . it—"

It is an awakening. A vivid flash of . . . of something like God, something more powerful than nature itself. And it is us.

And we know. We who have seen.

Drifting below and behind LM-1, the *Saturn*'s second stage dumped its fuel, creating a gentle concussion of expanding vapors that spread fifty miles wide and more. This was an added test, to see if residual fuel could be boiled off from the tanks (already insulated from the extreme temperatures of space) to make room for a crew that could, at some later date, go inside and turn the dead stage into an orbiting space station.

LM-1's spent ascent stage vaporized in the skies over Guam. The descent stage slipped into the atmosphere west of South America, and the plumbing in the heat exchanger, on which Artie Falbush and John Logalbo had expended so much time and effort, burst open again. Gold seals blazed briefly, became a spray of metallic smoke, then solidified into uncountable microspheres miles behind the ship. The beads would linger in the upper reaches of the stratosphere for several weeks, eventually washing down with the rain.

Not far from the heat exchanger, one of the titanium fuel tanks exploded and threw insulating material around a second tank. The insulation lasted mere seconds, just long enough to shield the tank until it came loose into open air. Lighter than the dying descent stage, the tank trailed out behind it, scorched, but slowing . . . slowing . . . slowing . . .

In the jungles of South America, the tank, bits of the heat exchanger, corner posts, and aluminum sheets were seen to fall from the sky. Expeditions went in to recover the debris, only to discover that most of the pieces had been immediately snatched up by the local tribespeople, who worshiped them as gifts from the gods. Nobody had as yet laid claim to the titanium tank, which had crashed through a tree and rolled into the underbrush. Brought home to Bethpage, a sheet was pulled from it and cut into one-inch squares, into which the characters "LM-1" were engraved. These were handed out to Grumman employees, and these too were worshiped.

EXCERPTS FROM INTERVIEW WITH
JESCO VON PUTTKAMER
Date of interview: May 8, 1983
Place: Stony Brook, New York

VON PUTTKAMER: I have spoken about the soul in the machine. It is an attempt to explain why machines, in my opinion, as they get more complex, do become more responsive to humans. They become more sophisticated. They become more automatic. They become more independent. *Voyager 2*, as it flew past Saturn, was in a sense very independent from humans. One command beamed up from Earth triggered a whole chain of commands, which were preprogrammed. So *Voyager* was kind of an independent machine, and *Viking* on Mars also. And the Shuttle, of course, is even more complex than that. It has five brains, five computers on board. Each one could fly the entire ship by itself. They do majority voting, and together they could fly the Shuttle automatically down to landing, without any crew at all. So if you look at the inanimate matter all these automatic systems are made from—sand, copper, steel, plastic, and so on—then we have here basic inanimate substances elevated to a higher grade.

PELLEGRINO: Do you mean, as biology has done with carbon, we are doing with plastic and steel? I've heard it said that *Viking*'s computers contain as many bits of information as are needed to build and operate a virus, and that the Shuttle's computers could do everything that the brain of a garden-variety ant does. What you're saying is almost spooky. A silicon chip moves electrons around in very precise ways, and isn't that what the brain does? Are we, in a sense, creating life?

JVP: In a sense, yes. The computer chip is still inanimate matter, but it is obviously something more than sand.

CRP: But what is it that is "more"?

JVP: My answer is a complexity, which shows itself in terms of a consciousness. The Shuttle obviously is conscious. It is not alive, but it is conscious in that it can sense its environment: up from down, air flowing over its wings, its height from the ground. And it can calculate its actions and the consequences of its actions, and make the appropriate moves. LM worked the same way, with its landing radar and sensor probes and so on. As you trace this capability of feeling the environment back into the Earth, back to raw minerals, there must have been a continuing chain of increasing degrees of consciousness, which started all the way at the simplest form of matter. It has to start somewhere, and I figure it starts at the electron. The electron could actually be the unit of consciousness. And electrons combine to hold separate atoms together, to build molecules, and molecules form biological systems—

CRP: —and animals direct pulses of electrons through nerves in very specific ways—

JVP: —and living beings invent technology. Without brains there wouldn't be any complex machinery—

CRP: —and computers direct pulses of electrons through circuits in very specific ways—

JVP: —so human brains are really the electron's way of reaching increased complexity.

CRP: You make it sound as if the electrons do this by design.

JVP: And who's to say there is no grand design?

CRP: I try not to view nature that way. There are plants that survive and multiply because humans like them and cultivate them. I do not believe they preadapted themselves on Earth with cultivation in mind. Roses developed the way they did for reasons that had nothing to do with human perceptions of beauty. They were here for sixty million years before man came onto the scene, and then their shape and color and smell became an unexpected advantage, an advantage that was exapted or exploited to greater use. It may be the same thing with electrons in our bodies, and in our machines.

JVP: You wear the badge of Darwin with too much pride, Charlie. Be careful. It can blind you. A good scientist leaves all possibilities open, even the possibility that there is a grand design. Look at us, for example. We are building more and more complex machines, and we really don't know why. We are just doing it. Somewhere we think it's the right thing to do, almost as if we were following some deep-rooted instinct. We build LM and the Shuttle, reaching on, and if somebody asks us why we are doing it, basically we have no answer. We are just supposed to be doing it.

CRP: I'm thinking about those electrons. They work in our interest, supposedly. They are the basis of every thought we have. Now, picture what you and I would look like with all the organic molecules in our bodies stripped away from this table, so we could see only the electrons. Our outlines would be sitting here in every detail—brightest at the brain and spine—but even the nerves in our fingertips and eyelids would show up as streams of electrons. Maybe it is the electrons who are speaking these words. Perhaps our bodies are little more than vessels serving *their* interests.

JVP: Isn't a computer a vessel for shuffling electrons around in organized fashion?

CRP: Yes. Strip away the plastic and the metal, make it invisible except for the electrons, and you'd see nothing but trails of electrons running through wires and silicon chips.

JVP: Artificial brains. We have certainly come a long way from sitting in front of caves and milking goats. I think by turning primitive matter into complex matter, we are giving the Shuttle a soul. And you see the ship standing there on the pad, and it exudes something. You touch it—people touch it—and they feel something like a spiritual touching. This thing has been in space five times, and somehow this gave it a halo. And the LM, with its complexity, also had this consciousness. And before that, submarines had it on a somewhat reduced scale. So humans have been building more complex machines all the time, the same way the cosmos has been building more complex machines, like humans. The machines are extensions of our brains and our bodies. The LM was just a member, an organ that we grew for a little while to enable us to land on the moon.

CRP: What kind of extension, then, is an ICBM? A consciousness created to destroy itself?

JVP: Nobody said everything has to be point up. A man can use a baseball bat for killing someone. It's not the bat's fault. The same man that can be trained to be a doctor, a healer, can also be taught how to build atomic weapons. And the weaponry he builds—say, a cruise missile—it doesn't "know." The same computer that can fly the Shuttle can also be programmed to seek a target. A machine can be used for good and evil. Either we will build machines that take us to the stars or we will burn our cities. I do not think we can do both. It's like Robert Frost's poem about two roads. The roads diverge here, in the twentieth century.

We are on the verge.

37. ZOND AGAIN

On March 2, 1968, the world's second restartable cryogenic stage rammed a highly evolved *Soyuz* completely away from Earth. Weighing about five tons, the unmanned *Zond* 4 assumed an elliptical orbit that took it more than a quarter of a million miles up, but it flew to the side of the earth opposite the moon. Like *Apollos* 4 and 5, this was an engineering flight, probably intent on testing the capsule environment at lunar distances and, above all, the performance of the Earth Orbit "Escape" stage. The presence of the moon's gravitational field would have provided an unnecessary complication. Gravity could be dealt with at a later date, when it came time to send the first living creatures into deep space.

As it turned out, *Zond* 5 would be the first spacecraft to carry life to the moon, and to return it safely to Earth.

38. POGO

On the morning of April 4, 1968, the unmanned *Apollo* 6 rose from its launchpad, taking a full ten seconds to climb only three hundred feet. *Saturn* V rockets were heavy, and slow ascents were normal. Absolutely normal.

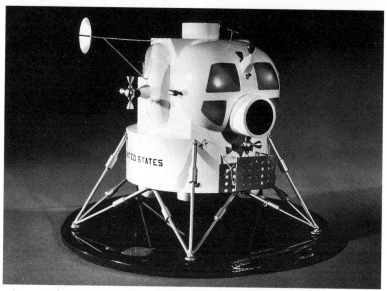

A very early stage in the Lunar Module's evolution is seen in this 1962 model.

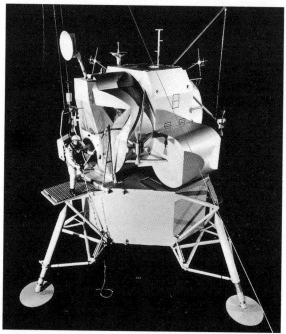

Clambering around on a full-scale wooden mock-up in 1963, astronauts were suspended from a "Peter Pan Rig" to simulate the moon's low gravity. Ed White found the knotted rope on the ship's face impossible to climb down (or up). Designers added a ladder and hand rails to the porch.

Wernher von Braun (very cautiously) steps down from the porch of Grumman's aluminum mock-up, in Bethpage, New York, on October 6, 1964. "You've got to go up there," he called to a friend. "Go in there, it's great!"

Astronaut Roger Chaffee (center), during a 1966 visit to the Grumman facility, insisted that the assistant plant manager for the LM descent stage, Milt Radimer (at his right), personally introduce him to all the people who were building the ship. On the stand behind him rests the frame of a descent stage.

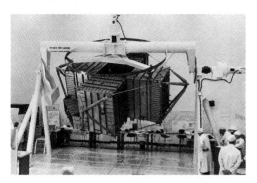

(A-C). A descent stage is rotated on the tumbler to shake out loose debris.

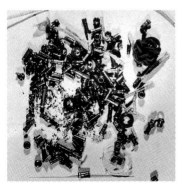

The result of a descent stage tumbling.

A Lunar Module descent stage is shown mounted in its work frame in the Grumman Clean Room.

Seen in the Grumman clean room—a nearly complete descent stage.

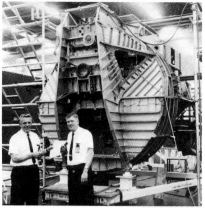

NASA quality-control officer Andy Weatherall (left) hands Grumman Supervisor Chet Senig his seal of approval for the frame of LM-2's ascent stage.

The ascent stage is shown with some of its tanks and wires added, prior to shipment to the Grumman Clean Room.

A nearly complete ascent stage (believed to be LM-8) is seen on its hoist in the Clean Room.

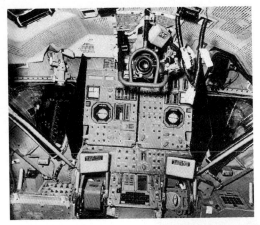

An astronaut's view of the LM cockpit. Note the notorious "eight balls" (center).

The two Lunar Modules shown here, with their jackets of thermal insulation added, are nearly ready for shipping from the Clean Room in New York to Florida's Kennedy Space Center.

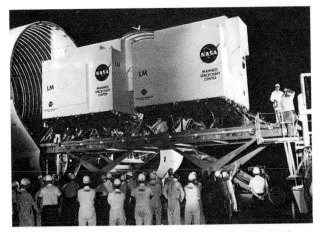

Crated ascent and descent stages roll off the giant "Guppy" airplane at the Kennedy Space Center.

The Lunar Module is sampled for bacteria prior to launch. Amid fears of contaminating the moon with organisms against which lunar life forms might have no natural immunity emerged a new question: Could death strike from the other direction? Nobody could provide a clear answer to that question prior to July 1969, so it was decided that the astronauts and the moon rocks should be isolated from Earth as soon as they set down upon it.

A finished Lunar Module is lowered into the frame of a *Saturn* launch adapter. Once in place, four panels will be erected around the LM to form a protective cocoon. The LM, being the first manned vehicle designed to be flown entirely outside the earth, must be shielded from aerodynamic forces during its ascent to orbit. On top of the cocoon (or LM adapter) will stand the Service Module.

The LM adapter, complete with LM, Service Module, and Command Module, is hoisted into position for mating with the *Saturn V* third-stage (Earth escape) booster in NASA's Vehicle Assembly Building.

LAUNCH
ESCAPE SYSTEM

BOOST
PROTECTIVE COVER

COMMAND MODULE

SERVICE MODULE

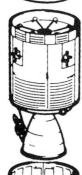

ADAPTER

LUNAR MODULE

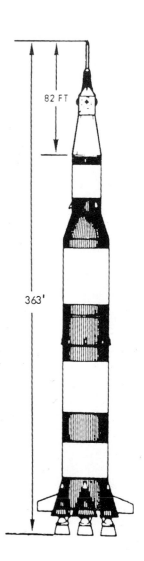

82 FT

363'

Saturn V launch vehicle.

Joseph Gavin, Lunar Module program manager, Bethpage (left), and George Skurla, Lunar Module program manager, Kennedy Space Center, stand at the feet of Saturn 1B-204, the rocket upon which the *Apollo I* firespill had occurred some months earlier. This picture was taken in April 1967, after SA-204 had been moved from Pad 34 (the site of the fire) to Pad 37 and prior to the flight of LM-1.

George Skurla (left) and Rocco Petrone, director of launch operations, Kennedy Space Center. "You know," says George, "I learned more working with that man in my first year at the Cape than I learned in the previous twenty years working in Bethpage."

Engineer Tom Kelly, the "father of the LM" (left), and Lew Evans, president of Grumman Aerospace Corporation, share a private joke at an Apollo prelaunch party.

LM builders in Bethpage watch the flight of *Apollo 11*.

Buzz Aldrin looked down to see the American flag caught in the blast of the ascent-stage rocket. He watched it fall.

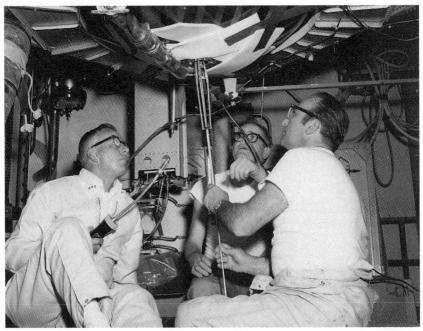

After a false fuel reading almost led to an abort of the *Apollo 11* landing, Grumman quality-control inspector Harry Walther (left) was called on to assist with the task of building baffles inside the *Apollo 12* fuel tanks, a job somewhat like building a ship in a bottle.

The LM over the moon…

…and on it.

Almost three years after *Surveyor* 3 set foot upon the Ocean of Storms, astronaut Charles Conrad, Jr., examines the robot explorer's TV camera. The *Apollo* 12 Lunar Module is seen 600 feet away on the horizon.

North American Rockwell
Space Division
Downey, California

CONSIGNED TO

INVOICE NUMBER
70-417

INVOICE DATE	PACKING SHEET NO.	DATE SHIPPED	PROJECT NO.		TERMS: NET FOR BETHPAGE, N.Y.
17 April 1970					
CUSTOMER ORDER OR CONTRACT NO	OUR ORDER NO.	BILL OF LADING NO.		SHIPPED VIA	

ITEM NO.	QUANTITY	DESCRIPTION	UNIT PRICE	AMOUNT
1	400,001 Miles	Towing, $4.00 first mile, $1.00 each additional mile Trouble call, fast service Battery charge (road call + $.05 KWH)		$400,004.00
2	1 KWH	Customer's jump cables		4.05
3	50 Lbs.	Oxygen at $10.00/lb.		500.00
4	1	Sleeping accomodations for 2, no TV, air-conditioned, with radio, modified american plan, with view		Prepaid
5		Additional guest in room at $8.00/night (1) Check out no later than noon Fri. 4/17/70, accommodations not guaranteed beyond that time		32.00
6		Water		N/C
7		Personalized "trip-tik", including all transfers, baggage handling and gratuities		N/C
				$400,540.05
		20% commercial discount + 2% cash discount (net 30 days)		83,118.81
		Charges for keeping this invoice confidential		100,000.00
				$417,421.24

One of the old, original (amazing multiplying) copies of Grumman's Apollo 13 towing bill to Rockwell.

— Charles R. Pellegrino

FORM REV. 5 8-89 ECM

PLEASE PAY LAST AMOUNT SHOWN

1970: A Space Oddity...In the final hours before splashdown, Grumman Aerospace Corporation (builder of the Lunar Module) sends North American Rockwell (builder of the Command/Service Module) a "towing bill" for *Apollo 13*.

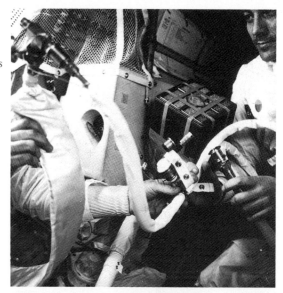

Astronaut Jack Swigert adapts *Odyssey*'s carbon-dioxide scrubbers to *Aquarius*'s life-support system.

Five hours before entering the earth's atmosphere, the astronauts jettisoned the dead Service Module and got their first glimpse of the damage caused by the firespill. Three and half hours later, they climbed out of their LM lifeboat/tugboat into the Command Module and jettisoned *Aquarius*. Following close behind *Odyssey*, the LM, which had not been designed for atmospheric entry, would plunge to meet its doom. A tired voice called up from the ground, "Farewell, *Aquarius*, and we thank you."

The last hurrah: The moon awaits *Apollo* 17.

A LM that never was. MO-LM (for Mobile LM) was to have no ascent engine. It would be landed on a descent stage, then used as a camper by astronauts descending in a second LM. The MO-LM mission was designed to last several weeks.

A full-scale version of MOLAB (Mobile Lunar Laboratory) was built and tested, but funding cuts ended all plans for a long-term human presence on the moon. MOLAB is now on exhibit at Long Island's Cradle of Aviation Museum.

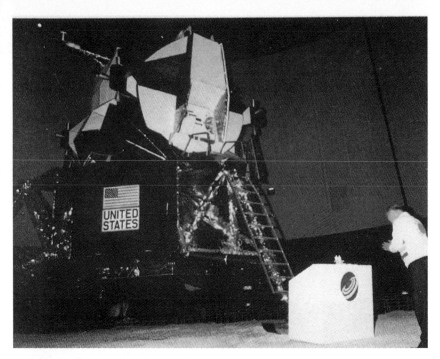

America's last LM was built for Japan's 1976 Space Exposition. After closing the Expo, the head of the exposition, Ryoichi Sasakawa, extended his sincere appreciation to LM-7½ (top), while in junk yards half a world away (bottom) moon ships crumbled in silence.

That was the last normal thing the rocket did.

Within seconds, at least two of the five first-stage engines began belching and burping unevenly, creating thrust fluctuations that, according to signals from the Command Module, ranged up to ± 0.6g. To anything in or on the rocket, this was like being dropped from the top of a two-story building—repeatedly. The ship bounced along its axis like a giant pogo stick.

Behind the Service Module, one of the four panels that enclosed a LM mock-up broke free. That's when Houston's ground controllers began receiving impossible signals from the LM test equipment. Readouts attested to the fact that the rocket was indeed climbing out of the atmosphere, but the air around the mock-up kept getting thicker . . . thicker . . . curiously thicker, as if time were running backward—which, in a sense, it was. The mock-up had fallen through the opening in the side of the rocket. The mock-up *was* running backward, dropping from space into dense air and scattering in pieces over the Atlantic.

The troubles deepened after the first-stage engines burned out and the five smaller second-stage engines took over. Two of the engines stopped, and the other three had to burn longer to compensate for the loss of power, which would have been well and fine if the fuel hadn't run out earlier than expected. The dead second stage fell away, leaving the third stage in a highly irregular orbit that dipped halfway into the ionosphere. Three hours later, Mission Control sent up the signals that would restart the third stage and simulate translunar injection. This too failed. The rocket that was supposed to propel American astronauts to the moon refused even to acknowledge the signal. Plans to hurl the *Apollo 6* capsule 300,000 miles out into space, where *Zond 4* had been, were dashed.

Mission Control then turned to an alternative mission: Separate the Command/Service Module from the crippled third stage, fly it out twelve thousand miles, and then crash-dive it into the atmosphere at six miles per second to simulate a return to Earth from the moon.

The USS *Okinawa* found the capsule floating northwest of

Hawaii, and above in the skies, pieces of the broken rocket were skipping off the outer atmosphere, like stones bouncing off pond water—all the way around the world. Some of the pieces, little pods, came down on parachutes. They were flight monitors, part of a program called "flight evaluation." They would aid the diagnosis of pogo and other *Apollo* ills.

Jesco von Puttkamer explains: "In the early rocket days, before Gemini and Apollo, test rockets were always wrecking themselves. We were used to that. It was just part of the game that missiles blew up. Then we decided one day that we'd had enough of that kind of thing. We had to put on enough telemetry to exactly tell what went wrong. You see, originally, rockets were just flown, and then out of pure guesswork the reasons for an accident were determined, because telemetry was expensive, and we really didn't know how to get intricate data down to Earth from a flight. In order to develop a reliable, safe rocket for *Apollo*, the *Saturns* were heavily instrumented and a new discipline called postflight evaluation came about. We had specialists who could glean any type of information from a few telemetry data. We had movie cameras on board that were ejected at high altitude and came down on parachutelike ballutes. We could develop the film and see actually how stage separation took place. At that time, there wasn't any television system capable of beaming clear pictures down to Mission Control for videotaping, as with today's Shuttle. So we mostly used movie cameras, and they came down in watertight pods with radio beepers in them. And sometimes you never found them again. I remember we found one about three or four years after the *Apollo 6* flight. It washed up on some South Sea island beach, having drifted there like a coconut. The film was still intact inside, showing separation of the second stage.

"So this art and science of flight evaluation developed, and therefore rockets, while becoming more expensive to build, also became much more reliable. And this is what you needed if you wanted to get them ready to fly people. We called it 'man-rating.' "

          *   *   *

"This is Jules Bergman, ABC, at Cape Kennedy. The troubles with *Apollo 6* almost certainly mean another delay in America's lunar-landing plan. But even if this flight had been a full success, the space agency is still in deep basic trouble. It is searching for its future, and it hasn't found it yet. Nor has it convinced Congress that it has a real future beyond the moon. NASA now faces new budget cuts of up to a half billion dollars as part of the austerity drive. The great goals in conquering space are still just as great, but Congress feels there are greater, more immediate goals to be conquered here on Earth: rebuilding our cities, solving our transportation problems, exploring the oceans. And even an end to the Vietnam War won't solve NASA's problems. The faith of Congress and the space agency's credibility remain shaken."

The USS *Okinawa* steamed toward Hawaii with the wounded *Apollo*. The capsule had spent ten hours in space, returning safely to an Earth that was still very much the same . . . very much the same . . . even as she flew, a monster had slouched into Memphis, Tennessee, and murdered Martin Luther King, Jr. And in 126 cities across America, other monsters were joining in an orgy of looting and maiming and burning. Patches of orange light began to stain the night skies in the directions of the cities, spreading there. Directly overhead, a false star fled toward the East Coast. It was the abandoned third stage. Viewed from the distance of that star, the normally yellow and unflickering American lights had taken on a crimson quality. They shimmered faintly, like glowing embers in a campfire. But this was not the shimmer of campfires.

39. A TALE OF WOE AND INTRIGUE

Six days later, the Soviet *Luna 14* entered orbit around the moon and began mapping the surface. Then, on April 15, *Cosmos 212* and 213 performed the world's second automatic rendezvous and docking.

In Bethpage, work continued on LM-5, the first ship that would actually land on the moon with a human crew. Progress was recorded almost minute by minute in logbooks whose covers proclaimed OPER. INSTR. Sometime between July and October 1968, a nameless LM builder, using a blue Magic Marker, subtitled the log A TALE OF WOE AND INTRIGUE.

EXCERPTS FROM THE LM-5 LOG

May 3, 1968
5:30 P.M.   Note: *we on the night shift* did not install rivets backwards on 116 shelf.

June 4, 1968
10:15 A.M.   *Astronaut-Pilot team inspection of cabin revealed discrepancies under floorboards (dirt and hairs).*

June 13, 1968
Resolved ITEM 3A. Held heap big pow-wow in ACE Room. CDC and NASA concurred that calibration history cards and annotated calibration sticker with specification numbers was sufficient evidence that the unit had been calibrated.

June 20, 1968

NASA *Quality Control was a little disturbed over the fact that the 4.5 Mc reading was crossed out a few times and had a stamp of verification on it. I think they are just busting chops. . . . Quality Control man just tripped over biaxial cables on the work stand. Beware of damaged cable or hot coupler when running R.F. check.*

June 21, 1968

1:20 A.M. *Can't install power amplifier for "S" Band antenna cause one NASA QC man (Baby) won't release it cause he wants to see something. No one on nite shift knows what—how come? Pray he doesn't die.*

3:20 P.M. *Left hand outer window has been received with scratches.*

June 25, 1968

5:30 A.M. *Picked up floorboard in cabin and vacuumed area.*

8:45 A.M. *Ross Fleisig called to find out how much dirt was removed from beneath the cabin floor. Floor was vacuumed with standard type vacuum (answer not available).*

July 8, 1968

3:45 A.M. *Getting many master alarms due to landing radar (malfunction). Stopped test for night.*

July 11, 1968

6:15 P.M. *Quality Control people found 1 pen and 1 flash light in cabin. NOTE: the only people in the cabin were Quality Control. They found only what they lost.*

July 12, 1968

3:10 P.M. *Called safety, to investigate crack found in fence post support. This crack found while making "Strict Search" about vehicle for unauthorized persons.*

July 16, 1968
Reviewing data from LMs shows the possibility that cosine
and sine readings may be reversed or not properly recorded.

LM-3 had arrived at the Cape with just over two hundred deficiencies, not the least of which was the newer, "better," and one-hundred-percent-spastic rendezvous radar. Even so, LM-3 was a better ship than LM-2, which was a better ship than LM-1. Experience was beginning to show.

Since LM-3 was better than LM-2, it was decided that LM-3 should be used for the first manned test flight of a lander. LM-2 might also have been suitable for a manned flight—perhaps even a moon landing—but it was rated for unmanned flight only. Since LM-1 had already proved itself, a second unmanned flight was viewed as an unnecessary expenditure of both time and money, so they shipped it to Houston, where it became a guinea pig for vibration tests and pogo simulations. Later, it would be sent to Washington for eventual display in the Smithsonian Institution.

By August 9, it became clear that repairs on LM-3 could not be finished in time for a 1968 flight. The *Apollo 7* mission was already past the planning stage. A *Saturn 1-B* would carry a Command/Service Module and a three-man crew into low Earth orbit: the same mission that *Apollo 1* was to have flown more than a year and a half earlier. But what to do with *Apollo 8?* Bob Gilruth and George Low wondered. Yeah. What to do?

(We choose to go to the moon in this decade.)

"The Command/Service Module is ready. . . ."

"Von Braun and Rees say they nearly have the pogo problem licked. . . ."

"Why not an orbital flight around the moon, a manned flight?"

"Why not?"

"Oh, God . . . can we do it? When *can we do it?"*

"December," Rocco Petrone answered. "Considering our workload, we can have her ready by December. You want a Christmas flight? You got one."

"One thing," Apollo program director Samuel Phillips said. "We should keep this plan secret until a decision is made by NASA's top officials. In the meantime, we will use the code name 'Sam's Budget Exercise' as a cover."

Five days later, on August 14—"Decision Day"—NASA's new deputy administrator, Thomas O. Paine, put forth the following question: "Not too long ago, you people were trying to decide whether it was safe to man the third *Saturn V*, the rocket you propose to use for *Apollo 8*. And now you want to put men on top of it and send them to the moon. Any comments?"

"I have one," George Low said. "Assuming *Apollo 7* is a success, there is no other choice."

"The design of the mission makes a lot of sense," said Joe Gavin. "It is one we should do."

"It is the only chance to get to the moon before the end of 1968, maybe even 1969," said Donald Slayton.

As he so often did, Wernher von Braun summed the whole question up with an obvious and powerful truth: "Once you decide to man a *Saturn V*, it does not matter how far you go."

The plan was on, with the requirement, at least for the time being, that it be kept secret, that none of the sixteen Apollo officials who knew of the proposed trip around the moon speak to anybody outside NASA and the White House about anything other than an Earth-orbital mission. If all went well, *Apollo 8* would head out for the moon on December 21.

As it turned out, the Soviets, too, were secretly planning a flight into deep space.

On August 28, with *Apollo 7* in preparation for an early-October launch, the Soviets put *Cosmos 238* into Earth orbit. Like the previous four *Cosmos* spacecraft, this was unmanned. Still, it carried a full load of equipment designed for use by a human crew. For four days this equipment was run through extensive and sometimes brutal tests, and it held together beautifully. This was the final qualifying flight for the changed *Soyuz*—changed by the *Soyuz* 1 accident sixteen months earlier. Soon, very soon, cosmonauts would return to the far sky.

Shortly after midnight on September 15, *Zond* 5 lifted off from the Tyuratam Cosmodome. The highly evolved *Soyuz* broke out of Earth orbit an hour later and flung itself at the moon. Radio telescopes in North America and Australia tracked the object while the Soviets remained characteristically silent about mission objectives. On September 18, *Zond* 5 flew within fifteen hundred miles of the moon's surface, and just before it swung around to the far side, something astonishing crackled down to Earth: a human voice.

Mostly as a test of the Earth-moon communications system, and partly as a rude joke, a tape recording of a cosmonaut reciting instrument readings had been sent along. Not far from the tape player, turtles swam in zero-gravity, accompanied by flowering plants, seeds, bottles of flies, and trays of bacteria.

Emerging from the lunar far side, the *Zond* immediately began its four-day fall to Earth, letting Isaac Newton do most of the driving. On the evening of September 21, it slipped into the atmosphere at just the right angle—not too steep, or it would explode into a shower of sparks, and not too shallow, or it would skip off air and back into deep space. The narrow reentry corridor took the moon ship over the South Pole, where its crew of turtles went from zero-gravity to more than twelve times their normal Earth weight. The ship had followed the simplest and safest trajectory to a splashdown in the Pacific Ocean: Russia's first water landing. Soon, another *Zond* would fly around the moon, returning through the atmosphere in a skip trajectory. It would make one shallow skip off the upper stratosphere, losing half its velocity and experiencing less than seven gravities, then touching air a second time, shedding the remainder of its forward momentum and parachuting down to the ground. One more flight, just one more. NASA could only hope that it would not be a manned one.

And in Bethpage, the work continued.

EXCERPTS FROM THE LM-5 LOG

October 13, 1968
12:30 P.M.   *I spent last night in the cabin of LM-5 with no breaks and no supper. Request that in the future we have adequate coverage, and if needed bring a man in from home.*

October 16, 1968
2:50 A.M.   NOTE: 23 MEAL CHITS NOT ENOUGH. *Need 28 a night.*

October 17, 1968
8:00 P.M.   *Start troubleshooting Bit Error Comparator (for on-board computers).*
10:00   *No progress.*
12:45   *New NASA man came on job. Other NASA man did not inform us he was leaving but had given Grumman quality control the go-ahead to perform test. New NASA man refused to stamp off test performed under go-ahead from previous NASA man. Requested he verify previous steps (preparation, switch positions, and cooling unit turn on). He refused to perform this 10 minutes of work. After arguing to no avail and calling his boss, it was decided to continue testing from step at which new NASA man came on job and try to get Grumman quality control to chase around for old NASA man, who should have bought off steps before leaving for home.*
1:00 P.M.   *No progress. Quick lunch.*
1:20 P.M.   *Continue troubleshooting Bit Error Comparator.*
7:00 P.M.   *Have been working on Bit Error Comparator all day and meeting called with Walt Martens and Ross Fleisig. Martens thinks no more can be done until RCA designer comes in at noon tomorrow.*
7:30 P.M.   *H. Friedman comes on duty and notifies us that RCA representative thinks he has computer problem*

licked. Count is up to 168 million bits with zero bit errors. Now to 200 million with zero errors.

October 18, 1968
The Landing Radar assembly is in trouble. It seems that it barbequed—fried to a charcoal finish. The 10 Amp breaker popped. Also, the cable connecting the Landing Radar assembly to the vehicle was overheated to a black charred mess. Ugh!

October 19, 1968
When new radar gets turned on, try not to burn it up! As we are the last RF system without any problems. Lots of luck.

October 20, 1968
4:00 A.M.   Master Alarm reported (in cabin) at 3:30 into Dynamic Run . . . observer (in cabin) said a crew light came on but couldn't remember which one. Recorder for observer's channel wasn't turned on till about 4 minutes into run. Clever, weren't they? Furthermore, recorder in RTDE Station wasn't recording that channel—another Boo Boo . . . the observer didn't think it was the Environmental Control System light, or the Glycol, Control Electronics System—AC, Control Electronics System—DC, or Abort Guidance System Caution and Warning lights that came on, but still can't remember which one. Oh forgetfulness, sweet forgetfulness.
11:00 A.M.   Power Failure—IN HOLD—

October 22, 1968
10:10 A.M.   Requested CDR man to state if docking hatch is open during the test. Answer: Yes, open. Question: How is docking hatch switch held in depressed (open) position? Answer: It is taped in the depressed position. The tape just fell off (loose tape was probably the reason for failure #62).

October 23, 1968
Nite Shift
 All alone am I, ever since you . . .
 Well you know the rest.
 I came, I saw, I left.
 No CES support, No George Handler, no nuthin . . .
  Boy am
 I lonely. I couldn't do anything.
 I herefore, decide I will switch to days.
 We are obviously not needed.

P.S. Remember the immortal words of
 Rocco Roy Robert Romeo:
 "NIL SINE MAGNA LABORE"*

3:27 A.M. STE requested we take a 20 minute break so
porter could mop floor.
4:56 A.M. Had to leave ACE Room so porter could wax
floor. Waited for floor to dry. Lost technical and quality
control coverage while floor was drying.

While all these things were going on, Wally Schirra, Don Eisele, and Walt Cunningham climbed into orbit aboard *Apollo 7.* All the equipment worked as it was designed to work. It was the humans who ran into trouble. For a start, the food was awful. Most of it was freeze-dried and tended to crumble into clouds of floating dust. Two days into the flight, the astronauts began arguing with each other over the more edible breakfast items. On Earth, Apollo Test Division chief Don Arabian, who had become famous for his surprise pizza parties and who prided himself on being somewhat of a human garbage can, couldn't understand what the astronauts were complaining about. He decided to live on astronaut rations for a few weeks and discovered to his disbelief

---
*Nothing without great labor.

that the sausage patties were about as chewy as granulated rubber and left an aftertaste like gasoline. The bite-size, freeze-dried ice cream was *right out*. Only foods that were half close to normal table dishes, such as the breakfast packets, were likable. Don began skipping meals after only four days. "They're right," he conceded. "It's awful." Which came as no surprise to Wally Schirra, a Gemini veteran who had sworn that he was going to bring some coffee with him if he flew on *Apollo*. And he did.

And—oh, God—the dehydrated meals. Not only was reconstituting them a chore; gas bubbles in weightless water did not rise to the surface and pop as they did in a glass sitting on a kitchen table. They stayed in the water, and that led to gas pains and cramps and feeble jokes about farting in space suits, and the possibility of diarrhea, which at zero-g was almost as unthinkable as nuclear war.

It was difficult enough to defecate in space when your feces were solid. These had to be collected in a plastic bag, affectionately called a "shit mitt," and they wouldn't just drop free, as they would in a toilet on Earth; they just hung there, at the exit. You had to reach back with the mitt and *pull* them free, making doubly and triply sure not to let one get away. Then, assuming everything "came out all right," you sealed the bag and broke a germicide capsule inside and spent the next few minutes kneading the bag in your hands until the germicide was mashed evenly throughout. The whole procedure required as much as an hour, and the astronauts looked upon it as something to be avoided. Most averaged only one bowel movement every three days. (For trivia enthusiasts, the record is eight days, held by an astronaut who kept it in all the way to the moon and back.)

Urination was much easier, if not downright *fun*. Urine could be collected in a plastic bag fitted with a rubber receiver that covered the penis. (The receivers came in three sizes: Small, Medium, and Large. But on the astronauts' insistence, they were reclassified as Extra Large, Immense, and Unbelievable.) The *fun* part came when, with the flip of a switch, the urine-collection service was emptied into space. With that, a spherical galaxy burst into existence all around the capsule. Released into vacuum, the urine first boiled, instantly, then froze into millions of tiny ice crystals: a snowstorm in orbit, a slowly expanding halo of twinkling stars. And a urine dump at sunset! It was a vision whose beauty rivaled that of Earth itself.

"Magnificent!" said Wally Schirra. "The constellation Urion."

Walt Cunningham agreed. "It's a real experience to see your own urine take on a cosmic quality."

It was also an experience to see and feel the cosmic quality that mucus took. In space, one of the worst things that can happen to you is the common cold. It happened on *Apollo* 7.

About halfway into the tenth orbit, Wally Schirra's nose gave out. During the next ten orbits, Cunningham and Eisele developed the same symptoms. A cold can make your life miserable enough on the ground; at zero-gravity there's no such thing as postnasal drip, and mucus cannot drain from the nasal passages. It just hangs there, accumulating. The only relief is to blow very hard, which is murder on the eardrums.

One week into the mission, the astronauts began to discuss their fears about reentry. Written procedure called for the men to wear space helmets, to guard against the unlikely (but still viable) possibility of a cabin puncture and resulting decompression. With the men unable to blow their noses, the buildup of pressure in the nasal passages could rupture eardrums during a seven-g reentry. Mission Control tried to persuade the crew to put on the helmets, but one of the great advantages of being almost two hundred miles out in space is that you can tell Mission Control to get stuffed and they can't do a thing about it (except maybe give you the wrong landing coordinates).

Apollo 7 ended its twelve-day flight southeast of Bermuda on October 22. Three pairs of eardrums came through the high g-forces intact, and as the crewmen stepped onto the deck of the USS *Essex*, *Soyuz* 2 was cleared for countdown. Three days later the ship lifted off, unmanned and unannounced. It was followed by Colonel Georgiy Beregovoy in *Soyuz* 3. An automated sequence brought Beregovoy within five hundred feet of *Soyuz* 2.

Then television cameras switched on and beamed the scene to Soviet living rooms. They saw *Soyuz 2* looming so close that they could almost reach out and tweak the rendezvous antennae. The two ships never docked, however, and it is unknown to this day whether or not docking was intended. For two days *Soyuz 2* and 3 approached and backed off from each other in a variety of ways. Then *Soyuz 2* pulled away and returned to Earth, while Beregovoy stayed in orbit to conduct further studies. He returned on October 30, just five days after the explosion in LM-5.

EXCERPT FROM LM-5 PHASE II RELIABILITY ASSESSMENT

October 29, 1968
Inner window failed under pressure test (vacuum testing of spacecraft) at 5.1 psig. The engineering investigation of the window failure is summarized in VDI APS #8. The LM-5 cabin cleanup, has been completed. It should be noted that the LM-5 cabin has been successfully proof pressure-tested to 7.7 psig on January 28, 1968. A complete analysis of LM window problems has been performed. The problem areas have been resolved. . . . Left hand outer window cracked. Problem has been resolved and window was replaced on LM-5.
Anomaly Description: Forward inner window panel. Structural crack under LM pressure proof test. Explosive decompression and loss of cabin pressure.
Subsystems Affected: Explosion may directly injure crew (Crew Safety).

Aside from providing one of 1968's great marvels of understatement, the LM-5 window explosion spread an unusual poison throughout the cabin. "All the glass wound up on the floor, and in little nooks and crannies," explains LM-5 team manager Ross Fleisig. "Unless it was cleaned up properly, in space the glass would float into the air, and it could be aspirated into the lungs. So we had a hiatus of about a week, when nothing was done to make progress on the vehicle. That week was used to clean out the vehicle. They went around with high vacuum pumps to suck out every microscopic piece of glass."

And then . . .

EXCERPTS FROM THE LM-5 LOG

October 30, 1968
4:25 A.M.   After approximately 10 hours of operation, radar performs as it did the first night (unstable, erratic, shudders, trembles and what not). Gyros not quite as bad as first go around. Antenna, within limits, seems to perform a little better than the first night.
P.S.   HAPPY HALLOWEEN—BOO

October 31, 1968
Crew Compartment Fit and Functional Team has $3,000,000 worth of equipment in cabin, and they are locking it up and posting guards around it (with machine guns), so I couldn't go inside.

EXCERPTS FROM LM MEETING HELD IN BETHPAGE

October 31, 1968
Addition of (American) Flag Kit to the first Lunar Landing vehicle: This item was approved by committee earlier this month and forwarded to Grumman for comment. George Franklin reported that the two flags, if made out of nylon, and their container would not exceed 1.25 pounds. Container concept is to vacuum pack flags in a teflon wrap and cover with Beta Cloth. If the flags were made of silk some weight savings could be recognized but would limit the method of displaying the flags to an under glass display. Stowage in the ascent stage is desirable and can possibly be done with no weight impact for stowage but requires a greater fuel

*budget. General Bolender will discuss this item with Mr.
Low on November 12, 1968. Decision is deferred until then.*

Two weeks later, while General Bolender and George Low
discussed how to plant an American flag on the moon, American
and Australian radio telescopes were scrutinizing still another out-
ward-bound *Zond*. Again crewed by turtles, a Russian, man-ready
spacecraft leapt over the lunar far side and boomeranged back
toward Earth. *Zond 6* executed two minor course corrections
along the way, then skidded into the atmosphere at seven miles
per second, made one shallow skip back into space, and dropped
safely into central Russia.

Close. It was getting very close.

Even as *Zond 6* flew toward the moon, NASA had finalized
and announced its plan to send three men all the way out into
lunar orbit. *Apollo 8* would be ready by December 10. She would
fly on December 21.

Zond 7 was ready. She would fly on December 8.

And LM-5 . . . LM-5 . . .

EXCERPTS FROM LM-5 PHASE III RELIABILITY
ASSESSMENT

Date: November 20, 1968
Place: Bethpage, New York
Portion Excerpted: Handwritten notes of Ross Fleisig
Gilruth is impressed with presentation—excellent. Getting
to crux of the matter. Impressed with some of the technical
problems left, but thinks they will be solved. Phillips—he
agrees with Low and Gilruth. Keep sharp to react quickly
to new problems.

We've built a 1st class vehicle.

Open problems include memory loss in guidance computer (non-recoverable: function may be critical) . . . De-

scent Stage "guillotine" malfunction (landing gear strap caught between blade and housing) . . . Anti-Bacterial Filter spelled wrong . . .

Sum up: Reportable failures have gone from 205 failures for LM-3, to 74 for LM-4, to 57 for LM-5. Significantly improved vehicle . . . this is very likely to be the LM to land on the moon—it should be.

On the morning of December 8, 1968, *Zond* 7 stood on the pad, with Pavel Belyayev curled inside. He was scheduled to be the first man to feel the gravitational tug of a world that was not his own. He would have been, if not for bad luck, if not for a glitch that showed up in the first-stage booster with less than four hours to go in the countdown. Belyayev was called out of the capsule, and after a thorough inspection of the rocket, *Zond* 7 was launched unmanned. About twenty-seven miles out, the pogo effect set in, and *Zond* was shaken apart and strewn about the stratosphere and blown up.

The race to the moon was over.

40. LINDBERGH AND THE ASTRONAUTS

If you ask George Skurla what his one major remembrance of his days at the Cape is (besides the first landing on the moon, of course), he'll tell you without hesitation of the day his staff assistant, Teddy Giannone, registered Mr. and Mrs. John Smith at the Cocoa Beach Howard Johnson's. That was on December 20, 1968, the day before the flight of *Apollo 8*, and "John Smith" was George's childhood hero, Charles Lindbergh.

He was with the Lindberghs, inside the highest point in the state of Florida, inside the Cyclopean cube known as VAB, when something uncharacteristic began to gnaw at the aviator. From atop one of the catwalks, Charles looked down upon a great white circle, and upon four bays where first, second, and third stages were being stacked. "My God," he said. "This is awfully high, isn't it?"

"Yes," George answered. "This bay alone is bigger than the United Nations Building."

"A city in itself," Anne Lindbergh said. "A city for giants."

George hadn't heard her. He was trying to interpret the expression that had passed over Charles's face. He couldn't.

"You know?" Charles said at last. "I'm not sure whether going to the moon really is the thing we should be doing."

Considering whence they came, the words struck George with all the numbing force of an electric shock. "Oh . . . oh . . . well, I think . . . you know, it's man's greatest drive, to reach out. I think your flight across the Atlantic opened up a whole new world in aviation, and I think our going to the moon is bound to do something like that."

"Well"—that puzzling expression was gone—"it certainly is a big, big facility."

Looking at it, Mrs. Lindbergh felt like Rip van Winkle. She turned to George and nodded. "Years ago, when Charles and I used to camp here, it was all jungle and pelicans and white herons, and the only structure for miles around was an old, striped lighthouse."

"The lighthouse is still there," George said.

"Yes, I saw it, dwarfed by this building, and by thirty-some-odd launching towers. It looks like a child's toy now. A relic."

No factories at the Space Center. That was one of the things that impressed Anne Lindbergh about the Cape. Thousands of firms all over America had manufactured the parts and put them together. This place was only for final assembly and testing and launching. And the support equipment! There were whole rooms of computers and television monitors, and Anne found herself trying to compare this world to the one she had seen in the New Mexico desert, more than thirty years ago, when she and Charles met a balding and often abused visionary named Robert Goddard. His ground-support equipment had consisted of a cinderblock wall shelter, a pair of binoculars, a home-movie camera, and an old alarm clock to drive a recording drum. His launch tower had been a converted windmill, and his wife sewed parachutes and recorded flight data. Anne looked about her now, and the world seemed to tilt irrationally, and she felt a strange longing for the homey, personal flavor of rocketry's pioneer days.

But the pioneer days had never really ended, just changed. There was a door leading to the astronaut's quarters. With her husband and George Skurla, she stepped through it, and passed under a sign that warned in big red letters:

NO ONE WITH A COLD OR SYMPTOMS OF A COLD MAY PASS
BEYOND THIS POINT.

There was a Christmas tree in the reception room, an aluminum one. Isolated from the rest of the world were disease-free conference and recreation rooms. Frank Borman, James Lovell, Jr., and William Anders were huddled around a long table covered with star maps and *Lunar Orbiter 1* photographs. It was almost noon when George Skurla and the Lindberghs walked in. The astronauts greeted them cheerfully and invited them to lunch, and George found himself sitting with Charles and Anne Lindbergh on one side, Borman and Lovell on the other. Then the back-up crew for *Apollo 8* came in: Neil Armstrong, Buzz Aldrin, and Michael Collins.

Lunch was filling and quite good; conversation was pleasant and relaxed.

"You know," Charles Lindbergh said, "I used to do some wing walking and parachute jumping, but I've never been in a zero-gravity environment. What is it like?"

"The sensation of weight decreases steadily with altitude until, to an astronaut in orbit, it hardly exists," Lovell explained. "There is no up or down in space, with Earth simply *out there*. Once, on *Gemini*, I squeezed a blob of Tang breakfast drink through a straw. It formed a perfect sphere at the end of the straw, and when I pulled the straw away, the ball of juice just hung there. I could bat it gently back and forth with my fingers, being careful not to hit it too hard and break the surface tension and splatter it all over the walls. I could have spent a whole week tweaking that little ball and watching it vibrate, but finally I pushed it to my lips and sucked it down. Someday it would be fun to take a goldfish up there and have it swim inside a big globe of free-floating water. One good, hard swish of the tail and it would find itself outside the water, swimming in thin air. I wonder if it could find its way back."

"Poor fish," Anne said.

"A very surprised-looking fish," Charles said.

George said nothing. He preferred it that way. He just sat there, taking in the moment, wanting to preserve in his brain every detail, as the old hero spoke with the new heroes-to-be. Charles Lindbergh seemed to him a young man—filled now with a childlike fascination for rockets.

He always had been.

"My husband goes back forty years to his early encounter with rockets," Anne explained. "In the years after his flight to Paris, he began wondering how the limitations of wings and propellers might be overcome. He asked engineers and scientists about strapping rockets on airplanes to reach higher velocities and altitudes, and they explained that rockets burned fuel too rapidly, and reinforced combustion chambers would be prohibitively heavy, totally impractical. And then a newspaper article about this 'mad scientist' whose rocket tests had been banned in Massachusetts caught Charles's attention. At last my husband had found somebody who saw the possibilities: Robert Goddard. I remember an evening sitting on a screened porch, while my husband and this quiet, intense professor talked of space exploration. Flying was then a new adventure to me; I had just won my pilot's license, and these two men were talking of a step far beyond flying: ascent into space."

"Goddard had ideas and dreams far outdistancing his designs," Charles said. "He had envisaged man's landing on the moon and even traveling to the planets, but he was cautious and practical when talking about the next step. 'Theoretically,' he said, 'it would be possible to design a multistage rocket capable of reaching the moon.' But he figured it might cost *a million dollars*."

There was a chorus of laughter, and when it subsided, Charles cocked his head at Frank Borman. "What you were saying about the amount of fuel needed just to lift the *Saturn V* a dozen feet off the ground—were those figures accurate?"

"Yes. Very."

Charles did some mental calculations and started shaking his head. "You know, in the first second of your flight, you'll burn ten times as much fuel as I used flying the *Spirit of St. Louis* from New York to Paris."

"That's tomorrow," Frank said boyishly. "Just think—it's hard to believe—this time tomorrow we'll be on our way to the moon."

That night, the Lindberghs stood a mile west of *Apollo 8*. Floodlamps threw brilliant white spokes on the ship, and into the sky beyond. The extreme cold of the liquid fuels had covered the rocket with a glaze of ice crystals, which sparkled in a million points of light through plumes of ground-seeking vapor.

Seen from this dark field tonight, it has curiously biological overtones, Anne thought, with tears beginning to well in her eyes. As with the newborn, there is something astonishingly tender about it. Vulnerable and untried, this is the child of a mechanical womb, of a scientific civilization—untried, but full of promise. Radiating light over the heavens, it seems to be the focus of the world, as the Star of Bethlehem once was on another December night centuries ago. But what does it promise? What new world? What hope for mortal men struggling on Earth?

The noise hit Anne Lindbergh with such shocking force that she dropped her binoculars. In the intervening miles between her and the rocket, the air was suddenly filled with wings. A great cloud of ducks and herons and unidentifiable small birds had risen from the marsh. The wild flight streamed out in every direction, dashing haphazardly and in alarm, as if this were the end of the world. Anne watched the birds, and during those long seconds, she missed the rocket clearing the launch tower.

Isaac Asimov did not notice the birds. His attention was on the rocket, which, beamed *live via satellite* into his New York living room, now placed him in the unaccustomed position of being too conservative. In 1939 he'd written a science-fiction story describing what was in essence this very mission. But he had placed it in 1973, and he supposed that if someone had asked him in 1939 if he really thought people would fly to the moon and back to Earth in 1973, he'd have said, "Not really, but it makes a good story." Well, they were doing it in 1968, and he was tickled silly as the television camera looked up and up and up, and showed, at an immeasurable distance, the slowly diminishing comet that was *Apollo 8*.

An orbit and a half later, after all systems had been checked and rechecked, Michael Collins opened up a new age when he sent up the first order for men to leave Earth Orbit. As dramatic as the moment was, the conversation was most undramatic. The astronauts got their instructions in five words: "You are go for TLI," meaning Trans-Lunar Injection, and they responded with one word: "Roger."

*   *   *

By late afternoon on December 23, the earth's gravitational pull had slowed the outward flight of *Apollo 8* from 7.0 to 0.8 miles per second. Normally, the ship would have continued to decelerate, until at last its rate of climb leveled off at 0.0 miles per second and then clicked backward to −0.1 . . . −0.2 . . . −0.3 . . . But presently the moon was moving into its path, yanking it away from Earth. Slowly, the ship began to pick up speed, to fall up, tail first, into lunar space.

The astronauts could not see the moon through the Command Module windows. They took it on good faith that it was sweeping up behind them, that Isaac Newton and Ground Control had done their homework. Looking out the ship's nose, they saw the earth receding: "A beautiful, beautiful view," Borman shouted. "A predominantly blue background and just huge covers of white clouds."

Down there, California curved north into Oregon, Alaska, and the North Pole; and south into Mexico and South America, all the way to Cape Horn. Borman saw whole continents wrapped around the surface of a sphere so distant that he could cover it, and all its inhabitants, with his hand. The good Earth, beautiful and . . . and *alive*. Glittering waves of clouds were advancing on Tierra del Fuego. "Better tell them to put on their raincoats," Borman called down to Michael Collins. "Looks like a storm out there."

Lovell turned away from the window. "Frank, what I keep wondering is if I am some lonely traveler from another planet what I would think about the earth at this altitude, whether I'd think it would be inhabited or not. I was just curious if I would land on the blue or brown part of the earth."

"You better hope we land on the blue part," Anders said.

Christmas Eve, 1968:
Ten two-hour circuits round the moon, sunshine and Earthshine, a sky blacker than the deepest mineshaft, with the moon covering a third of it. Names for new craters: Low, Gilruth, Shea,

Chaffee. . . . When flight controller John Aaron was the only man to see through all the excitement that the environmental-control system needed a slight adjustment, Crater Aaron was named on the spot. The crew resisted the temptation to announce the discovery of a huge black monolith. (Oh, yes, they'd seen that movie before they flew.)

"We don't know if you can see this on the TV screen," Anders reported. "But the moon is nothing but a milky waste. Completely void."

Borman interjected, "This is *Apollo* 8 coming to you live from the moon. We've been flying over it at sixty-mile altitude for the last sixteen hours. The moon is a different thing to each of us. I think that each of us carries his own impression of what he's seen today. I know my own impression is that it's a—a vast, lonely, forbidding expanse of nothing."

—they named the Crater Grissom—

(Our God-given curiosity will force us to go there ourselves because in the final analysis only man can fully evaluate the moon in terms understandable to other men.)

"It looks rather like clouds and clouds of pumice stone."

(. . . in terms understandable to other men)

"And it certainly would not appear to be a very inviting place to live or work. It makes you realize just what you have back there on Earth. The earth from here is a grand relief."

"I think the thing that impressed me most was the lunar sunrises and sunsets," Anders said. "These in particular bring out the stark nature of the lunar terrain, and the long shadows really bring out the relief. The relief is very hard to see in this very bright surface that we're going over right now. . . . We're coming up on a sea filled with dark rubble. There is a fresh, bright impact crater coming right towards us, and a mountain range on the other side."

"Ground Control to *Apollo* 8: We're reading you loud and clear, but we have no picture."

"How about now?"

"Loud and clear and the picture is real fine."

Borman said, "The contrast between the sky and moon is a vivid, dark line."

"The mountains coming up now are heavily impacted with craters," Anders added. "There is a dark area which, umm . . . could be a old lava flow. . . . The crater you're seeing now is about thirty or forty miles across. . . . We're now going over the Sea of Tranquility. It might be one of our future landing sites. It's smooth in order to be clear of having to dodge mountains. And you can see the long shadows of the lunar sunrise. . . . We are now approaching the lunar sunrise, and, umm . . . for all the people back on Earth, the crew of *Apollo 8* has a message that we would like to send to you:

"In the beginning, God created the heavens and the earth . . ."

42. THE DRESS REHEARSALS

Two weeks later, *Soyuz 4* and *5* linked up in space for an exchange of crews while work on the Russian LM continued in secret.

In Florida, LM-3 was on the launchpad and ready for fueling. That was when Wernher von Braun caught Grumman's rocket expert, Manning Dandridge, by the arm.

"The things that stand out in my mind are the things that sound humorous," Dandridge recalls. "You see, this LM sat on top of von Braun's third stage, and he wanted me to assure him that not one drop of propellant would fall down on his rocket. I told him that in every case we had redundant valves in the engines, and in addition to those valves we had what we call isolation valves in the propellant tanks. We had triple protection. And

that relieved his fears, fears that *our* fuel would drip on *his* rocket.
It struck me as funny."

Tommy Attridge had pasted together a poster showing the two
men who would fly LM-3: Jim McDivitt and Rusty Schweickart.
And—*crack!*—there it was: the LM, and Grumman's first men
in space.

Tommy held the poster in his hands and shook his head. "It
was kinda something that the people in Bethpage didn't realize
was going on," he says. "We had the F-14 program coming up.
We had the A6 program, the EA6 program, the E2 program. There
were a lot of programs going on in Bethpage besides that thing
over there in Plant 25, and all of a sudden, Hey! These two guys
are going to be our first step in space. McDonnel-Douglas had
been in the space program for a long time. Rockwell had been in
the program for a long time. They'd fired people up and down in
Mercury and *Gemini* and the *Apollo* Command Module, and here
we were about to send people out there on a very critical mission.
So I decided to take this poster around and get everybody on the
Grumman team to sign it. The guys down at the Cape signed it,
and I brought it back to Bethpage and a bunch of guys in Bethpage
signed it. It went to Houston. It went everywhere. Then I talked
it over with Jim McDivitt: 'What can we do? We want to send
this into space—not the actual poster but something we can make
replicas from after the flight.' And he said, 'Gee, that's neat. We'll
make a color negative and take it into space with us, and then,
after we get back, we can make some life-size prints.' "

It wasn't quite good enough just to have the poster reproduced, Tommy thought. I can get a picture of the launch, and
we can add a few other pictures that will really put the mission
in perspective. And we'll do the same for the other LMs.

LM-5. They would not do it quite the same way. Her crew
would carry *two* negatives into space. One would be returned to
Grumman for reproduction. The other would be left with the
descent stage on the moon. And, among all the hundreds of
signatures, two hand-drawn boxes would enclose the names Larry

Moran, Joe O'Neill, Lawrence Schlobehm, John Post, Sal Giuata, Milt Purdy, Al Declue, and Ray Rodriguez—eight people who had touched the ship, built her, or directed her building. Their brains had imagined the LM-5 flight, but like Moses, they were permitted only a single glimpse of the Promised Land.

Two little boxes.

They were an epitaph.

On March 7, McDivitt and Schweickart crawled through the Command Module's roof hatch and into the Lunar Module, where the "floor" and "ceiling" were orientated in the opposite direction from the ship they'd just left. This compounded the orientation problems and queasy feelings that had already gotten the *Apollo* 9 mission dubbed the "zero-gravity vomiting championships." Schweickart started throwing up almost as soon as he began to feel the sensation of weightlessness. Given the combination of bad smells and desperate scrambles for empty fecal bags— *cheeks full of vomit*—it almost became contagious.

"Space sickness," says astronaut Joseph Allen, "has something to do with what the eyes see. I don't want to make too much of this, but in one case one of our crew [on STS-5]* was putting up the shades to go to sleep, and he regurgitated when he looked up and saw the earth in a place he didn't expect it. In another instance, he was taking the sun shades down and had the same problem."

"It seems to be a sensory contradiction in the brain," explains Jesco von Puttkamer. "The eyes tell the brain something different than the fluid-motion sensors in your ear tell it. The inner ear has a sensory system that measures, first, linear acceleration (for example, accelerating forward in a car) and, second, angular acceleration. In weightlessness, however, the fluid is all over the place. As soon as you start turning your head, the fluid is pushed out by centrifugal force in opposite directions. Up becomes both sides of the head at the same time. So the brain gets all kinds of

---

*Space Transport System (i.e., the Space Shuttle).

conflicting and constantly changing messages about where up and down are. And these messages get in conflict with the eye message, which says, 'Everything is fine. I'm just sitting in my seat here.' And the seat of your pants also has a message: 'I don't feel anything.' One cue in the brain is different from the other. They don't agree at all. And the brain has a direct line down to the stomach, and for some reason it says, 'Get rid of food.'"

"They were flying around the world catching that throw-up in fecal bags—*in fecal bags*," says Tommy Attridge. "Christ! There's a picture of Jim McDivitt rummaging around LM-3 in this area called 'fecal storage,' and he thought he'd left some food in there. And he found a bag of food he put in there by mistake. He ate it. He was hungry in space. Dave Scott used to stick his head into the LM while the guys were checking it out to get some water, because the water in the Command Module was artificially extracted from the air and was crummy-tasting, whereas in the LM it was real water, mineral water from Earth. And he'd lean down and squirt some water in his mouth. It was good-tasting water, I guess."

"For the first LM-CM rendezvous in Earth orbit," recalls Arnold Whitaker, "they were a very taciturn crew. They really didn't speak much, and it was clear they were under tension. They just spoke in phrases. There was no conversation, no bantering back and forth. It was a very businesslike operation. McDivitt and Schwickart crawled into the LM and they separated out to 110 miles. It must have been scary, flying away from the Command Module in a machine that was incapable of returning you through the atmosphere to Earth.

"And they started rendezvous. The thing about rendezvous is that it's a very slow process. It's not time-critical. It's not like landing a plane, where you have to do everything right or you crash. If you make a mistake during a rendezvous in space, you just do it over again. You have plenty of time. You're just floating around, and if you make a wrong control action and you see that things are slowly getting worse instead of better, you go around and change it. So it doesn't matter in rendezvous if you take a half hour or an hour and a half. Halfway through this first rendez-vous, the astronauts were at a point of 'What am I gonna do?' That is, it's all working very smoothly, so they got to talking to one another."

A little flat ring drifted in front of Jim McDivitt's face. He called down, "There's a washer between the outside and inside docking windows."

In the Manned Spacecraft Center, Chris Kraft turned and pointed through double windows to Tommy Attridge and Lew Evans in an adjoining room. Tommy took a pad from his pocket and wrote "That's how we keep the windows clean."

Kraft's nose wrinkled.

Tommy wrote three more words: "One extra washer."

In space, the LM-3 pilots were probing the laws of orbital mechanics. Flip the ship over and fire your descent-stage engine against the flight path, then watch the earth flex its gravitational muscles and pull you down. Closer to Earth, confined to a tighter orbit, your angular momentum picks up and you start covering more ground, eventually pulling out ahead of the Command Module. If you don't want to lose your mother ship, you have to thrust yourself forward and swing up to a higher, slower orbit. In essence, you have to speed up to slow down.

From an orbit below the Command Module, McDivitt fired the ascent-stage engine and sent the descent stage tumbling end over end toward South America. He noticed, as it receded, that the ascent stage's small attitude-control rockets had burned holes through the insulation. Plume deflectors—panels designed to catch the exhaust—would have to be fitted to LM-4 and LM-5 before they flew.

"The whole pattern of the mission had changed," says Arnold Whitaker. "The astronauts began to joke with each other, just to pass the time, and you knew the tension was gone in this flight. Everything was running smoothly. And when they went to dock, the darned docking probe wouldn't latch. Well, that could be serious, right? But they were so relieved at this point, they were joking about what would happen if they were never able to get this thing to latch. You know, I was listening to this and saying, 'That's really not the way the mission started, right?' "

Finally, the ascent stage was dumped. Ground Control sent up a signal that fired the ascent engine, raising the ship to a 4,000-by-150-mile orbit. As he watched the glow of the departing thrusters, Schweickart called down, "I hope I didn't forget anything aboard it."

"We do, too," Mission Control said. "You sure McDivitt is there with you?"

"I didn't *forget* him. I left him there *on purpose.*"

Two months later, on the exceptionally clear afternoon of May 18, 1968, Rocco Petrone's launch team sent Tom Stafford, John Young, and Eugene Cernan on mankind's first return to the moon. For a time, it seemed as if they'd never make it. Pogo crept into *Apollo 10*'s first stage—a resonance that had all the frightful qualities of being thrown down one flight of stairs after another. Slammed forward and backward in his couch, Stafford watched instrument dials double and blur and found himself speechless when the first stage finally spent itself and separated. Then the second stage developed the same symptoms, and he began to fear that the ship would come to pieces, especially LM-4 below him, which he imagined might now be leaking hypergolics onto crimpled skins. Something groaned down there. It was the third stage coming to life, spitting and lurching and resonating as it rammed the three men into Earth orbit. That felt and sounded very unright.

They shut the engines down on schedule. A review showed that the LM and all other systems had held together. They were go for TLI. According to standard, written procedure, there was no need for helmets and gloves, but the astronauts wore them anyway—small comfort when Stafford restarted the third stage and it growled and shook all the way into translunar space.

That growl. There had better be a way to get back to Earth if we have to abort the mission on our way to the moon.

Stafford wondered.

Less than halfway to the moon, Young separated the Command/Service Module from the spent stage, executed a 180-degree roll, and watched the four panels that enclosed the LM float away. He docked nose to nose with the third stage and pulled LM free, then continued the long coast to the moon, with the empty stage trailing not far behind. On May 21, the crew fired the Service Module engine against the direction of flight, a braking maneuver that allowed the moon to capture *Apollo 10* in a circular orbit. The next day, John Young inspected LM-4 through the window of the Command Module as Stafford and Cernan danced her around on her axis.

"Okay," Cernan announced. "We're ready to go down and snoop around the moon."

"Roger."

"Don't get too lonesome, John. And don't go off and leave us."

Young used his attitude-control thrusters to nudge the Command Module two miles below LM-4. Then Stafford fired the descent engine against his flight path. The ship slowed, and the moon tightened its gravitational fist, yanking it down to an altitude of eight miles and tossing it ahead of the Command Module.

The moon has only one sixth the earth's gravity, so you must orbit it six times slower than you would orbit the earth or you go flying off into space. The astronauts appreciated the slower pace. It gave them time really to look at the Sea of Tranquillity, to describe the area where the next *Apollo* was expected to land two months later.

"It looks sort of like a volcanic site I saw in Arizona," Stafford said.

They flew along the *Apollo 11* approach path, along a "highway" dubbed by the engineers as *U.S. 1*. "It's much like the desert in California around Blythe. If they touch down on the near end, they'll have a smooth landing. But if they wind up at the far end of the sea, extra fuel will be needed for maneuvering around craters and boulders to a clear spot."

"You ready to drop the descent stage?" Cernan asked.

The rim of the moon tilted crazily, like a dish.

"SONOFABITCH!"

The ship was in seizure, lurching and wobbling and snaking along its orbit.

"We're in a gimbal lock!" Stafford yelled.

Gimbal lock—is that what it was? Had the descent engine swiveled over to one side and stuck? Oh, God, no. Oh, no.

Gimbal lock!

One of the pilots had mistakenly flipped a lever that switched the computer from "attitude hold" to "take over the guidance system and start searching for the Command Module," and the poor computer . . . the Command Module was nowhere in sight!

"Thrust forward! Thrust forward!" Stafford shouted. He punched the abort button to jettison the descent stage and fire the ascent engine, and . . . Oh, no . . . How high are we? That mountain sweeping up ahead. It's at least three miles high!

Attitude-control thrusters fired wildly in odd directions. The master alarm sounded.

—coming at us—

Stafford overrode the computer, took manual control, pitched the ship forward

—BIGGER'N SHIT—

and began working the attitude-control rockets. The gyrations abated.

—calm down, boy, calm down. You've got *plenty* of room—

The mountain passed beneath his feet.

—miles to spare—

It was time to go home to the Command Module, almost four hundred miles away.

Young first spotted LM-4 through a sextant at a distance of 160 miles. By then Stafford and Cernan had got a radar fix on him. The gap closed to one hundred miles, and with unaided eyes, the LM-4 crew could see Young's ship glittering out there in the sunlight. They passed through lunar sunset and into darkness and did not see the Command Module again until they were fifty-five miles closer. A single light flashed on and off, on and off in the night, and the distance shrank at last to twenty-five feet, with the relative speed between the two modules falling to zero. Stafford positioned LM-4 for docking, took aim, and fired her thrusters forward. The capture latches closed with a loud bang. The astronauts crawled through the docking tunnel to the Command Module and cast off the ascent stage.

Later, Mission Control restarted the ascent engine. It burned for four minutes until it ran out of fuel, shooting LM-4 completely away from the moon and into solar orbit. The three men watched it fly up and vanish.

And out there, 1.344 seconds away at the speed of light, Soviet leaders, watching the flight of *Apollo 10*, and knowing full well that, had they wanted to, Stafford and Cernan could have landed their ship on the moon, were now voting to shelve their manned-lunar-spacecraft program. The Russian LM was almost ready, but not ready enough. Officially, the newspapers would claim that Russia had never planned to send men to the moon. And privately, men and women who had labored these many years— under the same aura of excitement and with the same detriment to family life as the Bethpage LM team—would die a little.

43. SOME DEMANDS OF DESTINY

They called LM-5 *Eagle*. Julian Scheer, NASA's public-affairs administrator, had seen to that. He'd had a gutful of less dignified names. Gus Grissom had started the indignities after the sinking of his *Liberty Bell 7*. He'd proposed naming his next ship *Molly Brown*. The suggestion was turned down. His second choice, *Titanic*, was equally unwelcome. After that, missions were named *Gemini 4*, *Apollo 8*, and so on, but then came 1969, and with it *Apollo 9*. Mission Control would have to talk with McDivitt and

Schweickart as they tested LM-3 in Earth orbit, and to Scott in the Command Module. So to avoid confusion, separate names were needed for the two ships. Scott's ship, when it was first delivered to Florida, looked like a candy-wrapped cone, and somebody suggested the name *Gumdrop*. It stuck. For obvious reasons, LM-3 became *Spider*.

Give them an inch, the saying goes, and they'll take a mile. LM-4 was christened *Snoopy*. Its Command Module was *Charlie Brown*. Contributors to the project were given Silver Snoopy Awards.

When it came time to name LM-5, proposals included *Mickey Mouse, Lucifer, Sour Puss, Thing*—even *Titanic* resurfaced. Scheer put his foot down, insisted that with all the world watching, something a little more dignified would have to be used for the first lunar landing. *Eagle* came up and was accepted. When Neil Armstrong suggested Jules Verne's fictional moonship, *Columbia*, for the Command Module, Scheer clapped his hands in approval.

By this time, Grumman was as deeply into plans for space-shuttle hardware as it had been with LM in 1962. However, the company was also turning its attention to diversification in the commercial area. Having just completed design studies for a permanently manned space station, Al Munier sought and received the assignment to look into the development of high-technology products for commercial markets. For him it was "Goodbye, *Columbia.*"

Anne Lindbergh would have appreciated his reasons. "It was different," he says. "It had by 1969 become very bureaucratic. It was typical. In the early days there were some of the best people in the country, all coming together with a desire to accomplish something like the moon landing. It was very personal. By the time we got to the last proposal, there was one chap who went before interrogation (they always had an interrogation before they made a final decision, in what looked for all the world like the Dr. Strangelove Room), and he had some very good things to say, and, well, I don't know. The staff just sat there and didn't say anything. It had gotten bureaucratic, just like everything else does in Washington. And I figured, well, it *was* interesting. I think I'll go onto something else."

The bureaucratic machinery was having a field day. A bloody damned field day. Geologists, chemists, and physicists were almost to the point of slitting each other's throats to get their favorite experiments onto the moon's surface. And then there was that question from the biologists, that nagging question: What if there were microbes in the lunar soil, and what if they were unhealthy for humans and other living things, and what if the astronauts brought them back to Earth?

"Nature doesn't work that way," someone said. It was Lewis Thomas, chairman of pathology at Yale Medical School. "It takes a long and familiar interliving before one organism can cause illness in another and thus become a disease. We needn't begin by fearing the aliens (if they exist) or by deciding how best to kill them. Most associations between living things seem to be cooperative ventures, to one degree or another. If there is a microbe or a strand of RNA or a lost molecule of protein out there in the lunar dust, it will have to wait a long time for acceptance to membership on this planet."

But H. G. Wells had written a novel about octopi that arrived from Mars and conquered the earth with automatons so strange in appearance that they could have passed for LM's cousins. In the end, the Martians were laid low by disease and putrifactive bacteria to which we had long since become immune. Now, with Earthlings about to step onto another world, the roles could reverse irrationally: We could suffer the Martian death. Yet, what if Lewis Thomas was right? What if disease was merely symbiosis gone awry? We'd be safe, then, wouldn't we?

Sure. But what if it turned out that there was more science in Well's fiction than in Thomas's theory?

Okay, what if?

The whole outer skin of the Command Module will be sterilized by the bright flame of reentry.

Okay. What next?

Transfer the capsule, unopened, into an airtight quarantine facility.

Can't do that. The Service Module has to be jettisoned before reentry, and without the module's life-support equipment, the astronauts will suffocate inside the capsule before it can be recovered and loaded into the quarantine area.

The next-best option: Put on biological-isolation suits and climb from the capsule into a rubber raft, breathing through bacterial filters. A helicopter can lift the astronauts from the raft and transport them to a quarantine trailer aboard the recovery ship.

This option was only slightly better than doing nothing at all. If in fact some otherworldly version of the Black Plague lived on or in the lunar dust, *Homo sapiens* would have been doomed from the moment the hatch door banged open. Moon dust tracked into the LM on dirty boots would fill the air as soon as lunar orbit and zero-gravity were achieved. Passing through the docking tunnel with Neil Armstrong and Buzz Aldrin, some of it would settle inevitably on the raft and biological-isolation garments. Gusts from the recovery helicopter's rotor blades would have spread the disease to all points of the compass, and on their way to the quarantine trailer, the astronauts would have infected the helicopter pilots, the aircraft-carrier recovery crew, and, later on, President Nixon.

The *Apollo* Back Contamination Control Panel did not have an exclusive claim on xenophobia. In Bethpage, John Papin, who sculpted many of the little titanium parts that went into the LM, learned that two of his coworkers were FBI agents. Fear of Soviet sabotage was that great.

"It was getting *so* close to the wire," Milt Radimer recalls. "And the closer it got, the more people began to worry about, you know, 'Jesus, if the Russians landed on the moon a couple of days before us . . .' "

Doc Tripp: "There were a lot of stories from people who presumably knew what they were talking about, who could tell you what the Russians were doing and what they weren't doing.

There was always a lot of interest, because the Russians were really the forcing function. We had to get that thing on the moon by a certain time, if not earlier, for the threat was always there that the Russians would beat us to it. If that happened, it would have been like throwing cold water on our part of the program. Because they'd been there already. I don't think we would have necessarily canned the LM program, but it would have certainly been taken off the high speed."

Looking over the plans for the *Apollo 11* mission, Max Faget frowned down on the fact that the first step on the moon would be seen through an ordinary black-and-white television camera with what seemed to be the lowest possible resolution. "I don't believe it," he said. "It is almost inconceivable that the culmination of a twenty-billion-dollar program is to be recorded in such a stingy manner."

He was lucky to be reading about any television coverage at all. At times when little slivers and even molecule-thin layers of metal were being shaved from LM, the television cameras, which had no engineering value, were the first items to go, and at least two camera-shy astronauts had practically begged to fly without them.*

With less than sixty days in the countdown, and LM-5 in the stack, inspectors began to find peculiar crystals in the ship's water-glycol system. This system was responsible for cooling the electronics and the cabin environment. "Fortunately," Joe Gavin says "we had the ability to attach ground equipment to the system and give the ship a complete glycol transfusion without opening the LM up to the point where we had to retest the whole thing.

---

*The original mission sequence had called for only one of the two LM pilots to climb down in front of the camera. The other man would remain on board to tend the lander's systems and await his companion's return. However, a Grumman study indicated that both men could safely leave the ship, and raised questions about the psychological impact on a crewman of landing on the moon, opening the porch door, and not being allowed to step out.

Unfortunately, after we performed the transfusion and began running the old glycol through strainers, we learned that the more we strained the fluid, the more crystals we found. And then we found another batch of crystals growing inside the LM. Finally we had, I think, every damned dish in Grumman in use. We had little batches of glycol sitting all around; we were trying to determine, first of all, what the crystals were and what was causing them to form. We had been testing for six or eight years without having seen this particular phenomenon. And this went on and on as we got closer to the flight date, and we began to get help from a number of research establishments. A number of outside chemists got into the act.

"What we finally did—we were running out of time—was to run a test on the thing we were concerned about: the pumps and valves in the system. We set up an identical LM glycol system here in Bethpage and ran it for an amount in time equal to two missions and showed that even when the glycol was so thick with crystals that it looked like orange juice, everything would work."

Apollo 11 flew with the "orange juice," and it was learned later that, as Tommy Attridge liked to say, *better* had become the enemy of *best*. At the beginning of the LM program, Grumman had bought enough glycol to last beyond *Apollo 20*. They'd bought it from a small company in New Jersey at a total cost of about one hundred dollars, and it was the best stuff anybody could have asked for. Then, in 1969, Eastman Kodak came up with a better idea: a purer solution with an anticorrosion agent added, which produced just the right conditions for seeding billions of tiny, needlelike crystals. *Apollo 12* through *17* would fly with the proven cheap stuff.

Al Beauregard was alone with LM-5, and feeling not all too useful. They'd summoned him down to Florida, and he'd been attending all the important meetings, but he didn't have a hell of a lot to say in matters—in fact, almost nothing at all.

Now, it isn't as if George Skurla is deliberately shutting you off, Beauregard thought. He has his own team down here and he doesn't want any interference, and you really can't blame him. Can you?

Alone and lonely, Beauregard looked down and began to laugh. There was a picture he always carried with him—his little girl's picture—and well, why not? He wedged it under the insulation. It's still there, right behind the American flag, on the right side of the descent stage, on the Sea of Tranquility. The extreme temperatures of the lunar days and nights will, in time, alter chemicals in the film, causing the picture to fade, to one degree or another; but there is no rain or oxidation on the moon, and, though faded, her image will endure, a ghostly stain etched into silver emulsion. Her smile will live long after you and I and the towers of Manhattan have crumbled to dust, long after the *Mona Lisa* and the works of Shakespeare and Homer have ceased to be even a memory.

She will outlive the Sphinx.

Perhaps even Mount Everest.

EXCERPTS FROM INTERVIEW WITH
ARTIE FALBUSH AND JOHN LOGALBO
Date of interview: June 23, 1983
Place: Bethpage, New York

ARTIE FALBUSH: As far as I was concerned, LM-5 was a real ulcer job. At the last minute, they called me down to the Cape. They found a manufacturing error on squibs—little explosive valves that actuate the propulsion system—and they were on a countdown a few days from launch. Well, John Logalbo and Paul Dent and I always tried to be one jump ahead, just in case. So we'd been playing around in the shop, and I made this—we called it a mini-fitting. It had been laying around the shop a long time, this new brazing tool that looked like a gold-filled, stainless-steel ring about a half inch long and a half inch wide: a simple way to mend pipes once you opened them to do some last-minute job, like replacing defective squibs. I had only a few of these things, and they were real crude. We'd made them just to see if they would work, and they'd never had any fatigue tests done in a mock-up or anything like that. But there weren't very many choices. There was a little door in the side of the rocket, and one behind that, in the top of the LM descent stage, and there was no room to do repairs conventionally. It was either fix it or the whole launch was going to be scrubbed. They would have had to take the rocket back to the VAB, demate the Command Module, demate the LM and take it apart and wait until August or September for the next launch window. So my bosses agreed that this new tool looked good, and I went down to the Cape to make sure it would fit. The only fittings I had were the ones I'd made, so while I was at the Cape, Paul [Dent] and John [Logalbo] turned the machine shop on and worked night and day making these rings and testing them. To really see if it would work, we practiced on LM-7, and found that there were squibs on that one that were no good. And our practice came out good. It worked good. In the meantime, Grumman was trying to prove to NASA that these new tools were acceptable, and then John came down with the finished rings and one of the big wheels [Rocco Petrone] gave us a lecture: "If you goof this up, Grumman's gonna look like—you know what Grumman's gonna look like, don't you?"

JOHN LOGALBO: That's encouraging. That's very encouraging.

AF: And then he says, "Well, go to work."

JL: One day—I was on the day crew—I walked to the launchpad and I saw Artie up there. "For crying out loud, why the hell don't you go home," I said. "Leave me alone," he says. He was white as a ghost, working all night. And here you've got this thing on a countdown that's gotta go to the moon and you're nowhere near it. And he's working hard with these people, he's trying to get them organized, and he's skipped the point, in my estimation. This tool that he's talking about—he had to redesign the machine that brazed it in. Every time he heated this thing up, I said, "God! Is it or isn't it?" And I didn't know what we were going to come up with. And God was with us. We had four good shots. We got four of these rings into LM-5.

AF: We were up there working on this thing that runs out to the rocket like a diving board. I had my head in the side of the ship and somebody tapped me on the arm and said, "How you doin'?" I said, "Well, we're comin' along." And who was it but Neil Armstrong? That was his bird, so he was up there with Aldrin. He wanted to make sure we did a good job.

Later that day, Tommy Attridge sat down and began pulling silver LM replicas off little Gumman tie pins—one hundred of them. When he finished, the miniatures occupied a volume small enough to be contained in a three-inch plastic envelope. He gave them to Jim McDivitt, to give to Neil Armstrong, to fly to the moon and back. They'd split the pins fifty-fifty between the astronauts and Grumman.

Cocoa Beach had by this time drawn crowds that would put New York's upcoming Woodstock Festival to shame. Seats closest to the launch site were, not unexpectedly, in very great demand. In order to establish priorities for who got these seats, NASA set up a schedule based upon level of significance, as reproduced here by Bob Watkins, logistics-support manager for the LM program and assistant to George Skurla:

IIP: Incredibly Important People. This group included kings and queens and shahs.

VIP: Very Important People. This group meets the criteria that we all understand as VIP.

RAM: If you weren't an IIP or a VIP, then you were one of the Raggedy Assed Masses. I'm afraid most of us were RAMs.

It was a U-shaped building. Bob Watkins recalls, "The astronauts were in one leg of the U and we were in the other. The astronauts all parked inside the U. That was the VIP parking area. I remember one night, when we had only a few days left in the countdown for *Apollo 11*, I came out of the building to go home, pick up a clean set of clothes, and come back. As I walked into the parking field, a rented car came in and I knew it was an astronaut just by the way the guards waved him through. It turned out to be Mike Collins. I watched him walk up the steps to his side of the building, and suddenly he turned and came back. I stopped and introduced myself to him. I said, 'Mike, I'm from Grumman and we built a good spacecraft and wish you Godspeed on your trip. And I wonder if you would autograph this for my son, Bobby.' He did, and I realized why he had come back to the car. He had a rented car and he came back to check the mileage. I looked at the moon and I had to stifle a laugh.

"I was talking with his sister at a party and I mentioned that— that here's a guy going to the moon and he's worried about the mileage on a rented car. I would think it would be the last thing on his mind. And she said. 'That's exactly the way he was ever since he was a small boy. Our mother told him to make his bed once, and for the rest of his life she never had to tell him to make his bed.' He's a very disciplined, very organized kind of individual. So in his order of priorities, the fact that he had a rented car demanded that he write down the mileage, like you're supposed to do, before you go to the moon."

"What kind of script are you going to have?" Joe Kingfield asked. "Can we have some idea of the kinds of questions you're going to ask us? Being on national TV and all that, I mean, we at least want to know what you're going to say."

"I don't believe in scripts," Walter Cronkite said sternly. "I work right from my mind. Whatever comes into my mind—that's the way it will be."

The next two days at Bethpage are going to be a real dilly, Joe thought.

He was absolutely right.

"Now," Joe began to explain, "the ship's rockets work on hypergolic propellants—"

"Cut!" the director yelled. "What's a hypergolic propellant?"

"I was just getting to that. You take these two chemicals. One's a fuel and the other's a fuel oxidizer, and they ignite each other without having to be lit by a flame. Now, nitrogen textroxide is a very good oxidizer. The nitrogen really wants to get rid of that extra oxygen in a very bad way, and—"

"Cut! Never mind the hyper—hyper . . . whatever they are. Let's leave them out. Nobody in the audience is going to have any idea what you're talking about. Don't get too technical for the people."

And so it went, for hours . . . and days. Every time Joe tried to explain something, it seemed, the director yelled, "Cut! . . . Now, Joe, you really don't want to say that. You really want to say this. . . . And don't wait for Walter to ask you the question. Try to anticipate what he's going to ask you."

—I don't believe in scripts—

"Try to anticipate what he's going to ask you."

—Whatever comes into my mind—

"But—"

—that's the way it will be—

"But—but . . ."

"Now, Mr. Kingfield," Walter Cronkite said, "would you please explain this Clean Room to us. Use your own words, and tell me what you think."

"Well, here's where quality control really comes to a head. They say you have to have a back like a crocodile to be in my business." Joe looked around and swallowed hard. He talked for the next five minutes.

"Cut! I didn't like anything you said. Now, do you remember when you said you watch over everyone and how your job is to pry into their work? I want you to say your job is somewhat like the monitor in a high-school hallway. And remember what you said in the very beginning? I want you to say . . ." Joe didn't remember the beginning of the damned thing, much less what this film director wanted him to say. The whole production was turning into a horror story, and if it continued for much longer, Joe thought, he'd soon be too confused to remember his own name.

And it did continue. "Cut! Mr. Kingfield, you just blocked out Walter from the camera!" Joe Kingfield and Walter Cronkite were walking toward a LM, and someone stepped on Cronkite's wire and yanked him backward, snapping the microphone off the back of his head. Joe was seized by the giggles.

After two full, unendurable days of filming, Joe and his co-workers logged about ten seconds on television. Joe guessed that they'd all been so terrible that Walter had to fill in the whole thing: "*Apollo 11* is ready for flight. That's the official word from the astronauts' doctor, after the day's final major prelaunch physical.

"How can a society, which seems to have difficulty building a reliable washing machine, dare to build a spacecraft to land on the moon? Part of the answer lies in a technique called QC, or quality control. Our example is the Grumman aircraft plant in Bethpage, Long Island, the builder of the Lunar Module itself.

"QC is a major function here, kind of like the monitor in the corridors of high school. I asked Joe Kingfield, QC program manager, do people take offense sometimes?"

"Well, generally they say they give us these black hats to match our black hearts. But I really don't think so. I think everybody recognizes the role we play in the program and they do their most, er, their best to help us."

"Quality control on these Grumman moon landers is undeniably impressive. Yet even the men in charge here point out that quality control is basically a human technique, and therefore only as good as the people carrying it out. Just in our two days of filming this story, we saw several violations. A worker on a scaffold called for a tool. Someone below tossed one up, and it struck the fragile skin of LM-7, scheduled to fly with *Apollo 13* sometime next year. A cabin monitor stopped a worker without gloves from approaching a LM. They argued, and the monitor backed down.

"Nevertheless, as LM-7, looking like a jolly Japanese Christmas-tree ball with all its red tags, rolled out of the Clean Room for Florida and the moon, there was no question that despite human fallibility, quality control has achieved a phenomenal record of performance in the Apollo flights. Certainly, if Detroit built automobiles this way, the price might be considerably higher, but so would the trade-in value. Walter Cronkite, CBS News, Bethpage, New York."

44. IGNITION

George Skurla finished a hearty breakfast with the *Apollo 11* crew, and then, perhaps predictably, fell silent. He just couldn't shake the thought that in two hours these guys would be dead, or they would be way out there.

"Okay, guys, we're gonna go now," someone called from the door. "Time to suit up."

Everybody stood. The chaplain would walk with them down the long corridor, and Neil Armstrong turned to shake George's hand and—and, gee, what do you say at a time like this?

George wondered.

He said, "Good luck. Don't get your feet wet."

Below, on Earth, a needle of white smoke stood away from southern Florida. A point of light shone at its tip, and as the seconds passed, it shifted perceptibly, deliberately toward the east. Climbing outside the atmosphere, the light ceased to leave vapor in its wake. *Apollo 11* became a lone firefly, streaking toward Europe in low Earth orbit. Soon, the third-stage engines would cut off, and the glow would go out.

Far away to the northeast, another firefly had risen suddenly from central Russia and traveled on. An American satellite saw the infrared flash, and presently the hotline between Washington and Moscow was alive with voices.

45. UNBELIEVABLE NEWS

Peggy Hewitt's grandmother was visiting her in Florida when *Apollo* 11 lifted off. Peggy had invited her down from Philadelphia to see the launch because at ninety-eight, she could remember when the first automobile had been driven. She had been witness to the most astonishing decades that *Homo sapiens* had ever known, or probably ever would know: the conquest of air in flimsy, kitelike planes, the undoing of the sound barrier, and now the bridging of worlds.

"She thought it was great," Peggy Hewitt recalls. "She was probably more impressed with *Apollo* than I was. She thought she was a very, very fortunate woman. She was born right after the Civil War, with an outhouse, a horse and buggy, a cooking hearth, and no telephone. Cars and gas stoves and telephones didn't exist. And when she died, we'd been to the moon and back, and everybody had a telephone and television and everybody drove a car. She didn't drive, though. I tried to teach her how to drive when she was about eighty, but she didn't really take to it very well. Still, to have lived in such a vibrant time, she felt so lucky."

"Try to picture what *Apollo* must have been to a person who was born in the 1880s," Tommy Attridge says. "My wife had an aunt who was. She could comprehend going from horse-drawn carriages to electric cars to gasoline-powered things, and she actually drove her own car. And she understood the telephone, and electric ranges as opposed to coal stoves. But going to the moon was just a little bit too extreme for her. She couldn't deal with it. And she never believed it. She thought the media was putting her on.

"I can understand that. I really can. We're living through an incredible century. Things are just happening so quickly. Today you talk about integrated circuits and—I have a tiny, credit-card-size calculator now, which cost me ten dollars, which does more than the Texas Instruments calculator I bought in 1974, which did addition, multiplication, subtraction, and division, *period*. That's all it would do. It cost one hundred dollars and it weighed about a half pound. That was the state of the art in 1974. I suppose even the LM, in retrospect, is a primitive thing.

"Yeah, I can understand how my wife's aunt must have felt. She watched it happening on television, and to her it was like a hoax, a science-fiction movie."

And the news on the television *was* unbelievable: "We've just received an update from the Jordell Bank Observatory in England," Frank Reynolds announced. "The observatory is presided over by Bernard Lovell, who we've heard a great deal from lately. He tells us how they have sighted a significant change in the orbit of *Luna 15*, which is the Russian spacecraft now flying around the moon. And he said it meant the Russian spacecraft was either doing reconnaissance or preparing to land on the moon. They don't know which. And we don't either. We'll find out, in time, but we don't know at the moment. They said *Luna 15* and *Apollo 11* are still far apart as they circle the moon. No danger of their getting in each other's way. They thought, um . . . there might be some chance that *Luna 15* would settle down someplace where it could watch, electronically—this unmanned craft—where it could watch the *Apollo 11* landing. That's all we know, and we don't even really know that. But we'll find out the facts and pass them along as soon as they're available."

As he separated from *Columbia*, Armstrong called out, "The *Eagle* has wings!"

Landing would be difficult, but Armstrong's big concern was with the complexities of lifting off from the moon's surface, locating a mother ship in space, and docking with it. Watching from his home on Long Island, Bob Ekenstierna, who had supervised the day-to-day construction of *Eagle*'s descent stage, was concerned about landing an untried vehicle. If they got past the landing, he thought, the rest would be clear sailing. But there were too many what-ifs in the landing part. What if the ship pounded down at some odd angle in soft powder? What if there wasn't enough fuel to land safely? They had to land upright. *They had to*. If they tilted or tipped over, there would be no leaving. Eky knew these things, and more. There was no contingency plan. If the astronauts landed wrong and could not get off the moon, NASA would immediately cut its lines to the public-communications network, maintaining its own contact with the doomed men, and that would be that.

Eky listened to the live transmissions—listened, and prayed. Nobody knew how soft the ground was going to be. Nobody knew what was going to happen next. Truly nobody. *Surveyor 1* had made a safe landing; that much was true. But the weights weren't the same. It was not the same as going down with a big thing like *Eagle*, and it was not the same as going down in the Ocean of Storms.

Mike Collins's voice crackled down from *Columbia*: "I think you've got a fine-looking flying machine there, *Eagle*, despite the fact that you're upside down."

"*Somebody's* upside down," Armstrong called up.

"Okay, *Eagle*, one minute to T. You guys take care."

"See you later. Going right down U.S. 1, Mike."

"Chet Huntley here, at the NBC newsroom. The Russian spacecraft has changed its orbit somewhat and is now in an equatorial orbit around the moon, which is virtually the same path as our mission, um, is on; only *Luna 15* is considerably higher than Collins in *Columbia*. Now, this opens up all sorts of room for conjecture as to what *Luna 15* is doing, does it not?"

"Well, Chet," Frank Reynolds said, "before I let us get too far on that, I got some later information. The Jordell Bank Observatory provided a little more information, and the last word on it was that *Luna 15* is about ten miles above the surface of the moon, but it's not flying the equatorial path on its orbit. We're going across from east to west, er, just about where the equator of the moon is—about the middle of it—and they are coming from the southeast to the northwest. Er, so the two paths will intersect only above the landing site, and then only briefly, so far as any impact consideration might be concerned. But it is enormously intriguing to know—to *try* to figure out what they might be up to."

"Well, certainly we have no reason ever to conclude that the Russians plan in any way to interfere with the *Apollo 11* mission. That—there's just no basis for *that*."

"On the contrary, they've given us assurances that they will not."

"Certainly. However, there is every reason to conclude that they would, if possible, choose to observe our mission: photograph it, even televise it, I suppose. It's not out of the question. And, if we want to do some way-out thinking, I suppose, Frank, do you suppose they might be standing by for a possible rescue mission?"

"Boy! That's an intriguing thought. I don't—You said far out, but it *is* intriguing. But I would like to think—there's something in me that would like to think that they would undertake such a thing. I would not like to think that a rescue would be necessary. But if one were, and if the Soviet Union had thought that far ahead and was prepared to undertake such a thing, I think it would be enormously rewarding. Yes, of course. But, as you say, we have no reason to think anything like that."

Tom Kelly was too busy at Houston Mission Control to be thinking about *Luna* 15 or anything else but the garbled voices emanating from lunar skies. For some unknown reason, the master alarm (remember the master alarm?) was sounding aboard *Eagle*, and the Bit Error Comparator displayed computer overloads. Armstrong jiggled some switches and punched the instrument panel a few times. That stopped the master alarm, at least temporarily. Mission Control watched the out-feeds from the ship and assured the astronauts that there was no real problem.

"Eagle. *You are go. Take it all at four minutes. Roger, you are go—you are go to continue power descent. You are to continue power descent. Altitude forty thousand feet. We've got data dropout. You're still looking good. . . .*"

In Houston's Grumman Control Room, Ross Fleisig watched Armstrong's heartbeat climb steadily higher. The man seated next to him had introduced himself as the president of the company that had supplied *Eagle*'s landing radar. "That radar had better work right," he'd said, "because my neck is on the line." Presently, his knuckles were turning white.

"Altitude 13,500. *Eagle, you're looking great at eight minutes. Correction on that velocity, now reading 760 feet per second. . . .*"

The radar manufacturer passed out. Ross Fleisig didn't notice. Neither did anyone else.

Inside *Eagle*, more warning lights came on and had to be cleared. At seven thousand feet the ship entered *high gate*: pilot parlance for the beginning of the approach phase of a runway landing. The computer automatically fired the attitude-control rockets and kicked the LM into an upright, forward-facing angle to give Armstrong and Aldrin their first close-up view of the landing area. The moon filled almost the entire field of vision. It was less than a mile away, so they could see only a small fraction of its surface—and more and more of this fraction was slipping behind the horizon and out of view as they rode down U.S. 1. In seconds, Aldrin's eyes adapted to the bright lunar day. There was infinite detail below: a sea of hardened lava, colorless and astonishingly old. Every square inch seemed to be peppered with meteorite craters. Even the craters had craters. He suspected (correctly) that if he could get down on his hands and knees, he'd find dime-size craters, and he'd learn that even these were scarred with hundreds, perhaps thousands of microcraters.

This magical first view from high gate was broken by a sudden chain of warnings from the computer. The two men were still clearing alarms and watching cabin displays when Armstrong looked out the window and saw that only two thousand feet and about three minutes' time separated them from the Sea of Tranquility. A large crater strewn with automobile-size boulders was coming up at him.

He took control from the computer.

If he could land just on the lip of the crater, he thought, that might make a few scientists very happy. But the thought was only fleeting; he'd probably die trying. So he pitched the lander forward and fired the descent engine with the flight path instead of against it, picking up horizontal speed. He maneuvered to avoid parking on a mound of crater ejecta. Then, *"Five percent . . . quantity light seventy-five feet—"*

The quantity light flashed menacingly on the instrument panel. Its message was *You have barely five percent of your landing fuel left in the descent stage.*

Eagle's computer down-linked the news to Earth. A second later, racing between two worlds, the warning passed another signal flying in the opposite direction.

"Sixty seconds!"

Sixty seconds on a countdown to abort. If Armstrong did not have his ship sitting on the moon within a single sweep of the stopwatch, he would be ordered to fire the descent engine to full throttle, then fire the guillotine and ascent engine and—

Too late for that now, Aldrin thought. Altitude fifty feet. We've entered the *dead-man zone*. One wrong move and we'll be on the rocks before we can reach for the abort button.

"Things still looking good," said Armstrong. "Down in a half . . . six forward . . . light on . . . down two and a half . . ."

The lander started slipping to the right and rear—and there was no rear window, no way to see boulders or craters or other traps in waiting. Armstrong managed to push *Eagle* forward, but he could not eliminate her drift to the right.

It's always nice to have a gallon left when you read empty, Aldrin thought, but no such luck with the moon just beyond human reach. He felt no apprehension. Absolutely none. What he felt instead was a kind of arrogance, an arrogance inspired by knowing that so many people had worked for this landing.

"Forward . . . forty feet, down two and a half, kicking up some dust . . ."

The descent engine sent moon dust flying, not in a swirl of cauliflower billows but in a low-angle spray of high-velocity particles unimpeded by air. The spray fanned out in every direction, like rays of light, giving Aldrin the impression that he was descending into a fast-moving fog.

"Thirty feet, two and a half down . . . faint shadow . . . four forward . . . four forward . . . drifting to the right a little . . . six . . . drifting right—"

"Thirty seconds!"

Nobody was speaking at Mission Control. Tommy Attridge was looking at one corner of a LM console, anticipating a signal from one of the rod-shaped probes that poked down from *Eagle's* hind feet, a signal that would mean *I've touched something solid!*

"Four forward . . . drifting right . . ."

A blue light winked on. "They're down!" Tommy called.

"Huh?" someone said.

"Yeah," he said, pointing. "They're down. They landed!"

"Contact light. Okay, engine stopped . . . descent engine override off . . ."

(With seven seconds of fuel to spare.)

"Houston—er—Tranquillity Base here. The Eagle *has landed."*

"Roger, Twank—Tranquillity, we copy you on the ground. You've got a bunch of guys about to turn blue. We're breathing again."

Ascent-stage supervisor Chet Senig watched from the Grumman Clean Room. Half of the men were hooting and clapping. The other half were weeping. One of them pounded him on the back and said, "Well, Eky and his boys did a good job, right? Now, Senig, let's see what your half of the ship is going to do."

47. WHAT THE WORLD NEVER SAW ON TELEVISION

At Tranquillity, Armstrong reported that a tan haze surrounded the ship. Engine-scoured dust was flying out for miles in every direction. It settled quickly, unveiling boulders and bumps. The moon is only about as wide as Australia, so its curve is much sharper than the earth's. From the window, Armstrong looked out across the broad Tranquillitatus plain to a horizon that was only two miles away. Glancing down, he noticed that engine exhaust had apparently fractured some of the nearby rocks. Peeking upward through the rendezvous window, he saw Earth.

At the Grumman Control Room in Bethpage, engineering manager John Coursen and Manning Dandridge listened with the rest of the world to Aldrin's first descriptions of the landing area: "We'll get to the details of what's around here, but it looks like a collection of just about every variety of shape: angularity, granularity, about every variety of rock you could find. The colors—well, there doesn't appear to be too much of a general color at all; however, it looks as though some of the rocks and boulders are going to have some interesting colors in them."

"Roger, Tranquillity. Be advised that there are lots of smiling faces—"

"*Oh no . . .*" someone groaned.

John Coursen turned and saw one of his engineers staring into a console, his eyes beginning to bug out. Something was definitely ungood. John walked over to see what was going on. Dandridge joined him.

Incoming data showed that temperature and pressure had soared alarmingly in one of the descent-stage fuel lines. "Better get on the line to Kelly," Dandridge said. "Fast."

In Houston's Spacecraft Analysis Room, Tom Kelly had seen it happening on the readouts and was already on the phone with George Low: "We think cold helium did it. Froze a slug of fuel in one of the lines. The pipe is blocked solid, and we've got a bad pressure buildup between that frozen slug of fuel and a valve close to the engine."

The descent-stage engine had reached 5,000°F just before touchdown. Now residual heat was soaking back along the fuel lines. The pressure between the valve and the slug inched up even as Tom spoke.

"How bad is it?" Low asked.

"Don't know. What I'm really worried about is that trapped, frozen fuel. It's going to get hot, very suddenly, and it's a rather unstable chemical when you heat it up. There's no telling what it will do. We're not talking about a hell of a lot of it, but I just don't want to take a chance of having that slug go off like a little hand grenade inside there, right in the middle of everything."

"Recommendations?"

"We're working on a few. So far it looks like you might want to restart the descent engine at about ten percent power for a split second—sort of like burping a baby. That ought to relieve the pressure."

"Burp the engine? Can that be dangerous?"

"Probably not. We're looking into it."

"I'll have to talk with my team."

"Don't talk too long," Kelly warned. "We may only have about five or ten minutes."

As yet, the astronauts knew nothing about the crisis that was developing under their feet. During the first free minute in the postlanding checklist, Aldrin withdrew a wafer and a small flask of wine and took Communion on the moon. He read to himself a passage from the Book of John. He had planned to read his Communion back to Earth, but he submitted to pleas from Space Agency directors, who were already wading through a sea of protests from the American Civil Liberties Union, and at least one major lawsuit that had followed the *Apollo 8* reading of *Genesis*.

Okay, Aldrin thought, no biblical readings allowed. Instead, he announced, "Houston . . . I would like to request a few moments of silence. I would like to invite each person listening in, wherever or whomever he may be, to contemplate for a moment the events of the last few hours and to give thanks in his own individual way."

"Oh, God," John Coursen said. "We've got to get them out of there. Got to—" Blueprints had unfolded everywhere. Engineers were rushing from table to table, from phone to phone, searching for clues. Will it be a powerful burst? Powerful enough to damage the ascent stage? Nobody was sure, except that even a light burst might squirt fuel or oxidizer or both into the hot engine compartment, and there was no telling what that would lead to. "Get them out of there, back into space. Tell them to leave right away."

"No," Dandridge said firmly. "That's unwarranted. There are other options."

John thought about one of those options for a moment. Then for another. Sure, we can burp the engine. That's bound to relieve some of the pressure. Just crack the valves on the engine slightly, which might not be so good. *Or we can leave,* and leave the problem behind us in the descent stage. But that's not the option we want. We just got there.

Tom Kelly's voice blazed over the speaker system: "I think we've just about convinced Low to burp the engine, with some large number of people objecting down here because we don't know exactly what the LM's attitude is. If one of the footpads is sitting in a hole and we give the engine a sudden kick, they think we might just roll it over on its side."

Nobody knew, at this time, that the landing legs—originally designed to keep the LM steady on a regolith of deep dust or on a dome of ice—had penetrated barely two inches into the surface and found no ice. Now, with the possibility that *Eagle* would be tossed up from the ground at some odd angle, her overdesigned legs had become her safety net.

"We really think the spread of the landing legs is enough that the burp won't tip the ship over," Tom continued. "I'm more worried about that trapped fuel. If you heat it up above a certain temperature, and we're approaching that temperature, it just becomes unstable and nobody's sure just what it's liable to do. It might just sit there quiescently, but it might also detonate explosively. So we don't want to take a chance on that. We just want to get it out of there before it—"

"There it goes!" somebody yelled.

John Coursen saw it go. The pressure started down, then inched up again, then fell abruptly and stayed down. Either the ice slug and shattered and melted on its own, flying back toward the fuel tank before the worst of the back-seeping heat could reach it, or the pipe between it and the engine had ruptured and relieved the pressure. In either case, the problem had solved itself. And only a handful of people on Earth knew that there had been any problem at all.

Almost ten minutes had passed since Tommy Attridge saw the blue contact light wink on. Armstsrong and Aldrin were snatching bits of food between housekeeping chores. They liked the feel of one-sixth Earth gravity, and they wanted to go out for a walk.

Donald Slayton, presiding over the astronaut-training corps, had suspected that the men would want to skip their scheduled rest period. It was silly to expect them to land for the first time on another world and then to put their feet up and take a nap. They wanted to get out and take a look around. Mission Control agreed. Well, and why not? They'd be on prime-time television.

Armstrong knew that he had to be careful moving around the cabin in a pressure suit. One wrong turn and the backpack could bash half a dozen switches. Damn, he thought. We're so clumsy in these things, and it takes so much muscle just to flex an elbow that everything is—*wham!*

(*Snap!*)

"Oh, gosh. Er, Houston. I'm terribly sorry, but I just backed into a circuit breaker. It's for the arming switch and I . . . I think I broke it."

Wonderful, John Coursen thought. Just wonderful. There's the arming switch, which you turn on, *then* you push the button to start the ascent engine. Fine job, Neil. You just broke your ignition key. Okay. Blueprint time again.

Armstrong wanted to arm the ascent engine by sticking his pen in the circuit breaker, but that idea was *right out*. Stuffing a pen in there could short out any number of systems.

"Not to worry," Tom Kelly announced. "There's plenty of redundant wiring and plenty of time to work the problem out on a mock-up. We'll just find a new sequence of switches for them to throw. Piece of cake. We can tell the astronauts to go out and enjoy their walk and we'll work it out down here."

"And that's pretty much how we handled it," recalls Manning Dandridge. "We worked out a new sequence while the astronauts took a walk. That damaged arming switch did have me worried for a while, though. Electrical problems always worried me. I didn't worry about the engines themselves or the propulsion systems. The only thing I worried about were the little electrons in the wires. Were they gonna get to the right place at the right time?

"We managed to find a new path through which to arm the

ascent engine, to reroute the electrons and get them where they belonged. And somehow the public never learned about it. The public didn't know about a lot of things. In fact, the astronauts weren't told a lot, and probably with good reason, because why worry them until, you know, till you get everything all fixed up?"

Buzz Aldrin agrees: "As for the element of risk, that is present at every stage in a mission, and you can't eliminate it entirely. You just don't dwell on it unnecessarily."

They vented the air out of the cabin. Then Armstrong backed slowly, carefully, down the nine rungs of the ladder. At the second-to-last rung, he reached to his left and pulled a small ring that deployed a camera from the side of the ship. And thus began the first live (albeit fuzzy) telecast from the moon

"Neil, this is Houston. You're loud and clear. Buzz, this is Houston. Radio check and verify TV circuit breaker in."

"Roger. TV circuit breaker's in."

"And we're getting a picture on the TV!" Houston announced.

"Oh, you got a good picture, huh?" Aldrin said.

"Okay, Neil. We can see you coming down the ladder now."

Halfway to the moon, Mike Collins had asked Armstrong what he planned to say when he stepped onto the surface. He didn't know, and it was not until he approached lunar orbit that the words gelled in his mind. There had, of course, been a whole bombing run of suggestions, and Armstrong rejected them all. After all, nobody told Columbus what to say when he walked into a new world.

"I'm stepping off the LM now . . . That's one small step for man. One giant leap for mankind."

On NBC, Frank Reynolds looked puzzled. "I think he said 'One small step for man, but one giant leap for man.' I'm not certain."

"The, a . . . surface is fine and powdery. I can pick it up loosely with my toes." And then, seven months after the *Apollo 8* crew had looked down upon a world that was to them a cold and forbidding place, Armstrong spoke words that nobody expected to hear from the moon: "It's *pretty* out here."

Pretty?

Pretty . . . and alien, and fully describable.

(in the final analysis—)

It was Armstrong who spoke the first words on the moon.

(—only man can fully evaluate the moon—)

It was Aldrin who spoke the most beautiful ones.

(—in terms understandable to other men.)

It was Aldrin who scanned the horizon and summed up a whole world in just two words: *"Magnificent desolation."*

Aldrin broke out in gooseflesh as he stepped away from *Eagle*, and he immediately began to play with the dust at his feet. If he were to kick a clod of dirt on Earth, the lighter particles would become smoke while the larger, heavier ones traveled on. Here, all of the dust traveled the same distance. The excitement became too much, and Buzz Aldrin became the first man to pee in his pants on the moon.* More than one billion people were watching, but only Aldrin knew what they were really seeing. One of those billion viewers was Charles Lindbergh, whose attention kept drifting from Tranquillity Base to Mike Collins, alone in the sky.

Aldrin walked off toward a shallow crater, then started bounding forward, much like a child playing hopscotch. In lunar gravity, he and his suit and the bulky backpack weighed only fifty pounds. The slow, up-and-down motion produced a wonderful feeling of buoyancy, but he noticed immediately that his inertia was much greater than on Earth. Though he weighed less, he still carried the same mass that went along with three hundred Earth-pounds, so his forward acceleration was six times as sluggish as it would be on Earth. He could not simply sprint off at full speed in some direction. He had to build speed gradually with each successive hop—and when he wanted to stop, all that mass would still be there, wanting to continue forward. If he tried to

---

*Anticipating this, the engineers had provided each space suit with a urine-collection system.

stop in one step, like an Earth-bound runner, he'd wind up face-down in the dust, probably at the end of a long skid mark. On the moon, the laws of motion mechanics dictated that he had to use five or six steps to wind down to a stop. The physicists had said the moonwalk would be difficult, but his mind and body were adapting with surprising rapidity to the new rules. It was almost as if man belonged there.

Meanwhile, Armstrong walked over to the descent-stage panel that had deployed the television camera, reached behind, and began pulling out rock boxes, rakes, an American flag, and two experiment packages. His eyes paused at a handwritten message on the gold foil. *"What the h—"* and his better judgment told him not to mention it . . . for now.

Aldrin had stopped moving. He just stood there, looking around. The desert ranged from dusty gray to tan, depending on the slant of the sun's rays, and there was darkness all around the horizon. Here was unearthly beauty, made more unearthly and more beautiful by two apparitions. The first was his ship, blazing there in its thermal jacket of silver and black and gold. The second was Earth itself.

At Aldrin's feet lay rocks of almost inconceivable age. When they had formed, the remotest single-celled ancestors whose DNA ran in his veins had not yet appeared in Earthly seas. To feel the weight of time in one of those rocks, to understand them in terms of human lives, requires a thought experiment: If you started counting from the very second you were born, you would be thirty-two years old by the time one billion seconds had passed, one hundred twenty years old by the time you reached 3.7 billion seconds. Now, think up on this: 3.7 billion *years* had passed since the lava sea upon which Buzz Aldrin and Neil Armstrong stood had solidified, 3.7 billion years of meteoritic bombardment that had pockmarked every square inch of Mare Tranquillitatus. In all that time, Tranquillity had never known the stirrings of life. The sea had never lived . . . until July 20, A.D. 1969.

48. UFO

Ten miles away in the sky, a tiny star hurtled over Tranquillity Base.

On distant Earth, the Americans continued to speculate about the nature and purpose of the Russian spacecraft. Many had concluded that it was photographing the LM from low lunar orbit. A few were concerned that it might attempt a landing near *Eagle*, kicking up a potentially dangerous spray of fast-moving dust particles.

As it turned out, *Luna 15* never even cast an idle lens toward the Sea of Tranquillity. Flying directly over the American base, the little robot had ignored it completely, on its way to more important concerns.

After the *Apollo 8* and *Apollo 9* flights, the Soviet space agency had all but canceled its manned-lunar-spacecraft program and focused instead on accelerated development of robot landers. *Luna 15* and *Apollo 11* were in a race to return the first rocks from the surface of the moon, though neither the *Apollo 11* crew nor Mission Control knew, at the time, that there was a race. If victorious, the Russian planners would be able to boast that they had beaten the Americans at their own game without risking human lives.

Indeed, it did look as if the Russians were going to win.

49. A SEA OF CRISES

The rocks smelled awful, pungent, like spent gunpowder.

Armstrong and Aldrin found their lunar home cold, crowded, dirty, and too brightly lit. They were exhausted from their almost three-hour walk, and from more than twenty-four sleepless hours that had preceded Armstrong's first "small step." At last, their schedule called for sleep, but how the hell can you wind down for sleep after having just walked on the moon? And how do you sleep in a ship whose pumps and valves and circulating fluids make her about as noisy as a packing factory?

The astronauts put on their helmets to block out some of the racket and the stench of moon rocks, and to alleviate fears expressed by Tom Kelly that the aluminum shell could crack as they slept. Grumman had provided window shades to shut out the glare of lunar daylight, but even the horizon shone right through them. Armstrong could actually make out the bright outline of an outcrop on the Plain of Tranquillity. He shook his head and reclined against the descent-engine cover, hoisting his feet on a makeshift sling, so Aldrin could curl up on the floor. When Armstrong noticed that the light seemed to be getting brighter, he opened his eyes and saw the earth moving into the telescope's field of view, pouring blue rays into his face. Then the life-support equipment whirred louder, and it got colder, and . . . oh well, Grumman never was in the hotel business.

Luna 15 would not have to stop for sleep, nor would she waste precious time searching for and docking with a mother ship.

Passing again over Tranquillity Base, she began to change course ever so slightly.

In Florida, shortly before dawn, George Skurla stepped onto his driveway and picked up the newspaper.

"We did it!" he shouted to no one in particular. Of course, we've got to get off the moon, he reflected, but we got there, anyway, in one piece.

Then he unrolled the newspaper and read:

MESSAGE GOES UNANSWERED BY ASTRONAUTS

Whaaa—?

Oh, no . . . *oh no* . . . As George read on, he learned that during the previous night's celebration at the Cocoa Beach Holiday Inn, a woman reporter had joined the Lunar Module technicians and drunk right along with them. One man complained that the astronauts never responded to the message they'd left on the spacecraft—*on the spacecraft.*

Rule number one stated that NOTHING *goes on that spacecraft unless it's authorized.* NOTHING. *Not unless it's logged and it's official.*

Armstrong had deployed an equipment bay as he climbed down the ladder. Inside was the TV camera, a flag, rock boxes, experiment packages, and, taped to the left-hand wall of the compartment, a sheet of gold foil, on which a technician named Kupzyk had written the words

GOOD LUCK NEIL AND BUZZ, FROM THE GRUMMAN CHECK-OUT TEAM ON PAD 39.

Almost sixty signatures followed.

Kupzyk had done everything in accordance with the dictates of caution. He'd even weighed the damned thing. But the colonel would not take to it, George knew. *Knew.*

When he arrived at "Superchief" Rocco Petrone's office, he found the door open.

"George, come in. Congratulations. Sit down."

Rocco lifted a folded newspaper from his desk. "You've seen this?"

"Yes. I'm afraid so."

"What the hell is the matter with those goddamned Long Island guys you've got working for you? If they don't have the discipline to follow the ground rules after they've been here this long, then they don't belong here. I want every one of those sixty guys fired. *Today*. I want them off the Cape by sundown."

"No! You can't mean that."

The colonel looked at George severely. "They've got to go. They could have ruined that telecast, and you and me with it. We're very fortunate that the guy who put the message in there didn't screw up and tape it to the opposite wall of the compartment. Because if he did, it could have shifted and covered the lens of the TV camera and nobody would have seen Neil Armstrong climbing down the ladder."

"Hey, Rocco. Look. You know, nobody can be more hurt than I am. Here, my greatest moment. I've been working on this for four years. And it's . . . these guys *ruined* this wonderful moment."

"You know what's gonna happen?" Rocco said, standing up.

George knew. The colonel was concerned about *his* boss telling him he had no control over the people who worked for him — the contractors, the *Long Islanders*. He also knew that only a few hundred yards away, in the VAB, LM-6 and LM-7 were being prepared for flight.

Damn! George thought. These sixty guys, they're really good; they're the ones you want on the job. They're my angels with dirty faces. It doesn't make sense to let them go. LM-6 is almost ready for the moon, and these are the guys with the hot hands. The LMs are getting better all the time. The team is really learning how to assemble and test these things; you can see it in the diminishing number of discrepancy reports being written up. The maturity of the team is beginning to pay off.

"We can't let them go," George told the NASA management. "We can't do this."

"But Rocco is furious," the management said.

"But we can't do this."

"Give 'em hell," Bill Voorhest said. "You've got to give 'em hell. Let them know that after all these years of working so hard— the day that should have been the happiest one in your life— they just threw cold water over it. They really took the joy out of everything. Let them know how they stole your day of triumph, *our* day of triumph."

George walked up to the front of the room amid a chorus of clearing throats and shuffling feet. He surveyed his sixty "angels" with a clenched jaw, flashing laser beams from his eyes.

"You know," he began, "I've killed myself down here. And all of you guys have dedicated years of your lives to this thing at the expense of your wives and children. *How the hell could you do anything so stupid?*"

George knew very well how. Working closely with the astronauts, he had been able to send locks of his children's hair to the moon in one of the personal packets that astronauts had been carrying with them since the flight of Alan Shepard. His "angels" also wanted to send something personal to the moon, and George understood this, but he was also politic enough to know that the NASA management must be appeased. "Are you guys out of your goddamned minds?" George continued. "You don't know what you've done. You've embarrassed the company. Heaven help us if this comes out on Walter Cronkite's show.

"Who the hell told that reporter girl, anyway?"

He caught a glimpse of Kupzyk, whose face was drawn and sweaty.

"And Kupzyk!" George said, pointing an accusing finger. "You're the guy who pasted it in. *My God.* You used to be a tech on a nuclear submarine, and you were going to study for the priesthood and—How could you do something like this?"

"I—I have no answer, sir. I can't justify it."

"That's all you have to say?"

Kupzyk nodded.

"Well, that's all *I* have to say," George concluded. "Now, let's hope we still have jobs tomorrow."

"To make a long story short," George says, "Armstrong never said anything about the message, so Houston never heard about it and Rocco wasn't embarrassed by his superiors. He heard about my yelling session and was satisfied. He required me, subsequently, on every launch, to sign a special piece of paper. I had to personally guarantee that I'd made a thorough investigation, to the maximum extent humanly possible, and that there was no unauthorized stuff on the vehicle. And I had to sign my name to that.

"Of course, I got to keep my sixty 'angels,' and they got better and better, and they acquitted themselves. They turned out to be the best team you could ever get to do the final checkout and close-out of the LM, before Bill Voorhest and I kissed it good-bye through the mylar."

50. LUNA 15

Crashed.

51. HOW CHET SENIG'S PART WORKED

Now, Senig, let's see what your half is going to do.

"That's really how they put it," recalls ascent-stage supervisor Chet Senig. "It may be silly to think that way, but that's the way it was. The bottom half works, right? Now how good is the top half?"

The ascent engine, built by Bell Aerosystems and Rockwell's Rocketdyne Division, had been designed with an emphasis on simplicity. It had only four moving parts: two ball valves and their backups, which injected pressurized, self-igniting hypergolics into a bell-shaped thrust chamber. The whole assembly was small enough and light enough to be carried around on a man's shoulder. Like the rest of the ship, it had shed weight even during its last months on Earth. Some forty pounds of asbestos had been stripped out of the thrust chamber and replaced with a lighter, glass-reinforced ablator. True to the doctrine of Scrape and SWIP, the astronauts had removed all the frills from their space suits, taking their air through umbilical hoses in the ship's cabin while they vented the atmosphere, tore out every piece of excess baggage they could find, and pushed it out the front door. Empty food containers and fecal bags went first. They were followed by the bulky moon boots and backpacks. Film was removed from the surface cameras. The cameras were tossed out. Equipment-transfer bags, Beta cloth, and bits of netting—they were all thrown overboard.

At one-thirty on the Monday afternoon of July 21, 1969, William Kaiser dismissed his history class at Long Island's Hofstra

University and headed home on Hempstead Turnpike. He stopped for a red light and leaned over to adjust his radio. The astronauts were ready for lift-off from the moon. This was the point where the guillotine had to sever miles of wire and the ascent engine had to ignite right on time and keep burning. Kaiser knew that there was no backup for the engine, and he wanted to hear how this was going to work out.

The light turned green. The traffic started to move, and he followed, still trying to tune his radio. The car in front of him stopped—he never did find out why—and LM-5 would forever stick in his mind as the thing for which he banged up the back of another man's car.

Only a few miles away, in Bethpage, Lynn Radcliffe had gone pale and sweaty. In all his life, he could not recall wanting anything more than to have that ascent engine light up.

It did, of course. It burned for seven minutes, hurling Armstrong and Aldrin into an elliptical orbit of 10.5 by 52.2 miles. An hour later, Armstrong fired the engine again to circularize the orbit. Soon *Eagle* and *Columbia* were flying head to head only a few yards apart. Then, on the heels of triumph, another computer mishap surfaced.

"The astronauts forgot to turn off the LM automatic pilot," explains Jesco von Puttkamer. "So the LM automatic pilot and the Command Module automatic pilot started fighting. The LM computer was trying to respond to manual instructions, and the Command Module computer did not agree. The altitude-control thrusters were going like crazy, with both ships locked together and jiggling back and forth, breaking the docking covers. Quickly, somebody inside the LM threw the switch, taking out the automatic-control system. The docking hatch on top of LM-5 actually cracked, but it didn't leak yet, or it didn't leak enough for them to be worried, so the astronauts unloaded the LM, crawled through the docking tunnel to the command Module, and cut the ascent stage loose."

During his thirty-first pass over the lunar far side, Collins fired the Service Module engine into the direction of flight. *Columbia* emerged into Earthrise at lunar-escape velocity and began the long fall home. Behind, at Tranquility Base, a little plaque declared that the Americans had come in peace for all mankind, but up ahead, fully one third of mankind—the people of China, Albania, North Korea, and North Vietnam—could not know, as they looked up into the frontiers of the night, that men were flying near the moon, or that they had landed on it. Their leaders had kept the news back.

52. TASK ACCOMPLISHED

The Houston Mission Control Room contained nearly two hundred people, most of them with their eyes fixed firmly on the giant plot boards. For more than eight days, the boards had displayed status and trajectory data. Suddenly, the center board flashed a television picture from the recovery ship. A second board went blank, then lit up with the *Apollo 11* logo. A third showed the *Columbia* bobbing up and down on the Pacific. Words appeared across the center spread: "I believe that this nation should commit itself to achieving the goal, before this decade is out, of landing a man on the moon and returning him safely to Earth (John F. Kennedy to Congress, May, 1961)."

And then, on top of the mission emblem: "Task Accomplished—July, 1969."

Weeks passed.

Neil Armstrong went to Bethpage and palmed fifty silver LM pins over to Tommy Attridge. Tommy presented him with a silver plaque bearing eleven famous first words: "That's one small step for man, one giant leap for mankind."

Armstrong leveled a finger at the middle of the quotation. "Hey! They got it wrong. That's not what I said."

"What do you mean?"

"They got it wrong," Armstrong said. "Believe it."

Tommy sat there and waited for the punchline, tried to imagine what it would be.

"I said, 'one small step for *a* man.' Does one small step for *man* make any sense in that sentence? Somebody left out a word."

"You'll probably shoot me, but I think that that somebody was you."

Tommy played an MGM commemorative 45-rpm record of the flight—one of millions that had flooded the market within days of the astronauts' return. Tommy was right. No matter how many times he played the record, and no matter at what speed, there was no "a" before the word "man."

"But there must be an *a*," Armstrong insisted. "I *rehearsed* it that way. I *meant* it to be that way. And I'm sure I *said* it that way."

"And it will *read* that way," Tommy said. "We'll make a new plaque. Rest assured, it will go onto commemorative medals, and into the history books, the way you meant it."

Armstrong sighed. "Damn, I really did it. I blew the first words on the moon, didn't I?"

Indeed he had blown them, and the flag, too. The flagpole went into the ground with great difficulty. It penetrated less than six inches, and seemed unsteady. Armstrong and Aldrin were afraid that the Stars and Stripes would pitch forward into the dust as they saluted on global television. According to an aerospace engineer named Murphy, anything that could go wrong probably would, and at the worst possible moment. But the flag held out until lift-off, when Buzz Aldrin looked up from his instruments just long enough to see a shower of aluminum-coated mylar caught in the blast of the ascent engine. The flag was caught there, too, and he saw it fall.

Armstrong's first words were not the only item that needed correcting. The *Eagle* had landed on a countdown to abort, primarily because propellants were sloshing away from intakes and meters, giving off readings that the ship had entered the deadman zone with its tanks running dry.

Weeks of detailed, post-mission analysis had revealed a series of false alerts and driven engineers to design a system of plates or baffles that could be built into the tanks. Looking somewhat like the paddlewheel of a riverboat, the system would prevent propellants from sloshing around. Never again must indicators be allowed to read off figures even a few seconds lower than actual fuel levels. Never again must indicators trigger a premature countdown to abort.

The task of directing baffle construction fell to quality-control inspector Harry Walther. "It was like building a ship in a bottle," he recalls. "We put the baffles together piece by piece, through a three-inch hole in the bottom of the fuel tank. We pushed the core of the baffle in through the hole, then pulled a string that unrolled it like a piece of sheet metal. We kept rotating this core around, using tools that were attached to the ends of long probes, until we had the eight finlike plates bolted to it. Then we had to move the baffle and center it in the tank and anchor it. We tested our methods on a descent stage at White Sands, then moved on to the Cape, where *Apollo* 12 was waiting."

53. INTERLUDE

Up there on the Ocean of Storms, *Surveyor* 3 stood hard and silent over a dead world. In November 1969, a point of light parted the darkness, skimming low and bright—approaching purposefully as if on a collision course with the little robot. It stopped six hundred feet away, blazing there, hurling sheets of dust for miles and miles, and then dropping to the surface. LM-6, the *Intrepid*, had arrived.

Pete Conrad and Alan Bean removed *Surveyor*'s TV camera and some of the surrounding rocks and left the next day.

At the Lunar Receiving Laboratory, it was learned that high-speed grains of lunar soil, thrown up by the descent-stage engine, had impacted on the LM-facing side of the camera and dug out microcraters. There were no dents anywhere else on the camera, indicating that micrometeorites had not touched it during its two-and-a-half-year stay on the moon. Apparently, even microcratering events are rare, at least in respect to time scales experienced by human beings, meaning that fears of having one's helmet punctured while exploring the moon were unfounded. Not so the fears of pathogens in space. Years earlier, someone had breathed or coughed on the wires that went into *Surveyor*'s camera, and thus began the first documented instance of panspermia: the spread of living DNA to other worlds. For more than two years, hitchhiking *Streptococcus* bacteria had survived the rigors of vacuum, radiation, and the oven-hot, two-week-long lunar days, alternating with the extreme cold of the lunar nights. Brought back to Earth, they began to multiply.

Since then, three Soviet space probes have inadvertently spread the seeds of life to the Martian wilderness. The American *Viking* landers were carefully sterilized prior to launch, but each of these spacecraft had an orbiting component, which was not sterilized, and which will eventually crash down upon Mars's surface. Our DNA may actually be hurtling out of the solar system altogether, aboard the *Pioneer* and *Voyager* spacecraft.

"They changed when they came back from the moon," says Frank Messina. "I was deputy program manager on the LM, which brought me into close contact with the astronauts. I knew them before they went to the moon, and it was an experience for me to witness the way they reacted or acted when they returned. I don't know quite how to put this, but I thought that in some cases the personalities were a little different. They were not as outgoing as before they went. They seemed more pensive."

"No man I know of who has gone to the moon has not been affected in some way that is similar," says astronaut Edgar Mitchell. "It is what I prefer to call 'instant global consciousness.' Each man comes back with a feeling that he is no longer only an American citizen; he is a planetary citizen. He doesn't like the way things are, and he wants to improve it."

Tommy Attridge had sent fifty gold pins along with Pete Conrad and Alan Bean. They were round, like the moon, and heavily cratered, with the Stars and Stripes (the wrong number of stripes) in the foreground. On their backs were engraved the words FLOWN TO THE MOON BY AN INTREPID CREW.

Conrad and Bean were permitted to keep twenty-five of the pins, to hand out to whomever they chose. Tommy Attridge kept one, and passed the remaining twenty-four to Lou Evans, who handed them out, one at a time, to George Titterton, Howard Wright, Tom Kelly, Bob Mullaney, Joe Gavin, Al Beauregard. . . .

Add to the list of Lunar Module mementos several hundred Tom Stafford autographs, many of which are forgeries. You see, Tommy Attridge and the *Apollo 10* commander could have passed for brothers, and to the public all astronauts looked alike anyway. So it was that when someone in the Alvin Theater ticket booth noticed that Jim McDivitt and Tom Stafford were in the audience, a finger of light pointed down on the back of Tommy Attridge's head as the house lamps dimmed for Act I of *Promises, Promsies*.

Tommy leaned over to McDivitt and said, "I think they must have that spotlight on for you and Stafford."

"Well, Stafford's not here yet, and I don't know what the hell it's all about, anyway," McDivitt said.

"Okay. I'll get up and you get up with me."

The two men stood and waved to the audience, then turned and took their seats. A minute later, Act I began, and Tom Stafford came down the aisle with his wife.

More than four hundred people descended on them during intermission, all of them wanting their *Playbills* signed by Tom Stafford, so Tommy Attridge signed Tom Stafford, Tom Stafford signed Tom Stafford, Jim McDivitt signed Tom Stafford, Mrs. Stafford signed Tom Stafford. . . . At one of Cocoa Beach's seafood restaurants, Tommy Attridge found himself surrounded by a growing knot of people. "You're Tom Stafford," one of them said.

"Yeah, sure," Tommy said.

"Oh, please sign this . . . and this . . . and this . . ."

Tommy signed them all. Sitting on his right were Alan Bean and Pete Conrad, who had just walked on the moon. To his left were Jim McDivitt, Rusty Schweikart, and Tom Stafford.

Tom Kelly: "I used to give a lot of public talks. So did most of the people on the LM program, and it used to disappoint me that people would think that the ship was too technical to understand. Some of the details might have been technical, but the basic mission was really very easy to understand if you just applied yourself to it at all. Yet I found that most people wouldn't even make the attempt. I mean, going to the moon was just some kind of magic show to them. They really didn't have the foggiest notion of how it was all happening. I don't know if we've advanced at all today in technical literacy, but it was pretty low in the LM days. The desire to think about anything that might be even remotely technical just wasn't there. That was kind of sobering to me as an engineer."

Doc Tripp flashed a picture of *Surveyor 3* onto the screen. There came a sprinkling of oohs and ahhs, and polite applause from the audience. An astronaut stood next to the robot, dwarfed by it—and LM-6 stood on the horizon.

"Just before they put LM-6 down on the surface," Doc Tripp said, "the crew took control away form the computer and finished the landing by hand. They did that on this mission, and they did it on the one before. And I'm betting they'll do it every time. Our man on the LM simulator, Mike Solan, works with the astronauts. He helps NASA train them to fly our ship, and he believes they take control away from the computer because they are out of the pilot community, and they trust a computer to get them just so far. And when it comes to that last critical moment, their backside is on the line, and they want to be in the loop. If it's gonna screw up, they want to be part of it.

"One of our consulting pilots, a man named Tom Gwynne"—the slide changed, showing three space-suited figures walking into a mission simulator—"also works in close quarters with the astronauts. And, well, the ship can actually fly itself if you let it. In the fully automatic mode, you just watch it do its thing all the way down. The question is, since you have a fully automatic capability, will any astronaut ever allow the system to land the vehicle? Tom Gwynne doesn't think so, and his argument makes sense. Here you've got one shot in your life"—the slide changed again—"to make a landing on the moon. Are you gonna let an autopilot do it for you or are you gonna do it yourself? The Consulting Pilot's Office has a whole case of champagne riding on a bet that *all* of the astronauts will take over at the end and land it manually. And I think they're going to win."*

The lights came on. There was applause, a brief question-and-answer period, and then more applause.

Afterward, while refreshments were being served, two elderly ladies approached Doc Tripp.

"Oh, we're so thrilled that things have gone so well for your first two landings," one of them said, smiling.

"And we want you to know," the other added, "that our friends will continue to help you."

Doc swallowed hard and set his cup down. "Friends?"

"Oh, yes. Our friends. We have connections with some space people, and they have been watching over your operation, especially when you're outside the earth's pull. They made sure your

---

*The pilots won the bet. The Space Shuttle, too, can fly itself, yet, at this writing, though dozens of flights have taken place, the pilots have never once turned the landing over to a machine.

first landing was safe. When you go to the moon, there will always be somebody there to make sure that everything goes well for you."

Doc looked at them closely. They were sincere, he was sure. There was no question in his mind that these two ladies were convinced that they had some friends up there. He listened, and nodded, and began to wonder about the rest of his audience.

"So don't you worry about that next flight," the more talkative of the two said. "Everything is going to be all right. Believe me, everything is going to work out just fine. Just fine."

"Oh, what the hell," Doc said without much enthusiasm. "We'll take all the help we can get."

And they'd *need* all the help they could get.

The next flight was *Apollo 13*.

54. SORRY TO INTERRUPT THE FESTIVITIES, BUT WE HAVE A PROBLEM

Apollo 13 lifted off on April 11, 1970. LM-7, christened *Aquarius*, never made it to the moon's surface, which was just as well for mission commander James Lovell, Lunar Module pilot Fred Haise, and Command Module pilot Jack Swigert. In keeping with the principle of discarding what was no longer needed, LM-7's descent stage would have been left on the moon and the ascent stage jettisoned after its return from the ground. Eight years after Houbolt won his battle in favor of LOR, and in a way that few of LM's builders would have anticipated, "that dumb thing" proved its spaceworthiness. A vehicle designed to land two men on the moon and then return to an orbiting Command Module was modified in mid-course to sustain three men halfway to the moon and back. It became a lifeboat. It was also called on to become a tugboat.

"I had a lot of confidence in that vehicle," recalls Fred Haise. "I was confident because I *knew* my ship. I had been active at Grumman during most of 1967 and 1968 on all the LMs up through LM-6. But I never really met *my* LM until the tests at Cape Kennedy. The role I had was one of looking at the vehicle checkout with consideration from the astronaut's standpoint. The engineers who develop subsystems are very attuned to the features of their system but tend to ignore the human operator. I also wanted to be right on top of the changes that were going on. No two LMs were ever the same. There was a continual upgrading of the vehicle—baffles in the fuel tanks, changes in test procedures, and so on. I even became familiar with where the wiring paths were, with connectors and pin numbers and cables, and with how these things related to various functions. You do not have to know about this to fly the vehicle, but I had that level of knowledge about the LM, which gave me personally a great deal of confidence in it.

"I also had a lot of confidence in the workers' attitude, right down to the solderers. I got a feeling they felt that the vehicle was a part of them—it was a very personal thing. I remember one night, back on Long Island, I was in a test with one of the very first LMs; and one young technician who worked on the test end drove in from Brooklyn every day. He came over to me and said that he personally could not understand why I wanted to go to the moon, but if I was going to go, he wanted to make sure I had the best vehicle for getting there and back. That was a pervasive, comforting attitude. And the bottom line was that ten LMs flew, and each fulfilled all mission requirements—except mine, which did not land, of course. But we used it and actually abused it and milked four days out of a two-day vehicle."

Odyssey-Aquarius was one day from Earth and, looking back, Haise tried to come to terms with the human mind's ability to adapt. Only a few months earlier, millions had jammed southern

Florida to witness the departure of the first expedition to the moon. Now, front-row seats were available for the asking. There was none of the uproar that had accompanied *Columbia-Eagle*. The unbelievable had become commonplace, if not a downright bore. Soon, Americans would see live transmissions from the first robot on the surface of Mars preempted by reruns of *Magilla Gorilla* cartoons—an historic anomaly (?) almost as fascinating as space itself . . . as—

—space itself—

"We were really there, in space, on our way to the moon," says Fred Haise. "The only traumatic event—thus far—had been at staging. The launch vibration was very reasonable for any fighter pilot, but staging was like an instant stop. You had engine shutdown followed by separation, and there was a lot of clanging, and then the next stage kicked in and it was sort of like a minor train wreck. In fact, it would throw you against the instrument panel if you were not prepared and braced for it."

And then came the weightlessness. It had been with them from the moment the third stage shut down, back there in Earth orbit. Haise found it very unusual; not scary, just unusual. He could play with flashlights floating around the cabin, pause them or spin them in midair. It made him queasy at first, especially if he rotated on his axis or swam in the air, but it was not like seasickness, because once he strapped himself down in a chair, it went away. He really couldn't understand why people were making such a big fuss over space sickness. Besides, zero-gravity made spaceships so much roomier. You could store things anywhere—on the floor, on the walls, on the ceiling—or just let them float around and snatch them out of the air when you wanted them. It was certainly unlike any dwelling he'd known on Earth, where half the space in every room seemed to be wasted. Zero-gravity actually *doubled* the usable volume of a spacecraft, which would become a godsend when Haise, Lovell, and Swigert were required to live in a lifeboat sized for two people.

For the moment, though, during this brief interlude between two worlds, Haise looked with anticipation toward his LM flight. With the ascent and descent stages fully loaded, his ship weighed about 35,000 Earth pounds and, according to Neil Armstrong, handled like a heavy transport or bomber. But as it burned off fuel it got lighter and lighter and eventually shed the descent stage and ascended into lunar orbit with its tanks almost empty. It would go from 35,000 Earth pounds to only 5,000, its mass and inertia changing as he used it, until, from the pilot's vantage point, it evolved into a little gnat fighter.

Transports and fighters: That's how Fred Haise saw space, as just another medium to fly in, except that the altimeter read higher.

Australia and New Zealand were down there in the bottom, but China was hard to see. Wellington Harbor caught the rays of the morning sun and threw them back into space. There was autumn mist in the Southern Hemisphere's only fjords—and through the ship's telescope, the crescents of green that surrounded Franz Joseph Glacier were still visible. The river of ice ran through a valley of its own creation, deep-cut into the earth, with carpets of tree ferns, tropical evergreens, and scattered palms on its walls. It was a scene that belonged in a science-fiction movie, but it was true: In New Zealand tropical plants lived almost on the margin of South Polar climate, shoulder to shoulder with ice.

Though he could not see them, Haise knew that penguins were walking in the shade of palm trees. The glacial valley and the rivers of the Cook Strait shrank with distance, even as Haise watched.

None of the science-fiction movies he'd seen, nor the ground-based simulators he'd worked in, nor the photographs from previous missions had prepared Haise for the view of Earth from space. The view became a problem, because all he and Swigert wanted to do—on their first flight into space—was look out the window. But there were system checks to be made, and housekeeping chores, and it was very tempting to sightsee when one should be working. Haise was reminded unexpectedly of the first time he'd ever seen a live elephant at the zoo. Even though his parents had already shown him pictures of elephants, nothing on Earth could have prepared him for an encounter with the real thing.

EXCERPTS FROM THE APOLLO 13 MISSION LOG OF DESIGNERS GRAY SMITH AND WILL BISCHOFF

April 12, 1970
30:55 [30 hrs., 55 min. into flight]   Noticed oscillation in fuel cell (battery charger) #3 after Service Module Propulsion System burn (bubble in loop?). Asking for engineering reports on possible corrective action.

April 13, 1970
54:25   Fred Haise has entered LM. (to perform equipment checks)
54:46   Transferred to LM power.
55:01   Transfer back to Command/Service Module power.
56:05   Problem with Command/Service Module fuel cell (lost power to main Bus B—main power supply).
56:06   LM/CM electrical umbilical essentially static (they're off main power supply) at 1.4.
56:09   Crew says they're venting something.

EXCERPT FROM THE HOUSTON POST

April 13, 1970 [morning edition]
Horoscope for Aquarius
Do surprises turn you on? Then this is your day for the unexpected.

It was almost a reenactment of the *Apollo 1* firespill—and it would have been, if not for the fact that the vacuum of outer space is a very good fire extinguisher.

At 55:53, an electrical surge from fuel cell number three sent sparks flying from a circulating fan in the Service Module's number-two oxygen tank. Teflon materials in the dome of the tank ignited, shot flares in every direction, warmed the surrounding gas, and expanded it. For two minutes the fire burned. Tank pressure spiraled up and up and up, until at last a titanium wall tore open, spilling out oxygen and sending the fire along with it. Wires, insulation, and black boxes burst into flame—but only briefly, for a whole side of the Service Module exploded away.

Men peering up through Earth-based telescopes noticed something strange: a faint yet unmistakable bubble of expanding vapor. Its radius was more than twenty miles, and *Apollo 13* was its focus.

Minutes earlier, Lovell, in *Odyssey*, had been playing *Also Sprach Zarathustra* (also known as the *2001* theme). Inside the LM, Haise opened a valve, then closed it with a loud bang. Both Lovell and Swigert flinched.

"What the hell was that?" Lovell said, a little unnerved.

"It's okay," Haise called up. "That was me, cycling the re-press valve."

They all laughed, unaware that a firespill had begun. Haise was drifting up to the Command Module when he heard the bang and felt the wall of the tunnel shiver. The master alarm squealed. Still chuckling about the noise Haise had made with the valve, Lovell poked his head into the tunnel with an expression on his face that said *Enough already; stop fooling around,* and saw Haise looking up at him with one that said *That wasn't me!* Almost simultaneously, Swigert yelled, "There's a warning light on!"

Haise continued through the tunnel and—oh, no—that sound accompanying the bang. Could that be true? Had it really been the sound of bending and crinkling metal?

"By the time I got back and closed the hatch to the LM," Haise explains, "one main-voltage reading was at the lower limit of the scale. Then we saw a very large debris field outside the window—just thousands of particles everywhere. The closest particles looked like ice, and you could see gold insulation floating around. Stuff continued to stream out from our spacecraft. We could see something streaming out behind us. James Lovell could see the sunlight reflecting off it. The oxygen was just shooting out from us."

"Okay, Houston," Swigert said. "We've had a problem here."

"This is Houston. Say again, please."

"Houston, we've had a problem," Lovell repeated. "We've had a main B Bus undervolt."

"Roger. Main B undervolt. Okay, stand by, Thirteen. We're looking at it."

"Okay right now, Houston. The voltage is looking good." Haise added, "And we had a pretty large bang associated with the caution and warning there. And if I recall, main B was the one that had an amp spike on it once before."

"Roger, Fred."

Outside the window, something was still venting, and the stars were moving. The explosion had put the ship into a spin.

Fred Haise: "There was a sickness in my stomach. It was the kind of sickness you feel the instant you turn around and realize that you just slammed your kid's hand in the car door. People ask if we were scared. We were never scared—only disappointed and sick that we could not land on the moon. We had lost a mission. We had worked a lot of years, and seemingly for nothing. The worst feeling was right away, when I looked at the meter and saw that the oxygen tank was gone, and knew that the landing had to be scrubbed. After that it got better.

"We were describing the problem to the ground, and trying to determine the extent of the damage. So we were giving all the pressure readings and light indications, and after about twenty minutes we realized that the Service Module's second oxygen tank was also damaged. It was leaking slowly, so we were going to lose both oxygen tanks. When that happened, the Command Module would have to be powered down. No problem there; it was losing power all on its own. The Service Module, which charged the Command Module's Earth reentry batteries, was dying. *Dying.* James Lovell and I removed the hatch to the LM and got ready to go in there, since we knew the Command Module was going to get dark pretty quick. Mission Control was a while behind us, and it took them another few minutes to figure out that the Command Module was a lost cause."

Jack Swigert: "The fuel cells [battery chargers] were all going.

It was only a question of time until we were without oxygen and power in the Command Module. I suggested that we start powering up the LM and getting its guidance system aligned. In very short order, Mission Control came back with the word that it was to be a LM lifeboat mission. We had fifteen minutes before our last fuel cell ran out. This was something we'd never done in training. We'd thought about losing one or two fuel cells and an oxygen tank, but we'd never trained for losing all three fuel cells and both oxygen tanks. If someone had thrown *that* at us in the simulator, we'd have said, 'Come on, you're not being realistic.' *This was real.* I've never seen the LM activated so fast. I could see that our last cell was going out, so I turned on a battery to keep the inertial-guidance system going while Lovell got the LM guidance lined up. Just as he got a good alignment, the last fuel cell quit. Mission Control told me to shut off the electrical power. We were going to need those batteries. I followed the steps, and in a minute or two the Command Module was powered down. It was eerie: no lights, no radio and [as pilot of the Command Module] nothing for me to do. I drifted through the tunnel to *Aquarius* and looked at James and Fred. 'It's up to you,' I told them."

EXCERPT FROM THE APOLLO 13 *LOG OF JOHN STRAKOSCH AND GRAY SMITH*

56:50 [45 min. after firespill]   Jim Harrigan starting the LM lifeboat effort. Will need electrical power subsystem people, environmental control system people, propulsion people.

Got Howard Wright and Tom Kelly. They will try to get down as soon as possible.

Preliminary Consumables
O_2:   *140 hrs. of useable for 3 men*
H_2O: *5.1 lbs/hr   66 hrs* ⎫
            4.1 lbs/hr   82 hrs ⎬ *assumes nothing*
estimated time to splashdown: 100 hrs.

*   *   *

The LM lifeboat plan demanded thought about a whole range of ideas never before imagined. It raised new questions about equipment performance and emergency procedures, and it demanded answers under a stopwatch. Who better to ask than the men who lived with LM-7 through design, development, building, and testing?

At midnight, Eastern Standard Time, practically everybody connected with LM-7 was awakened. Often, the voice at the other end of the line said little more than "Get down here fast." Dozens of cars swarmed onto the Long Island Expressway at eighty-five miles an hour. The police who stopped them ended up giving escort at a hundred miles an hour. By 1:00 A.M., a procession of unwashed bodies clothed in T-shirts and whatever pants had been close at hand was filing into offices at Grumman and its principal suppliers, which included Hamilton Standard, the builders of *Aquarius*'s life-support system.

George Skurla got the call at 12:15 A.M.: "There's been an explosion."

"Is it going down the tubes?"

"We don't know yet. Just come in, and please hurry."

Minutes later, as he drove down Florida's A1A, he noticed that there were more cars on the road than he'd normally expect to see in the predawn—and all of them were heading for the Cape.

Tom Kelly was at MIT, where he'd been teaching and developing space hardware. Fortunately, he'd gone to bed early that night. He'd need the sleep. It was almost 1:00 A.M. when he got the call from Harvard. It was Howard Wright, the electrical engineer who had worked with him throughout the LM program.

"Did you hear what happened?" Howard said.

"What?" Tom said, groggy, but waking up fast.

"Turn your radio on. They got a problem on *Apollo*."

Tom hit a switch next to his bed, and he heard it right away. *Oh, wow!*

"They want us to go down to Bethpage, to the Mission Support Center. There's a jet waiting at Logan Airport."

On the plane, Tom's anxiety went down a few notches. The explosion had occurred at a good time. The LM was full of consumables—plenty of oxygen and water and—oh wow, the lifeboat mission was happening, really happening, just as Al Munier had said it would be, way back in 1961, during the design-study days. He and Al had been talking about LM, and Al looked up from his notes and said, "Gee, I wonder, you know, suppose something happened on the way out to the moon? Suppose you lost your oxygen or water or engine power"—and now they had lost all three—"could the LM bring the Command Module back? I'm just curious. I wonder if the thing could bring back people, like a lifeboat."

So they made some calculations and, yes, the LM could bring the Command Module back, if you made the LM tanks a little bit bigger, if you put in a little more oxygen, a little more water, a little more electric power. At that point in the game, everything had still been on paper. Nothing had been built yet, so changing the specifications didn't really cost anything. It gave you more fuel to land with (lucky for *Apollo 11*), it let you stay on the moon a little bit longer, and it gave you a rescue option (lucky for *Apollo 13*).

Not to worry, Tom thought. The Service Module is shot. But the Command Module is okay. And the LM is okay. Everything is okay.

Floating inside the aluminum shell of LM-7, everything was not okay. Haise began wondering about the capsule's heat shield. Had the explosion cracked it? He didn't want to delve too deeply into that thought, or to discuss it with Mission Control. Anyway, if it was cracked, there was nothing anyone could do about it, so it wasn't worth talking about.

Near Houston, a telescope revealed the tiny fleck of light to be a comet. It was setting in the western sky, dimmer now, a wisp of vapor close on fifty miles across, with a tail that swept thousands of miles behind it in the solar wind. Someone in NASA had once said that a comet was as close to nothing as anything could be and still be something. Someone else had defined a comet as bad luck. In the early-morning hours of April 14, 1970, both descriptions applied. The apparition in the telescope was little more than a few pounds of gas, vented slowly through a puncture in *Odyssey*'s number-one oxygen tank, which was the core of the comet.

"It couldn't have happened on a worse night," recalls simulation engineer John Hussey. "We had an ice storm in New York. The roads were just glazed ice. I was home, asleep, when the call came through. I was to bring in all the people who worked with me on the LM simulator. At that time, nobody really had any details on the problem. I got most of my early information from the television in my bedroom while I was calling people. We had a network set up where I would call five people, and then those five people would each call five people, and the message would be passed down the line like a chain letter. Then, getting to work, I skidded through stop signs and traffic lights. I hit the front gate going in, skidded right through it and scared the hell out of a guard."

Tom Kelly arrived at 3:00 A.M., and already there were five or six hundred people at Grumman. Technician Rob Rowen was not one of them. He had the misfortune of looking like and dressing like what Rocco Petrone called the "typical Long Islander"—a bad way to look when you're going through a stop sign at sixty miles an hour, during an ice storm, in the South Bronx, about six blocks from the scene of a liquor-store robbery.

"What the hell is this all about?" Rob called from the cell. "What's going on? I only went through a stop sign! I gotta get to work. There's been a problem on *Apollo*."

"Shut up!" a mean-looking thing in the next cell demanded. "The spaceship!"

"Spaceship? Yeah. Right. Tell me about it."

*　　　*　　　*

They were 210,000 miles from Earth, on a trajectory that would bring them within sixty miles of the moon. The LM simulator became an ideal facility for practicing the engine burn that would add speed to *Apollo 13*. Passing once around the far side, the moon's gravity would be used to sling the ship on a glide path back to Earth.

John Hussey: "The only engines available to use were on the LM. It was important that the thrust vector go through *Odyssey-Aquarius*'s center of mass. You could gimbal the descent-stage engine during a burn, but you were limited in terms of what kind of angle you could gimbal to. It's the angle with which the thrust goes through the center of mass that determines the direction that the vehicle is going to go—and a few inches in the wrong direction, added up over tens of thousands of miles, could either crash you directly into the moon or swing you out into a weird, egg-shaped orbit. So that's one of the control elements you do in a burn: You control the angle at which you push through the center of mass—very carefully. Now, the LM was designed to handle a shifting center of mass within its own environment, but here we're talking about a combined vehicle where the center of mass was some fifteen or twenty feet ahead of the LM itself. It was completely outside the LM's environment, so the ability to swivel the engine to direct the thrust where you wanted it was limited. We would have to use the attitude-control rockets. But again, these small clusters of engines were meant to handle the LM's problems, not this stacked configuration.

"Our first attempt was to see if we could reprogram the autopilot that handled the sixteen little attitude-control rockets on the sides of the ascent stage. We very quickly learned that it was not feasible. Well, what *can* we do? We had done some testing about a year before, looking forward to future uses of the LM. One of these involved a space-observatory configuration, in which a telescope would be attached to the LM. The telescope would have weighed about as much as the Command/Service Module, and was to be attached in the same place. And there we had it! Procedures for flying the LM with a very bad center of mass location had already been worked out, so we went to our LM simulator and turned off the automatic-control system for the attitude-control rockets. The simulator showed us that by monitoring a certain display in the cabin, we could ask the pilot to fire the little rockets in certain ways until he saw a needle move to the center position, and his task was to keep that needle in the center position during the engine burn.

"We described the details to Houston, and they tried it on *their* mission simulator, testing both the procedure and *our instructions for its execution*, which would have to be voiced up to the astronauts."

EXCERPTS FROM THE APOLLO 13 LOG OF JOHN STRAKOSCH AND WILL BISCHOFF

65:50   Power. *Will be very tight.*
66:55   *Paine wants to be assured by Rocco Petrone that all subcontractors be on a "ready" status.*
66:59   *Tom Kelly—called him and passed the word on above item. Tom will implement. Tom said was not apparent why we had to keep the Service Module on board—looked like from reliability standpoint was to our advantage to get back as soon as possible: should jettison SM and go for shortest time. Said I'd check.*

Flight directors debated with Tom Kelly and Rocco Petrone the pros and cons of a possible fast-return strategy that could put the crew on the Pacific within fifty hours. To do so required that the dead weight of the Service Module be shed, reducing *Odyssey-Aquarius*'s mass by about half. Unfortunately this tactic would also require that *Odyssey*'s heat shield be exposed to the on-again-off-again temperature extremes of sun and shade in space for at least two days. Nobody was quite sure how the shield would react in such an unfamiliar thermal environment—expansion in the heat, contraction in the cold, and if the explosion had produced even one hairline fracture . . .

Petrone's team opted for caution, and recommended a plan that would return *Odyssey* to Earth in seventy-five hours.

Rob Rowen missed the engine burn.

The owner of the liquor store told the police that he was definitely not the man who robbed him. By that time, one of the arresting officers had taken a second glance at Rob's Grumman ID card. Then he turned on the radio and—*Oh, God*. "Hey, kid. You're telling me that this company out on the Island built that spaceship?"

"Yeah. We built it. Where have you been for the last ten years? Who do you *think* built it?"

"I thought NASA built these things, down in Florida. Who would ever believe that they built spaceships on Long Island? Jesus. We really created a problem here. Don't worry, son. *We'll* get you to work."

They got him to work, all right. They covered the forty-mile-long skating rink between Bethpage and the Bronx in what seemed to be half as many minutes . . . plus two 360-degree turns on the downslope of the Throgs Neck Bridge and a dozen stop signs that might just as well never existed and shrubberies on someone's lawn that no longer did. Oh, yes, they got him to work, but he was pale and sweaty and absolutely useless for the next six hours.

As the astronauts continued toward the moon, the need for a margin of safety guided the LM builders to a recommendation for strict rationing of power, air, and water—especially water. Their plan called for shutting down as much as possible of *Aquarius*'s electronics to lessen the draw on water supplies. Electronic equipment could generate a lot of heat in a LM, so it was kept cool by running chilled glycol through it during use. The glycol emerged from the electronics with stolen heat, and in turn it had to be cooled before it could be pumped back through the electronics bay. This was accomplished by running it through tubes encased in ice. The ice was made from the ship's water supply by exposing it at a steady trickle to the cold vacuum of space. As more hot glycol circulated through the pipes, more ice boiled away into space and had to be replaced. The problem was that the LM carried only enough water for a visit to the moon and then a return to the Command Module. There were 84 pounds of water in the ascent-stage tanks and 254 pounds in the descent stage. During the early hours of the crisis, water use rose to 6.3 pounds per hour. At this rate, LM-7 would have exhausted its entire water supply more than a day before reaching Earth, and every piece of equipment would be in danger of burnout. Everything became a candidate for shutdown to reduce heat production and thereby the rate at which *Aquarius* sweated her water into space. Consequently, it was going to get very cold.

NASA wanted to know if the power-down could be extended to include the heaters that kept the Abort Sensor Assembly (ASA, which monitored the performance of the descent engine) at 70°F. Could the fluid in the gyroscopes stand a temperature drop into the 30s? Would the ASA function after it was heated up again? These questions fell to ASA engineer Robert Fairbrother to answer. "We just didn't have time to run tests," he recalls. "We had to take the data at hand and analyze it in relation to the estimated temperatures and the time ASA would be soaked in the cold. Everyone was confident the assembly could start up at 38°F, but it had never been done before."

A supplementary water supply—perhaps twenty hours of it, if used carefully—was found in the Command Module, but transporting it at zero-gravity would be a problem (you couldn't just use buckets), and the Command Module water was chlorinated, whereas *Aquarius* worked on unchlorinated water.

Warren Pinter, engineering manager for Hamilton Standard's life-support system, says, "We went right to work on tests of whether or not we could use chlorinated water in the LM ice-maker [called a sublimater] by seeding LM water with chlorine and trying it out in the lab. It worked. At one point we were even seriously considering using urine to keep the system going."

As it turned out, the urine was never needed, but the plan was on the books, just in case.

It is often said that space travel is not inherently dangerous, but to an even greater extent than the sea, space is terribly unforgiving of any carelessness, incapacity, or neglect. *Aquarius* proved to be an exceptionally forgiving ship. Planners on the ground, poring over blueprints and schematics, were able to advise NASA on how to jerry-rig the life-support system to purify air for three men instead of the intended two. Mission Control voiced these instructions up to *Aquarius*. Then someone had to figure out how to use the LM descent engine to get *Apollo 13* into and out of lunar gravity and on a heading for Earth. Almost no one had seriously expected to be planning for that trick.

Will Bischoff: "NASA, in that environment, did the specific planning; the contractor (that was us) became the adviser. We spent a lot of time pumping a lot of information into them: 'You can't do this. You can't do that. This is what the alternatives are.' They ultimately planned the return mission."

John Strakosch: "We examined eighty-five what-if questions. What if the descent-stage oxygen system fails? Or what if we can't separate the LM ascent stage from the Command Module as we approach Earth? That's what I spent most of my time on: What do we *do* if . . ."

EXCERPT FROM THE APOLLO 13 LOG OF JOHN STRAKOSCH AND WILL BISCHOFF

April 14, 1970
What if we run out of water or water flow is stopped during low power operation? How long can we last?
   If lost H_2O—4 hours to dry out boiler. 5°/hr glycol temperature rise. Assume boiler dries out at glycol temp. 60°. 80° glycol temperature limit—4 hours for boiler dry out.
   Time that will take crew to get in a state of heat collapse.

½ *hour at* 100% *relative humidity and then no more*
, *sweat and crew begins to store heat.*
    : *stat at* 65%/100%   4 *hours to the point where they've*
stored all the heat they can.
    Crew can last 4½ *to* 5 *hours.*
    Could lower relative humidity by open flow O_2 *dump to*
3½ *pounds per square inch but cost* 6 *lbs.* O_2.

Strakosch and Bischoff assigned teams to the eighty-five questions, and the eighty-five generated a whole crop of subquestions
that needed answering.

Years later, the thing Strakosch would remember most was
that the job required one hundred percent concentration, working
harder than he'd ever worked in his life for longer than he'd ever
worked and never feeling tired until it was over. Then he collapsed. He'd recall this period as being about eighteen to twenty
hours in duration, but his entries in the *Apollo* 13 log show that
it was actually three days.

On the second day, still en route to the moon, the astronauts
fired LM-7's descent engine as prescribed by Earth-based simulations. Minutes later, Lovell's sextant readings confirmed that the
maneuver had worked. *Apollo* 13 was on a *Zond*-like trajectory
that would swing the three modules over the lunar far side and
back toward Earth rather than into lunar orbit. A very relieved
John Strakosch took a moment to write "Completed burn" in the
mission log.

James Lovell: "Nothing in the Lunar Module had been designed for the work we were now asking it to do, so there was a
big feeling of relief when that engine fired for thirty seconds to
boost us up and take us around the moon at an altitude of about
130 miles instead of 60 miles. Now we had our free ticket home,
if our consumables held out: oxygen, electricity, especially water.
That first burn of *Aquarius*'s descent engine put us on a course
that would land us in the Indian Ocean, but that was the very
least of my worries at this point. I didn't know until after I got

back that so many nations had volunteered to help in a recovery operation, but any old ocean would do as long as it was on Earth."

Jack Swigert: "We adjusted to our routine readily enough. We started referring to our spacecraft as a two-room suite. The Command Module was the bedroom. Whenever Mission Control would ask where so-and-so is, we'd say, 'He's up in the bedroom.'"

Fred Haise: "Now at least we were going in the right direction. People were working on Earth, trying to figure out the rest of the plan: how we could power up the Command Module before reentry, how to correct our course for Pacific splashdown, how to extend the life of the LM. They didn't have exact answers. We'd never trained for a double failure such as this. We'd trained for the loss of one oxygen tank, but never two. It was never supposed to happen. They figured that if you lost two tanks, it was something catastrophic like the ship blowing up and we were supposed to be dead, so why train for it? It's all academic. That was their philosophy."

John Hussey: "Fred Haise happened to be a very special person to most people here at Grumman, because he was always here. He was very friendly and well liked and he had spent some time in our simulation facility prior to the flight. He was the Astronaut Office's interface at Grumman, responsible for LM, so a lot of times when we were flying a test function [in the LM simulator], Fred Haise was the actual subject. Everybody liked the man, so as a result there was a personal interest for the people. They really wanted to help, and that personal aspect generated an intensity to get the job done. People pretty much stayed here. I think that whole crisis lasted maybe three or four days, and I couldn't get people to go home and get some sleep. I was literally having to kick them out of here, demanding that they go home for eight hours and then come back. In the simulation area, we were normally a group of people staffed to work one shift, so we didn't have a lot of spare people working different functions. What we did was to trim ourselves down to a condition where we could at least stay in an operational mode and try to send people home for eight-hour stints, and still stay in a readiness state for twenty-four hours. But even still, I'd go in a back room and see somebody flaked out on a cot. He was really supposed to be at home."

Tom Kelly: "Some people, nobody asked them to come in; they just came in, to see if there was anything they could do to help. So, as they came in, depending on what their specialty was, we put them to work. We thought of something for them to check on, or asked them to call some supplier to get more information on a part they'd built. There were plenty of things to be taken care of; that was for sure. But it really was a spontaneous outpouring of concern. And it was amazing. Really amazing."

TO PRESIDENT NIXON: I WANT TO INFORM YOU THE SO-VIET GOVERNMENT HAS GIVEN ORDERS TO ALL CITIZENS AND MEMBERS OF THE ARMED FORCES TO USE ALL MEANS TO RENDER ASSISTANCE IN RESCUE OF THE AMERICAN ASTRONAUTS.
PREMIER ALEKSEI N. KOSYGIN

TO PREMIER ALEKSEI KOSYGIN: I WILL LET YOU KNOW FAST IF WE NEED YOUR GOVERNMENT'S HELP.
PRESIDENT RICHARD M. NIXON.

TO THE CREW OF THE AMERICAN SPACE SHIP "APOLLO 13" J. LOVELL, J. SWIGERT, F. HAISE: WE, SOVIET COSMO-NAUTS, ARE FOLLOWING YOUR FLIGHT WITH GREAT AT-TENTION AND ANXIETY. WE WISH WHOLEHEARTEDLY YOUR SAFE RETURN TO OUR MOTHER-EARTH.
ON BEHALF OF THE PILOTS-COSMONAUTS OF THE USSR.
V. SHATALOV

The Russian news agency Tass, in a rare display of support for the United States, reported that four Soviet ships were steam-ing toward the anticipated splashdown area, among them a "fish-ing boat" and the helicopter-equipped *Chumikan*.

France, the Netherlands, Italy, Spain, West Germany, South

Africa, Brazil, and Uruguay put their navies on alert. Australian television superimposed *Apollo 13* Mission Status Bulletins over an episode of *Lost in Space*. In Italy, Mayor Vito Bellafore, surrounded by his advisers, looked up from earthquake-devastated Santa Ninfa and said, "My friends, all our worry is for those three lonely men."

In Houston, Mary Haise kept the children home from school. The family gathered around a NASA squawk box, which had been installed to relay every word from the ship. Al Beauregard's wife and astronaut Gerry Carr were with them.

Fred Haise's son looked up from some paperwork and announced, "My daddy's not coming back." He had been working out how long the LM's electricity would hold out, and his figures came up short. His announcement began to erode Mrs. Haise's courage. She turned to Gerry Carr, and he sat down with the children and sketched out the ship's parts, jotted down numbers, and noted rates of consumption. He answered questions, patiently and truthfully, and explained exactly how the LM lifeboat mission was going to work. Finally, the boy turned to Gerry Carr and said, "You're right. He's gonna get back."

"You bet he is," Gerry said.

"But all those reporters in front of the house weren't very encouraging," says Mrs. Beauregard. "And they wouldn't go away. Mrs. Haise went out and talked to them. There she was, expecting a baby any day, and she stood on the lawn and told them that everything was going to be all right. That satisfied them. Here were guards trying with no success to keep them away, and she went right out and talked to them. And then they were gone. She was terrific."

On Tuesday, April 14, the U.S. Senate adopted a resolution that urged "all business and communications media to pause at 9:00 P.M., their local time, to permit persons to join in prayer for the safety of the astronauts." More than ten thousand joined Pope Paul in St. Peter's Basilica. Special prayers were said at the Wailing Wall in Jerusalem.

Feeling now like snails with beards, the men in Grumman's

Mission Support Room didn't have time for prayers. They were busy trying to save three men about to boomerang round the back of the moon. *Aquarius* would approach the earth's atmosphere with the Command Module, or capsule, attached. Somebody had to figure out how the astronauts were going to separate the capsule from the LM and nudge it into the atmosphere at just the right angle: no small task, when you consider that the LM would have to do all the maneuvering, up to the last minute, just before the astronauts crawled into the capsule. Then there was the problem of backing the capsule away from the LM when you had no attitude-control rockets. Somebody on the ground suggested that you could overcome this problem by building up pressure in the crawl space between the capsule and the LM, pop the latch a few minutes before contact with the atmosphere, and hope pressure in the compartment would thrust the two modules apart.

77:08

Something monstrous, a half mile across, at least, had splashed down on the surface. They saw it in England, on the evening of June 18, A.D. 1178. The giant meteorite disintegrated in a searing white glare, throwing up a flaming torch and hot boulders and sparks. The rim of the moon blurred and danced behind a veil of hard-flung dust. Tight swarms of broken rock jetted out of the lunar highlands. Some of the spray arched back, carpeting the moonscape with long, bright fingers of fine powder—all pointing away from a twenty-mile-wide crater named Giordano Bruno. Haise aimed his camera and began shooting the fresh-appearing scar in excruciating detail. Why not? he thought. We'll be going forty-five minutes round the back of the moon, and we have a lot of film aboard. No point in bringing it all back blank.

Haise did not know, at the time, that Giordano Bruno was only 792 years old, or that from the cauldron of its creation had come a splatter of moon rocks that fanned out to the orbits of Venus and Mars and touched the earth. Soon, a moon rock would be found lying on the Antarctic ice cap, and it would be learned that the moon itself was still ringing from the impact, with a period of about three years and an amplitude of ten feet. As yet, nobody on Earth knew how close an asteroid had come to snuffing out the bright flame of civilization. Even so, as Haise surveyed the destruction, it occurred to him that Ray Bradbury had been right all along: the Earth was too small a basket for humanity to keep all its eggs in.

To James Lovell it was the same wasteland he'd beheld during his *Apollo 8* flight, except this time he found the moon even more uninviting. Now, he'd live with the distinction of being the only man to go twice to the moon and not land on it once. But it could have been worse, he knew. This could have happened during *Apollo 8*.

EXCERPTS FROM THE APOLLO 13 LOG OF JOHN STRAKOSCH AND WILL BISCHOFF

79:44   *Water freezing not a problem.*
80:25   *Cabin temp. 65°F. What can we maintain?*
        Relative humidity 55%—Crew will be leaving comfort zone at about 60°F.
81:50   *Consumables*
        498 Amp hours remaining.
        215 lbs of water useable.
        LiOH (to clean CO₂ from cabin air) 192 hours of LiOH in Command Module. 44 hours remaining in LM (includes secondaries in back packs).
        Oxygen: 120 hours of O₂ left.

Fred Haise: "I figured the electrical power we were going down to would be sufficient to get us back. We would make it on power using the LM electrical system. We had plenty of oxygen in the ascent and descent tanks, in the backpacks intended to be used on the moon, and their emergency supply (even that would have lasted a day). I didn't even have to really figure it out; there was plenty of oxygen. The water was a problem. As you already know, the water cooled all the electrical systems; without it they would all burn out. I made my first calculation using the LM-5 water data, which I had on board. It showed that we would fall short by five hours. We would run out of water. But on LM-5, which they left in orbit around the moon, Armstrong and Aldrin shut off the water valve in the sublimator before they crawled into *Columbia*. They deliberately let the critical electrical systems burn out to see how long they would last. The first critical unit that overheated and failed was the computer, and it failed at eight hours. So I figured that even if we ran out of water five hours before reentry, it would be eight hours before the first critical system failed. It looked like the water situation would be okay, but marginal.

"We unconsciously, voluntarily, rationed water to ourselves— to save it all for the electronics. We had that mentality. We quit eating food that required water in order to be eaten—which was just about everything. It was all dehydrated. We mixed up the drink bags, grape juice and the like, from the water in the Command Module, because we knew that the Command Module water was eventually going to freeze. We pressurized the Command Module's water tanks and we filled every drink bag we had on board, so we didn't use any LM water for that. In fact, we had a big mess, because Swigert let the bags get loose. We had all the drink bags in a big sack, and they all got out and were floating all over the place. We only ate things like bread cubes and peanuts. Even if we had enough water to reconstitute the foods, it wouldn't have worked, because most of the food, like the scrambled eggs, required *hot* water, and the LM had no means for heating water, even if we could spare the electricity. Powdered eggs and cold water? It would have been terrible! We ate some cold beef stew and frankfurters, and we did become dehydrated, which probably contributed to my getting sick with a bladder infection on the way home."

EXCERPT FROM THE APOLLO 13 LOG OF
JOHN STRAKOSCH AND WILL BISCHOFF

82:25   Lovell: *only other concern is* CO_2 *rise up to 10.7. Capcom is watching it, have medical go to 15. Lovell: "There's a medical first for you!"*

Fred Haise: "The other problem was how to clean the carbon dioxide out of the air. I had missed this problem in my original calculations; I didn't even consider it. And it *was* a problem, because the LM environmental-control system didn't have enough carbon-dioxide-cleaning cartridges. The LM had only two of these lithium-hydroxide cartridges. There were more cartridges in the Command Module, but they were a different size and shape and would not fit the LM environmental-control system. The engineers had not designed interchangeable cartridges for the LM and Command Module because the basic philosophy was that the Command Module would never die.

"Houston recognized the problem and worked it out off line— on a LM simulator—before calling us. They worked out a way of adapting *Odyssey's* cartridges to *Aquarius's* life-support system using the materials we had on board. We used checklist covers, which were stiff and cardboardlike, and wrapped them in cellophane and adhesive tape to make a box. They called up instructions, telling us how to attach LM hoses to the makeshift box, how to suck LM air through it and the cartridges it contained. We had plenty of Command Module cartridges. It was just a matter of replacing them as they wore out. From then on, as far as scrubbing the air was concerned, we were home free."

EXCERPTS FROM THE APOLLO 13 LOG
OF JOHN STRAKOSCH AND WILL BISCHOFF

April 14, 1970
82:56   *Crew sees something coming (venting) out of side of Service Module. Ground will give camera setting to take*

picture of venting if practical from crew standpoint. Fred unlimbering movie camera and a Hasselblad surface camera.

April 15, 1970
85:10   *Info: Saturn 3rd stage impact 74 miles from Apollo 12 landing site; detected major seismic activity; lasted 4 hours with decreasing amplitude.*
86:24   *43,262 Nautical mile distance from moon.*
87:30   *Consumables Status*

	H_2O	O_2
remaining	*195.4 lbs.*	*92.24 lbs*
present rate	*3.25/hr*	*.97/hr*
time remaining	*60 hr*	*95 hr*
splashdown (est)	*55 hr*	

94:38   *CO_2 procedure is working great.*
97:02   *Estimate Command/Service Module potable water gone.*

James Lovell: "Eventually it dawned on me that somehow we all had to get some sleep, and we tried to work out a watch system. We weren't very successful. Events kept upsetting it and making a sensible rotation impossible. Besides, the inside of *Odyssey,* our bedroom, kept getting colder and colder. It eventually got down pretty close to the freezing point, and it was just impossible to sleep in there. Fred and I even put on our heavy lunar boots. Jack didn't have any, so he put on extra longjohns. When you were moving around, the cold wasn't so bad, but when you were sitting still, it was unbearable. So the three of us spent more and more of our time together in *Aquarius,* which was designed to be flown by two men, standing up, at that. There wasn't really sleeping space for two men in there, let alone three, so we just huddled in there, trying to keep warm and doze off by turns."

Fred Haise: "It was actually helpful having three people in the LM. The body heat helped keep you warm. It was between thirty-two and forty degrees in there. It was not that cramped, however. Two guys stayed up near the windows and one stayed back over the ascent-engine cover. We were not jammed against each other. It would not be an ideal size for a space station that you would live in for a few months, but for four days it was like camping. The chill was bad. I'd been a lot colder before, but I'd never been cold for so long. And then I got the infection, which developed into chills and fever. James and Jack did not get sick but were exhausted since our sleep was very sporadic. We were constantly being awakened to do things. There were no normal sleep periods. Normally we would get eight hours after work. We were continually awakened every hour or so to do something. James and Jack slept for only eight hours each in four days. I slept for a total of ten hours.

"The ground controllers—and this was a gap in our understanding of each other—requested that we not use the overboard urine-dump system for a number of hours, because they wanted to get accurate track data, and these explosions of urine mist were fouling up their Doppler readings. We misunderstood. We thought they meant forever: not to use the urine dump again. So, on board, we tried to figure out where to store all this urine, because there were no accommodations on the LM or Command Module for storage of urine. We ended up using a fiberglass container in the LM, which was originally intended for catching excess water when you filled up your backpack on the lunar surface. We figured that you could hook a hose up to it and squeeze urine into it from a bag. One mistake we made was that a relief valve on top popped when we were squeezing the bag and a big glob of urine started to form. We had to push the urine back into the container, and tape that valve down. We soon filled the container. Then we went to every rubber bladder bag we had—each space suit had one of those. We went through those, and then we filled some backup Gemini bags. We were going to use the small plastic drink bags, and we would have to tape the tops down on those, but when we mentioned this to the ground, we learned that we had misunderstood. They wanted to know what we planned to do with all those bags of urine."

*   *   *

The burst came at 108:54. The pressurized helium, which forced fuel and oxidizer into the descent-stage engine, was warming and expanding. Normally, at this point in the mission, the pressure of all that helium would have been vented during the moon landing, but now, less than a third of the LM's fuel had been used, and there were fears that the helium tank might explode. A burst disk finally relieved the pressure, venting helium into space in what looked to James Lovell like a stream of sparkles. Gone was the worry of another major explosion. Gone also was any possibility of using the descent-stage engine. Not to worry, though: The remaining course corrections were so slight as to be within the capability of *Aquarius's* little attitude-control rockets, and, if it became absolutely necessary, the descent stage could be jettisoned and the ascent engine called into action.

EXCERPT FROM THE APOLLO 13 LOG OF JOHN STRAKOSCH AND WILL BISCHOFF

April 16, 1970
108:54   Helium tank burst disks blew—Hallelujah!
Lovell: Got a fast yaw out of it. Actually reversed ship's yaw and put in a little pitch.

Depression was gnawing slowly at the three men. They began to believe that the Apollo Program would be canceled as a result of their failed mission, and that, in a way, they might be personally responsible. They were on "live microphone" when Lovell said, "It will be a very long time before anyone goes to the moon again." Then the news media bit down hard and repeated his words as headlines.

"No!" the engineer said. "If they are right, if this is the fall of Apollo, it will not be the end of the missions to the moon." He led the general toward a building that housed a Soviet version of LM-1. "We can revive it," the engineer said. "If Apollo fails, we can have a manned *Zond*."

*   *   *

EXCERPTS FROM THE APOLLO 13 LOG OF
JOHN STRAKOSCH AND WILL BISCHOFF

109:33   Separation Procedure
- *Shut LM hatch*
- *Shut CM hatch*
- *pressurize tunnel to 0.5*
- *monitor pressure to insure integrity*
- *Blow pyrotechnics with tunnel pressurized*
- LM takes off

(option—crew suited? I would vote yes!)

112:06   Aquarius "go" for Battery charge.

Jack Swigert: "On the way home, Mission Control gave me a procedure for getting LM electricity to run the Command Module. That was something that had never been done before. By following the new procedures, we got LM power into the Command Module. We used it to recharge the reentry batteries. After that, we knew that we had a good Command Module electrical system, but we still didn't dare use it until the last couple of hours. Thanks to Mission Control and the guys who worked it all out in the simulators, the procedures worked perfectly. That last morning I was back in my element. I had something to do, and every switch and circuit breaker that I turned on in *Odyssey* just made me feel that much better. I forgot (for a while) about being tired, and I didn't even notice the cold. James and Fred were the same. Our teamwork was fantastic. We were one body with three heads and six hands. As tired as we were, there was never a cross word. Everybody meshed. Everybody took his share of the load."

EXCERPTS FROM THE APOLLO 13 LOG OF
JOHN STRAKOSCH AND WILL BISCHOFF

112:39   *Hurricane 500 miles west of landing site does not pose a problem.*

121:45   *University of Toronto estimates overpressure peaks during LM-CM separation 7 pounds per square inch (psi)*

on the surface of the CM hatch. Equivalent to 10 grams of
TNT. University of T thinks shock wave plane is fully devel-
oped on LM hatch and not necessarily on CM hatch. Univ.
of T says we are better off cutting our pressure (in the tunnel)
as much as possible.
122:50 *Velocities of pressure waves may reach 10,000 ft/*
sec. U. of T. says the pressure in corner of Hatch 10-25 psi.

At Mission Control, Donald Slayton, one of the "original
seven" astronauts, told Jack Swigert that he really ought to be
getting some rest.

"Well, if I get everything done, I'll try," Swigert said. "But I'll
tell you, it's almost impossible to sleep. All of us have the same
problem. It's just too cold to sleep. It's just awful cold."

For a moment, Slayton was afraid to answer. Swigert's tone
worried him. The astronauts were getting cranky and depressed.
This was a moment the physicians had hoped to avoid. The ever-
worsening environment was exacting a potentially deadly toll. The
crew might falter, become careless. He meditated for a few seconds, and then made a suggestion. "I know that none of you are
sleeping worth a damn, because it's so cold, and you might want
to dig out the medical kit and pull out a couple of Dexedrines
apiece."

"Fred brought that up," Lovell said. "We might consider it."

"We wish we could figure out a way to get a hot cup of coffee
up to you. It would taste pretty good now, wouldn't it?"

"Yes, it sure would. You don't realize how cold this thing
becomes in a passive thermal-control mode that's slowing down.
The sun is simply turning on the engine of the Service Module.
It's not getting down to the spacecraft at all."

"Hang in there. It won't be long."

The up-link went quiet for a while. It was now 2:30 A.M.,
Houston time, 132:30. Slayton could understand now why primitive men worshiped the sun. He tapped the microphone. "Okay,
skipper, we figured out a way to keep you warm. We decided to
start powering you up now."

"Sounds good," Lovell said. "And you're sure we have plenty of electrical power to do this?"

"That's affirmative. We've got plenty of power to do it."

EXCERPTS FROM THE APOLLO 13 LOG OF
JOHN STRAKOSCH AND WILL BISCHOFF

April 17, 1970
133:32   LM being powered up early to warm up cabin.
133:36   Frost on windows—OK to turn on heaters? OK to turn on—can be left on indefinitely.
133:37   Current up to 60 amps.
134:01   Lovell: getting warmer in LM now.
135:00   14.6 hrs. water left
135:46   LM cabin "warmed up" almost comfortable. LM 48,000 miles away; coming in at 9,000 feet (1.7 mi) per second.
136:20   Everybody happy

John Hussey was happy. He was sitting with his simulation team, having coffee and buns, when Swigert's voice came down: "I'm looking out the window now and the earth is whistling in like a high-speed freight train."

"Well," someone announced, "looks like it's all a matter of sitting around and waiting to see what angle they enter the atmosphere at. Looks like it's all up to Rockwell's ship now."

"Rockwell!" a stern voice called. The man stood up and stared around the room, feigning antagonism. "I think we ought to send them a bill! We towed their damned ship in, didn't we?"

"Wait a minute. *Wait a minute*," someone said. "I have a purchase order around here somewhere. Aha! Got it!" He pulled a piece of paper from his pocket and unfolded it on the table. "Okay. What do we put in the column where it says 'part number'?"

"Your boo-boo," John Hussey announced.

A flashpoint had been reached, at which twelve sleepy men became slap-happy and self-sustaining.

"Okay. Towing at four dollars for the first mile, one dollar each additional mile . . . four hundred thousand miles. It was a trouble call . . . fast service. We've just given them a battery charge. That comes to—"

"Aw, be a sport. Throw in the battery charge for free."

"Okay. Free battery charge. But they did use our jump cables, which should be worth, say, four dollars and five cents."

"Oxygen at ten dollars per pound . . ."

"Fifty pounds."

"Sleeping accommodations for two, no TV . . ."

"Air conditioned!"

"Right! Air conditioned, with radio, modified American plan—*with view*."

"No charge! The room was *prepaid*."

"Yes. But they had an additional guest in the room. Tack on an extra eight dollars per night—checkout no later than noon today."

"Accommodations not guaranteed beyond that time . . ."

The room went silent for a moment.

"Er . . . right! Charges for keeping this invoice confidential?"

"That should be worth at least one hundred thousand dollars."

But the invoice did not remain confidential. Everybody wanted a copy, so one of the test pilots ran up to his office and asked his secretary to type it. She was immediately stricken by the giggles. She showed it to the other secretaries, and they all wanted copies, and that's when things became unglued. From hand to hand, the invoice began to multiply, seemingly by the square of the number of people who saw it, and by the cube of the number of photocopiers in the Grumman complex. And so, inevitably . . .

"Walter Cronkite reporting. An unusual piece of paper has just come across my desk. . . ."

During the next six months, envelopes containing anywhere between ten cents and twenty dollars would trickle in with Grumman's mail. Concerned citizens wanted to help Rockwell pay the towing bill. Grumman would eventually throw a party to "eat up the reserve cash."

At 138:02, still attached to *Aquarius*, *Odyssey* dumped the Service Module. Sweeping up ahead, the earth was little more than four hours away. They would want to be at least three miles ahead of the Service Module by then, for it contained almost nineteen tons of unused hypergolic propellants, and there would soon be a great deal of shrapnel flying around the upper atmosphere.

EXCERPTS FROM THE APOLLO 13 LOG OF JOHN STRAKOSCH AND WILL BISCHOFF

138:02   *Service Module Separation! Whole panel of SM is blown out right from front to engine. Looks like it got to the engine. Knocked the high gain antenna into the bell.*
138:06   *Taking pictures of SM. SM drifting in front of windows. Lots of debris hanging out to side in front of S-band antenna.*

The Command Module had only reentry batteries, which could power the ship for just a short time. The crew had to live off the LM almost to the last minute, and as they watched the earth's membrane of air rushing up at them, they became increasingly uncomfortable floating around in a vehicle that could not possibly make it to the ground.

Fred Haise: "It was time to leave the LM. We wanted to take back some pieces of the ship—anything that was loose and could be removed quickly. We took out all the netting from the LM, its inner wall that hides the tubing and wiring. I took one armrest—that was easy—but there was no time for anything else. [The armrest is currently on display in Grumman's Plant 5.] There wasn't even time to get into our space suits."

EXCERPTS FROM THE APOLLO 13 LOG OF
JOHN STRAKOSCH AND WILL BISCHOFF

140:18　　*Lovell: Have new communications system known as yelling through the tunnel.*
140:20　　*Pyrotechnics armed.*

Fred Haise: "We were sad to see the LM go, from a point of friendship and from a practical side. It had proven itself. It had done all that it could do for us, and we were now shifting into a machine that had been powerless for four days. The Command Module was never intended to be powered down, and it was even frozen inside. There was ice from the water tanks. We were not sure that this machine could make it, but we had no choice. We were concerned that we were letting the good vehicle go—popping it off into space like a cork from a bottle—and we had to ride this other thing."

At 141:29, Swigert asked, "Can I proceed and kind of punch off early?"

"Jack, when you are comfortably ready to punch off, you can go ahead and do it," came the answer.

On April 17, at 11:23 A.M. (Houston time), Swigert punched off. LM-7 drew away from his docking window. It would follow close behind *Odyssey*, crashing against the atmosphere and pulling itself apart. From Houston, a tired voice called, "Farewell, *Aquarius*, and we thank you."

"She sure was a great ship," Swigert replied.

"She sure was," Milt Radimer says. "To have Fred Haise sit inside her and go around the moon and come back and tell us about how we built this lifeboat and it saved him—well, that makes you feel good. When I was a kid, I worked as a lifeguard and I pulled somebody out of the water, but building something like that and having it . . . from that far away, well . . ."

*　　　*　　　*

EXCERPTS FROM THE APOLLO 13 *LOG OF*
JOHN STRAKOSCH AND WILL BISCHOFF

141:30   *LM Jettison!*
        • *No change in cabin pressure.*
        • *No change in attitude.*
        • *Rock solid all the way!*
141:58   *Will Bischoff paid up on bet! Received this day $5.*
142:28   *Lost data on LM (loss of signal)*
142:31   *LM data back—still looks good!*
142:33   *CM Guidance and navigation is go!*
142:35   *Lost LM data again.*
142:36   *LM data back but spotty (comes and goes).*
142:39   *Loss of signal CM (due to ionized gas around capsule).*
142:46   *Voice contact with CM.*
142:49   *Drogues out.**
142:50   *Main parachutes out on TV.*
142:54   *Splashdown! 3½ miles from ship.*

Fred Haise: "The Command Module had gotten very cold and very wet, so when we got back in we got rained on during the first part of reentry. All the water came out from behind the instrument panels as soon as we encountered a g-field. We peaked out at about five gravities. There was no noise during reentry, except the tiny thrusters firing through the Command Module's hull, to keep the heat shield pointing in the right direction. Outside the window we saw a great white glow from the ionization, because we were moving at 36,000 feet per second when we contacted the upper atmosphere. It was like being inside a neon light. Lower in the atmosphere the ionization leaves a trail behind you—you can see it through the window. It changes into a smoky, reddish-brown fire trail. The g-forces felt pretty strong. Fighter

---

*Drogues are small parachutes used to slow down the craft before the larger, main parachutes are opened.

pilots often experience up to nine g's, and we had only five, but we were used to zero-gravity, so it felt like double. We did not hear the air moving outside, although there was a loud noise when the nose cone popped off and the drogue chute came out. It was like being inside a drum, like shotguns over your head. And then we were down on Earth."

In Houston, the cheering went on and on and on. In its midst, Lew Evans turned to Bob Gilruth and said, "Well, how many bonus points do we get for *that?*"

NASA bonus points: That's where all the profits were. One point was awarded for each major mission requirement fulfilled by your company's vehicle. LM-3, for example, had earned four bonus points, which brought Grumman several million dollars over the cost of the vehicle.

NASA's contract officer was sitting next to Gilruth when the question of bonus points came up. "What are you talking about?" he said. "The contract awards bonus points for a moon landing. You didn't land on the moon. Your ship didn't do a damned thing."

"The hell it didn't!" Tommy Attridge snapped. "Just look at that plot board. Look at that capsule floating out there. Look at those three men. Our ship saved their lives. What would you have liked us to do, Darryl? Would you like to think about what would've happened if we just said, 'Let's detach the LM in lunar orbit'? Then where would you be, Darryl, baby? You know where you'd be? Three guys adrift in space dying. It would really look neat on color television—three guys turning blue."

"Don't worry, Tommy," Gilruth said. "I guess we're going to have to renegotiate that contract now."

Within days, the contract was rewritten, and Fred Haise flew north to give the netting he'd pulled from *Aquarius* to Al Beauregard, who had become the supervisor for LM-7 after the flight of his first vehicle, LM-5. Haise, Lovell, and Swigert wanted to do something special for the people who built the ship, something that went a little beyond saying thank you, and they had a plan. Al Beauregard's daughter (yes, the same little girl whose picture is on the moon) cut the netting into inch-and-a-half squares and glued the squares onto blue cardboard plaques printed up by the *Apollo* 13 astronauts. There were hundreds of plaques to be made, and during the days that followed, Fred Haise began calling Beauregard's daughter "Miss Elmer Glue." The nickname stuck.

During the week of April 25, 1970, the astronauts handed out the plaques, each with a LM builder's name on it, each with a piece of *Aquarius*, and each bearing the words THANKS FOR A JOB WELL DONE! followed by the penned-in signatures of James Lovell, Jack Swigert, and Fred Haise.

George Titterton looked down at Swigert's autograph and knew that somebody in Grumman should now be feeling a strong kinship with the man at Decca Records who had turned down the Beatles. Jack Swigert had first come to Grumman in 1965, whereupon his test-pilot application was promptly declined. Two months later, NASA signed him on as an astronaut, and, try as he might, George never could learn who declined the application.

Never.

Nobody admitted it.

55. THE END OF THE VON BRAUN ERA

During the next six months, China launched its first satellite, another unmanned *Zond* flew to the moon and back, *Luna 16* landed and returned to Earth with a few ounces of lunar soil, *Soyuz 9* was used to simulate a ten-day lunar mission, and a series of unmanned tests of the Russian LM began. The LM's debut was a flight called *Cosmos 379*. First the descent-stage engines were fired into the direction of flight, swinging the ship out into high Earth orbit. Then the ascent stage separated and fired to simulate a lunar lift-off. A second flight tested the communications system using taped voices, and the ascent engine was fired to assist the two descent engines in a simulated landing abort, with both stages still attached—an added safety option that the American LM did not have.

The Apollo Program recovered in less than a year (or at least gave the impression of doing so), and, after Ed Mitchell and Alan Shepard brought LM-8 down on the edge of a four-billion-year-old lava sea, the Soviets quietly and mysteriously returned their manned-lunar-exploration plans to the shelf, where they were to remain, at least into the next century. They focused their efforts instead on urine stills and closed ecosystems and permanently manned space stations capable of generating up to ninety percent of the oxygen, food, and water used by "space colonists." If all went according to plan, by 1990, Soviet stations, equipped with their own propulsion systems, would develop the ability to leave Earth orbit, in favor of lunar and Mars orbit.

The first Soviet space station, *Salyut 1*, was launched in April 1971, slightly more than ten years after Gagarin's flight, a year and two days after the return of *Apollo 13*, and two years ahead of the American *Skylab*. After a twenty-two day occupation of *Salyut 1*, cosmonauts Georgi Dobrovolsky, Vladislav Volkov, and Viktor Patsayev became the first men to die in orbit. Their *Soyuz* ferry emptied all its air into space, and then traveled on to perform a perfect automatic landing.* Astronaut Tom Stafford served as a pallbearer at the funeral, and within a year, the first (albeit short-lived) effort to establish an international space-rescue capability,

---

*The *Soyuz* spacecraft has two manned components, the orbital module and the landing module. Prior to reentry, the orbital module is jettisoned and the cosmonauts return to Earth automatically in the landing module. In order to fit three cosmonauts, instead of the usual two, into the *Soyuz*, planners had to eliminate the space suits to save room. On *Soyuz 11*, when the crew jettisoned the orbital module, a valve designed to open after the ship had descended to 15,000 feet sprang open prematurely. Cabin pressure fell to zero within 45 seconds. The crew attempted to close the valve; but a subsequent investigation revealed that a full two minutes were required to crank it shut. Today the Soviets fly only two people in *Soyuz* . . . and they wear space suits.

including compatible U.S.-USSR docking systems, went from the preliminary-design phase to the manufacturing phase.

On July 28, 1971, Dave Scott and James Irwin landed the first extended-stay LM, the *Falcon* (LM-10, *Apollo* 15), near the collapsed roof of what had once been an underground river of lava. Budgetary considerations had precluded the flight of LM-9 (originally assigned to *Apollo* 15), and the ship eventually found a permanent home in the Kennedy Space Center's Mission Simulation Building. With *Falcon* came the first lunar-rover expedition. Man had gone beyond the stage of merely probing for hazards in the lunar environment. He was now an active explorer.

Nine months later, seeking rocks from loftier terrain, John Young and Charles Duke set *Orion* (LM-11) down on the Descartes highlands, where they discovered open fields strewn with asteroid-ejected rocks as big as houses. On December 9, 1972, Eugene Cernan and Harrison Schmitt landed the *Challenger* (LM-12, *Apollo* 17) in a lava-flooded crack that had opened up 3.7 billion years ago, when an asteroid as big as the state of Rhode Island carved out the Serentatis Basin.

And then the ships stopped landing.

Nine Apollo expeditions had gone to the moon, taking away with them 841 Earth pounds of rocks and soil and leaving behind seven descent stages (one dropped off by *Apollo* 10), six ascent stages (five dumped on the surface, one left in lunar orbit by *Apollo* 11), three lunar rovers, six American flags, and more than a hundred million dollars' worth of scientific measuring devices in five lunar laboratories, all of them designed to beam information back to Earth—all of them shut down in an economy move. Up there, on the moon, are the initials of Teresa Dawn Cernan sketched into the soil, a plaque and figurine commemorating fourteen dead American and Russian astronauts, a falcon feather, a wedding ring that accidentally got left in the cabin of LM-10, a shamrock, a photograph of Charlie Duke's dog, two golf balls, the lingering resonances and stamp numbers of hundreds of human beings who would never go to the moon, and the footprints of twelve who did.

*   *   *

America's last LM was built in 1976. It was wheeled down Long Island's Sunrise Highway, loaded onto a 747 freighter, and shipped off to the world's biggest shrine for *Apollo*, which happens to be located in Tokyo.

As America prepared for its bicentennial celebration, two Japanese businessmen arrived at Long Island's Cradle of Aviation Museum at Mitchel Field and knocked on director William Kaiser's door. They told him about an international show that would take place in Japan, a sort of World's Fair devoted to space, and they wanted to know if he could lend them a LM.

"We're designing a special building to house the vehicle," one of them explained. "We want to put two actors dressed in space suits inside and lower the vehicle one hundred feet to a simulated lunar landscape. The actors come out and walk around. They go back inside, and then we raise the ascent stage to the ceiling." They spread a pile of drawings across Kaiser's desk and showed him how the exhibit was supposed to work: On the ceiling, the audience would see motion pictures of an approaching star that became a LM in flight, with the screen parting and rolling away during a bright engine flare and the real thing descending to the surface.

Kaiser looked over the drawings and listened politely. The two men stopped talking. There followed a long silence. Kaiser eased back in his chair, grinning, and said, "You know, you can't raise a LM one hundred feet and separate the ascent stage from the descent stage once, much less eight times a day for something like three months."

"Well, who built the LM?" one of them asked.

"Grumman made the LM."

"Can we buy one?"

The question put Kaiser on the verge of hysteria. He turned to the window, trying to suppress the urge to laugh. Out there in front of the museum waited a black Cadillac limousine with three doors on each side. It looked about four times as long as Kaiser's Toyota.

"Uh, right," Kaiser said. "You do know that LMs are kind of expensive, and made for one-time use?"

"Well, can you arrange for us to meet the people who made them?"

The two men explained what a great thing their people thought space travel had turned out to be, and that their country was building a whole *city* just for the exhibit. They spoke as if they had untold billions to spend. Perhaps they did. Outside the office, someone called Kaiser aside and told him with whom he was dealing with: "His name is Mr. Sasakawa. You know, Bill, some people think Howard Hughes is a very rich man . . ."

Kaiser called Grumman vice-president John Rettaliata. He explained that he was bringing two Japanese businessmen over, and they wanted to buy a LM. John appreciated the joke. Convincing him was no easy matter, because Grumman had for years been peddling its E-2Cs and S-2Fs to the Japanese with never so much as a nibble. And now they wanted to buy a LM? Could that be true? If it was, maybe they'd buy airplanes, too.

Out came the red carpet.

Grumman rebuilt a LM mock-up for the Tokyo space show. "What we had to do," says LM "troubleshooter" Joel Taft, "was completely rebuild the old CBS-TV mock-up so it could handle an elevator hoist. We had to man-rate the vehicle so it would be safe. One guy from structural design was assigned to that. I was assigned to complete the exterior—to make it look as real as possible. I'm a bug for things like that. I just ate it up, and to this day I think it's the best-looking LM around. We did it right. For instance, the rendezvous strobe light on the front of the vehicle—it would have cost thousands of dollars to buy a real one. I found a company that manufactured school bus lights, and by luck they had a prototype light with a white lens, so for thirty bucks we got our rendezvous light. For the gold mylar insulation, we found a window-dressing place in Valley Stream that had a series of metallic films for about a dollar a yard. For the dishes of the antennae we needed something that wouldn't cost us a small fortune or require us to go to the machine shop and have them spun, so I knew where the scrap yard was and I found two LM descent-stage fuel tanks—titanium—and I thought if we cut the bottoms and tops off those suckers, they'd be perfect: perfect shape, perfect size, and free. Those tanks were about a week away from being scrapped. I said, 'Don't move them!' And we cut the dishes out of them and put them on the ship. And we put a real equipment pallet on the side of the descent stage. I found it lying on the ground outside one of the plants, and we swiped it. We rigged a handle to the porch, just like the one Neil Armstrong pulled as he climbed down the ladder, and when the Japanese astronaut climbed down, he'd pull the thing and—bingo!—down came the pallet.

"You know, I really admire those Japanese. I spent a month over there and I fell in love with the country. They assigned interpreters to each one of the American crews. I sort of pumped some of the Japan Airlines cargo reps for Japanese customs before I got there, so I wouldn't act like a dummy and insult them. I learned the words for 'this here' and 'that there.' We were un-packing the LM the first day, and they were attaching the thing to lift the ascent stage, and I said, *'Koray koko'*—'that here'—and every one of the Japanese workers stopped and turned. It broke the ice. I used the interpreter as a teacher. It was a cute situation. There was a little guy who was the lead man of the crew that was working for us. His name was Kono. He couldn't speak En-glish, but he could understand it a bit. We got to be pretty good friends. I asked the interpreter what the Japanese word was for 'friend.' She said it was *tomudichi*, and that's what I used to call him.

"In Bethpage I found some of the original LM brochures. They were the beautiful color ones with the plastic overlays. I took about a thousand of them with me to Japan. I asked the interpreter to go around and ask each of the workers how many children he had. Then I went around and gave them enough for their kids. From that moment, you couldn't catch them. They were working so fast and so hard.

"All the LM design drawings were stored in one of the warehouses, and we needed some. Because our funds in space were being cut so sharply, they had just been thrown in boxes. Most of the boxes did not match their inventory sheets, and there were four thousand boxes of drawings. Many were to be thrown away—they were throwing away history—but I managed to find drawings of all the outer features of the vehicle. We ended up calling this last of the LMs 'LM-7½,' because we used drawings of LM-1 and LM-15."

On July 12, 1976, Joel Taft rode LM-7½ during its first "test flight." A day later, he transmitted his Mission Status Bulletin to Bethpage:

AT 1515 HOURS, 12 JULY, LM 7½ MADE THE FIRST SUCCESS-FUL MANNED LANDING ON THE MOON OF JAPAN. ALL SYS-TEMS WERE GO. ASTRONAUTS TAFT-SAN AND SCHNEIDER-SAN RETURNED SAFELY TO THE EARTH BUT FORGOT TO PICK UP ANY MOON ROCKS. FLIGHT REPEATED FOR INTER-NATIONAL PRESS ON 13 JULY. AUDIENCE OVERWHELMED. THERE IS NO DOUBT OUR BIRD IS THE STAR OF THE SHOW!!

". . . four forward . . . drifting to the right a little . . . six . . . drifting right . . . four forward . . . drifting right . . . Contact light. Okay, engine stopped . . . descent-engine command override off. Houston—er—Tranquillity Base here. The *Eagle* has landed."

"Roger, Twank—Tranquillity, we copy you on the ground. You've got a bunch of guys about to turn blue. We're breathing again."

Dvorak's *New World Symphony* rose to a crescendo, and Joel Taft got the chills. He'd worked with Peggy Hewitt on the ground-support team, on the very ship that now appeared to be sitting before him in the lunar dawn. The musical score chosen by the Japanese triggered memories, more and more of them, rising like summoned spirits from Joel's subconscious. For a few moments, for just a few, it was 1969 again.

At the fair's end, Ryoichi Sasakawa, its sponsor, bowed before LM-7½ and declared that it would remain a permanent exhibit.

Meanwhile, across the Pacific, LM-13 (originally intended for the canceled *Apollo 18* flight) found a home at the Cradle of Aviation Museum on Long Island. She was the lucky LM. LM-14 (*Apollo 19*) was placed in front of Philadelphia's Franklin Institute, where rain, wind, pigeons, and kids with spray cans full of paint began an assault. LM-15 was broken up for scrap metal. An unidentified LM ascent stage, probably a test article used for astronaut training, ended up on a scrap heap in a Florida junk yard; it is still there. Another unidentified LM mockup stands amid a savanna-like growth of grass and scattered bushes behind the once abandoned Hall of Science in Queens, New York. Somebody stole the ascent stage, apparently ignoring the *Mercury* and *Gemini* capsules that stand nearby.*

LM Test Article No. 1 (LTA-1), the first LM ever built (on which Grumman workers practiced their manufacturing techniques), wound up in an old garage at Sands Point, New York. For more than two decades, it lay half buried in old dining-room cupboards, airplane parts, rotting papers, horse-drawn carriages, and a demolished lunar rover. Squirrels had nested under the

---

*The government originally ordered 15 LMs:

 1. Flew unmanned on *Apollo 4*
 2. Not used, now at Smithsonian
 3. Flew on *Apollo 9*
 4. Flew on *Apollo 10*
 5. Flew on *Apollo 11*
 6. Flew on *Apollo 12*
 7. Flew on *Apollo 13*
 8. Flew on *Apollo 14*
 9. Not used, now at Kennedy Space Center
 10. Flew on *Apollo 15*
 11. Flew on *Apollo 16*
 12. Flew on *Apollo 17*
 13. Not used, was to land inside Copernicus, now at Cradle of Aviation Museum, Mitchel Field, Long Island
 14. Not used, was to land near Tycho, now at Franklin Institute, Philadelphia
 15. Scrapped

ascent stage. In 1999 LTA-1 was finally transferred to the Cradle of Aviation Museum, where it now stands in the company of MOLAB (Mobile Lunar Laboratory) and the world's largest collection of LM ascent stages—all in various phases of construction, all rescued from scrap heaps. LTA-8 is on display in Houston. An unidentified LTA is on display in Huntsville. Elsewhere, a LM footpad has been used as a bird bath,* gold foil as tinsel for a Christmas tree, and an attitude-control rocket as a paperweight.

In the bicentennial year 1976, while Japan unveiled a space city and made LM its focus, former LM engineers were selling hot dogs on Manhattan's streets. The fall of *Apollo* left more than discarded LMs in its wake. There was the human wreckage—hundreds of space engineers whose profession had disappeared overnight. A few, very few, were working with Rockwell on the Space Shuttle, which would fly three years behind schedule, thanks largely to a Congress that knew no end to budget cuts. For reasons that will probably never be clear, America had begun to despise its engineers and scientists. Men like Bob Watkins, who had once been among the proudest people on Earth, now found themselves turning up their coat collars and slouching a little bit on the way home, because their neighbors just didn't understand that all those billions of Apollo dollars had been spent right here on Earth, that space technology had put people to work just as surely as the construction of railroads and steamships used to put people to work. They just did not understand that Apollo had given America a permanent space port, and so many medical and technological spinoffs that a whole book could, and would, be written about them.† They just did not understand that all of these advances, even during the height of Apollo funding, were gained for less money than Americans were spending on cosmetics, or recreational drugs, or the defoliation of Vietnam.

---

*The bird bath was finally donated to New York's Cradle of Aviation Museum because sparrows kept drowning in it.
†NASA *Spinoffs*, U.S. Government Printing Office, 1980.

And still, cries that the space program's budget should be spent on "the people" became an argument that simply refused to go away.

"Around that time, part of what I was doing was speaking before groups and defending the space program," says Ozzie Williams, who had been in charge of the design, construction, and testing of LM's attitude-control rockets. "There was a lot of public disaffection for the space program. We had beaten the pants off the Russians. We proved we could do it. 'All right,' the public said, 'so that's the end of it. Let's stop throwing money into space.' Well, I had done quite a bit of research, and NASA encouraged us to talk to consumer groups, chambers of commerce, church groups, and so forth, to convince them that money sent into space was not thrown away. The big, 'in' cry in those days was, 'Kill the space program!' I had statistics showing that in 1972, the year of the last Apollo flights to the moon, the space budget was $4.5 billion, and the amount of money in the soil bank was $7.2 billion: That's money the government was giving farmers *not* to grow crops. *Completely* thrown away.

"How we ever got things like Viking and Pioneer and Voyager through, I don't know. The money we saved, the money that *didn't* go into space—where did it go? I don't know that either. Certainly it didn't go into human resources, which is what the public wanted. 'Take care of the people,' they said. 'Never mind space.' Where did they think hurricane warnings and crop analyses came from?

"I remember how the public got what it wanted. They got NASA to shrink into a very tiny thing, and the great people who made Apollo were . . . *are now* out selling insurance, or they're retired, or they're teaching. But they're not doing the kinds of things that could solve some of our problems today.

"I read in a book that in 1980, America spent more money playing Space Invaders than it spent on the Space Shuttle. I wish I had had *that* statistic in '76. The feeling, back then, was that the space program was being run by eggheads. I had the strong impression that grassroots America was with the program only as long as it was entertaining. And they had the feeling that the scientists were not to be trusted. They seemed to feel that the moon landings were, if not a trick, something that had been put over on the man on the street by these superscientists. And the answer is that the man on the street never had the time to get enough background to really understand what was going on. And those who opposed the expenditures found their chance to kill it, once the stunt was over. There was Senator Walter Mondale, who wanted to kill the Space Shuttle, absolutely kill it. Even the Congress was thinking that way. They didn't understand the nature of technical progress."

"And that was our fault," says Lynn Radcliffe. "Grumman, NASA, the total space business blew it with the people who pay the bills—the American public. We had the people in the palms of our hands, looking at the tube witnessing the most amazing achievement in the history of man, and we lost them. We seemed to be putting on a great show and perhaps doing too much breast-beating, and people couldn't see what was in it for them.

"As close to space as I am, I truly do think it's going to save the world ultimately. I'm thinking in terms of hundreds of years, but things have a way of happening a lot sooner. When I was a kid looking at *Collier's Wonder Book*, which came out in 1920, they were talking about atomic energy and airlines to Europe and trips to the moon, and I thought these things were hundreds of years away. But it all happened while I was still a relatively young man. And when Apollo came along, we never really told the people what space could do for their future. People have self-interest, and you've got to show people the microelectronics that came out of LM, how they would soon be able to bring computers into the home, and what *that* could mean. We didn't keep the people on our side, we never helped them to understand, and I think we only have ourselves to blame. That's the worst part of it."

"They never understood us," says rocket technician Leon Gurinsky. "After all the layoffs, after I turned in my badge and was escorted through the Clean Room for the last time, I visited LM-2 in the Smithsonian; people were standing around and looking at it, and still they didn't realize the significance of the program, or they didn't really care. That bothered me. I stood there and watched people and listened to their interpretations of it, and they were way off."

On October 4, 1957, on the day *Homo sapiens* became adult, Isaac Asimov decided he would start writing more science for the public, even if it meant he'd have less time for science fiction. "And that's exactly what I've been doing for the last twenty-five years," he says. "I didn't think I would make a difference all by myself if I wrote popular science. I thought that I, plus all the other science writers, might make a difference, and I wanted to contribute. *Sputnik 1* set up a vast feeling of inadequacy of American science education (like now, except that Americans no longer care), and I wanted to reverse that.

"Then came our withdrawal from the moon, and from space. I hoped the Russians would do something like *Sputnik* to us again and wake us up. After *Apollo 17*, it became clear that the attitude toward expeditions to the moon was 'We scored a touchdown; we won the game; now we can go home.' It struck me as stupid thinking. Then again, I began to think, that's how it was presented to people all along. There was hardly any concentration on the gains in technology or the joy of discovery. It was a matter of beating the Russians. On the other hand, if it was not presented that way, one wonders if Congress would have provided a red cent."

Jesco von Puttkamer: "In 1967, which was also the height of the Vietnam disappointment and the internal domestic problems, Nixon cut back the space program. *Apollo 20* was canceled in 1967, the *Apollo 19* and *18* in 1968, and so by the time we landed, in 1969, we were already living with the bitter feeling that this was just one of a few landings, even though the hardware had already been paid for.

"We all had stiff upper lips, like good soldiers—especially the older members, the Germans who had been through a lot of letdowns in their lives, like the result of the Second World War, when everything went to pieces for them. They ended up living with the blame of building V-2s for the Nazis. And so it wasn't the first time they had to face intense disappointments, and they were able to swallow it. But they were bitter anyway, because the pace of the space program slowed down to an extent where they just gave up. They said, 'This is just impossible. These Americans here, they started so beautifully, and everything was so full of promise, and all of a sudden the people have taken a 180-degree turn.' I think most of the immigrants couldn't understand that—that a nation actually would shut down this tremendous capability, that they would let so many skilled people go.

"Von Braun, when he went to Washington, when he left Huntsville, he was already in a mood which—he used to be very optimistic all his life. Prior to the retreat from space, he always seemed gratified. He was always encouraging everyone. Every time the team was depressed, he was the one who supported everyone, with his jokes and so on. But later on he got quiet, and more serious about things. He never really joked that way anymore. He wasn't really the center of fun, like he used to be. He went to Washington, and he had a few more years, doing nothing essentially. On the one hand he was supposed to do long-range planning. He was the focal point of NASA's long-range planning effort, and he had the job of assistant associate administrator, which was very high up. But he wasn't given any work, because there wasn't any interest in long-range commitments. He was told, 'You are our long-range planner, but don't you dare do anything, because we can't commit to any new program.' And he said, 'Let's go to Mars.' On August 4, 1969, right after the lunar landing, he presented a full-fledged manned Mars-landing concept to the President's Space Task Group. It was part of an integrated space program, which did not just include the Mars project but also development of a Space Shuttle, a space station, a lunar base with mineral-refining facilities, and a Mars flight to be launched from the space station—*a totally integrated program for the next twenty or thirty years.*

"And he was laughed at, and told to go home and forget it.*

"So, it's essentially like telling a long-range planner that his plans were shit. And he quit NASA and went to Fairchild, where he sold helicopters. It was something he didn't understand too much about, but his image in the world was good, so he sold helicopters to South America. And I definitely think that his cancer was related to this depression, to this constant depression, this aura of gloom that was around him, there, when his disappointment really became too large."

Wernher von Braun died on the Thursday morning of June 16, 1977. He was sixty-five years old. Among his personal papers was found a clipping, yellowed with age and barely readable for all the handling it had received in the end. It was a statement by Pearl Buck:

The truly creative mind in any field is no more than this: a human creature born abnormally, inhumanly sensitive. To him, a touch is a blow, a sound is a noise, a misfortune is a tragedy, a joy is an ecstasy, a friend is a lover, a lover is a god, and failure is death. Add to this cruelly delicate organism the overpowering necessity to create, create, create—so that without the creating of music or poetry or books or buildings or something of meaning, his very breath is cut off from him. He must create, must pour out creation. By some strange, unknown, inward urgency he is not really alive unless he is creating.

---

*In May 1983, President Reagan asked NASA to provide design studies for a space station and a Mars flight. It had all come full circle, back to Jesco von Puttkamer, von Braun's protégé, NASA's program manager for advanced planning. One of the first places he went to was von Braun's long-discarded plans—discarded by just about everybody except the Russians, who had made his integrated program the cornerstone of their own space effort. "In America," says von Puttkamer, "the only thing we salvaged from his integrated space program was the Shuttle. That is the only souvenir, or the memory we got from the von Braun days. He pushed for the Shuttle as part of many other things, and that is what—how do you call it?—almost a legacy. His legacy."

56. EMERGENCE

More than a two thousand people had gathered in the Mojave Desert.

An Air Force drummer began a long, unwavering roll. Something was about to happen.

When the ship nosed around the corner of Plant 42, with the word "Enterprise" painted on its side, the drum roll came to an abrupt stop and the band struck up Alexander Courage's *Star Trek* theme. It caught two thousand by surprise. They jumped up as one and yelled, and more than a few stern-faced politicians were seen to laugh. A dozen of them, more, were seen weeping. The shuttle orbiter *Enterprise* and the hint of the starship *Enterprise* had triggered a rare and beautiful mental twist. Something had dropped away. Fact and fiction touched, and even the most pragmatic minds probably saw into the future.

Was it just a space connection between the two? von Puttkamer wondered. Or was a deeper chord struck? Is it that *Star Trek* reflects the hopes of people for a brighter, open future for humankind, and that the space program, with its inherent potential to bring out man's greatest qualities, holds up the promise of upward, outward growth, both physical and mental—of a true humanization of the world we live in, of space?

By May 1983, von Puttkamer was following an official directive of the White House: the study of space stations.

"Space stations can come in all sizes, in many shapes and at many prices, just like Earth-bound homes," von Puttkamer explained. "In NASA we want one that has a future. We want one that has growth potential."

"But Congress is a problem," said one NASA planner. "They'll start taking us apart, and usually you've got congressmen who pretend that they are engineers. They start redesigning stuff for us, and that's when we get mad."

"Let me elaborate on that," said von Puttkamer. "The situation is that on one hand you have a Congress composed of men from all walks of life, but rarely are they engineers or scientists. The basic problem is not so much technical but political. It is the fact that whatever we do must be approved by Congress, and what they are faced with is approving taxpayer funds for high technology. Information flows between the executive branch, where we are at NASA, and the legislative branch, which is Congress, which makes the laws by way of hearings. But there is always the problem of understanding what our engineering designs are all about. For that purpose, Congress has its own Office of Technology Assessment (OTA). That's kind of a technology watchdog office with people who are studying our technological capabilities and requirements.

"Lately, the Congress has been asking us why we need to put a human crew in the space station at all, and they are happy when they find out that a manned space station will have some near-term uses for satellite repairs, making pharmaceuticals, and so on. The importance of a space station is mostly seen for its contemporary or near-term applications. But it is at least as important, if not more so, for its long-range aspects. It becomes a beachhead from which we can begin to build a whole new world for ourselves, not only 'up there' but on Earth as well. Earth, you see, is a limited resource. Populations are soaring; there will be over a billion new people in the next twenty to twenty-five years, amounting to the population of one hundred New York Cities. These people will need jobs, food, clothing, shelter, a little corner of the world for themselves. To support this population, to provide it with a reasonable standard of living, Earth-based industries will have to expand. If industrial expansion comes to a halt due to the limits of Earth, the future will quite likely be characterized by scarcities, deficiencies, defensive resource policies, regressions to intensified battles for survival, and a new fragmentation of mankind. The industrialization of space, however, appears to offer a solution. Such a move could generate new products and services, and eventually could shunt energy- and pollution-intensive industries into space, where both energy and waste reservoirs are plentiful. The resources of space could be used to create wealth for all mankind without detrimental effects on the environment.

"So a space station becomes a beachhead. It's not just a point from which you can spread out. It makes near-Earth space a neighborhood. Even today, when I give speeches, eleven-year-old kids ask me. 'When is NASA going to fly into space?' And I say, 'We have been flying in space all along. Didn't we fly in space with the Shuttle?' 'Oh, no,' they say. 'This isn't space.' You see, they are so used to Shuttle flights, and the earth looks so huge from near-Earth orbit, that it's not really space in their view. Even the moon is too close. It's like their back yard. They are used to space as they've seen in *Star Wars*, with home being very small and very far away. The young people are a pretty good example of the speed with which our culture had adjusted to the Space Shuttle and lunar landings. For those kids the lunar landings are history, just like Napoleon.

"But the space station . . . the point is, once you are there, the future is no longer a narrow road leading to the moon or Mars or the industrialization of space. It is *all* that. It is a multiplicity of options, not just a single goal. Some people will remain in low Earth orbit, developing larger science capabilities. Others will develop the geosynchronous orbital regime for commercial applications, and others will push for lunar industrialization, and a Mars sample return as a precursor to a manned Mars mission. Unmanned robot probes will continue to be launched on immense voyages, and they will continue to carry to other stars our greetings and descriptions of our cultures on metal disks. These are not machines in the traditional sense but our extended sensory organs, parts of *ourselves*—an early hint perhaps at the cybernetic beings of the future who will come after *Homo sapiens*.

"So you will have all these things, and they'll be done almost simultaneously. This is what this beachhead situation means: a multi-dimensional progression from Earth orbit. Compared with Apollo, this is an increased complexity in understanding. It is more difficult to convey this to a politician or a farmer, to talk to him about a space station. It was much easier to tell him that we would land on the moon and return safely to Earth. That's easily understandable. That the space station is a springboard to all kinds of things—that's not so easy to explain. It's a tougher program to justify.

"As for the design of the space station, it must have growth potential. It must be evolutionary. You don't walk in with a big one all at once. You start with a few building blocks, a few modules at a time, and you can buy it 'by the yard.' "

—and once we have the basic space-station architecture, we can go back to the moon—

"And we *will* go back to the moon," von Puttkamer predicted. "Probably around the second half of the 2020s."

There followed visions of men going down to the moon, not merely to explore it but to use it, to mine and refine its minerals and to build from them outposts and mass drivers and stepping stones to the frontiers of the night.

"But I don't foresee any of the giant colonies that were popularized in the 1970s," insisted von Puttkamer. "A colony housing several thousand people requires decades of construction before it is ready for occupancy. It is very monolithic, and any program that takes that amount of time to mature can't survive in a society that is as ever-changing as ours today, with a new president every four or eight years. In those decades of development, you might have a dozen different administrations. They would not necessarily feel obligated to maintain the program. After all, national priorities tend to shift. Monolithic programs are very risky, very shaky. Even the Apollo Program, which took only eight years—by the time we landed on the moon, it was out of tune. In 1969, we were doing our 1961 thing. What seemed to be correct in 1961 for the national psyche, for Camelot and the Bay of Pigs, was questionable for the Vietnam era. Apollo was doomed, just because it wasn't flexible enough.

"So space colonization will have to be flexible, just like living things. It has to be evolutionary. It cannot be monolithic. It has to grow like a coral reef. A coral reef can live through a bad period, through a storm, and it doesn't matter. It depends on the environment. Sometimes it does grow; sometimes it just stagnates for a year or two and then keeps on growing again. The individual polyps that make up the coral reef just keep growing. Huge space systems, large space technologies, will have to become more and more like coral reefs. They will have to be separate living systems, as they grow, in order to survive changes in the environment. Anytime somebody cuts our budget, the monolithic space program is dead. A modular, evolutionary space program can survive: You just don't add anything to it during bad times. We want the space program to be international, but that requires flexibility. Some nations might want to detach their portion and take the module back down to Earth. Other nations could join in midstride. This is what evolution is all about, and what space settlement really will be like—modular, like life itself.

"It is our destiny, in the long run. In space, on one hand, we can address near-term problems, and on the other hand we can help globalize mankind, uniting people more and more under common goals, peaceful goals, and in the long run we can continue growing and advancing civilization in directions and in ways not yet even touched upon by any science-fiction writer. It is difficult to believe that the coincidence in time of the explosive growth of the world's population and the advent of space exploration in the twentieth century should be an accident. Life is a force which has persisted on Earth for two to three billions of years, which has spread out across this planet like a grassfire, which has already gone out to touch the moon and the planet Mars, and is even now stretching its tendrils and sensors out toward the galaxy. This life, evolving under the pressures of its own making, will survive for many millions of years more—and to do so it will continue to expand and to weave its way out. Almost instinctively, man will follow this push and settle on other worlds . . . *to boldly go where no man has gone before.*"

EXCERPT FROM AVIATION WEEK AND SPACE TECHNOLOGY, August 8, 1983

Washington — Heads of eleven companies interested in private space investment told President Reagan last week that a space station is the most important element needed to stimulate and advance U.S. commercial operations in orbit. The President was quoted as saying, "I want a space station too, I have wanted one for a long time." But he qualified the statement by commenting on the realities of federal budgeting. The White House is actively exploring both space station options and how a station could fit into an even larger national space objective that could be announced by President Reagan. A list of specific space station options was completed at the White House August 4 and is scheduled to be presented to the Administration's Senior Interagency Group for Space this week. Following review by this group, the options will be presented to Reagan within the next few weeks as a prelude to White House decisions on the Fiscal 1985 budget.

George Skurla knew long before the White House meeting that the president would love to have a growing, active space program, but he couldn't. The deficits, education, unemployment, and welfare had him boxed in. But George also knew that there was probably more than rumor behind the Soviet Mars expedition, apparently intended for launch (from a space station) before the end of the decade. And he also suspected that the Russians had a shuttle system very similar to his—almost literally his. Photos taken by a high-altitude spy plane showed that a prototype shuttle orbited in June bore a haunting resemblance to Grumman Shuttle Proposal No. 518, which had been rejected in favor of Rockwell's design.*

---

*"518 went into the White House a winner, with our stamp of approval from NASA," von Puttkamer explained. "Then Nixon decided that it *would* be built in California, and that it would have those damned solid boosters—which no one in NASA wanted."

They've such an advantage over our Shuttle builders, George thought. They've seen that our system works. They know it can be done. All they have to do is get a three-view drawing and blueprints from *Astronomy* magazine and just go build the damned thing.

As he lunched with the president and his science adviser and representatives of ten other companies, that day's issue of *Aviation Week and Space Technology* was flying out of Washington aboard an Aeroflot jet. It would be fully translated before the plane touched down in Moscow. The translation would go immediately to press, and Soviet engineers would be reading it the next morning. Little need for spies or the KGB here: The Soviets obtained better than seventy-five percent of their aerospace intelligence from American magazines and public air shows.

"You know, George, I'd like to see us go up and *colonize* the moon," said Dr. Keyworth, the president's science adviser.

"You would?"

"Yes. I think we ought to go back, instead of building this space station that you're making noises about."

"Now, I really don't know what to do up on the moon. I'd rather see us go to Mars. Explore something totally new. But I guess that's not practical either. They'd never fund it."

"Well," said the science adviser, "I think it's time for you to say a few words. Try us."

His host watched anxiously as George spread his palms and became the focus of attention. "Now that we have the Shuttle going, I think we need another great space incentive in this country. We need another date goal, like the one Kennedy gave for landing men on the moon. The competition is catching up to us, the Japanese and the Europeans. And the Russians are already building a space station up there. Every time they go up, they bring another big barrel and they plug it in. They're working with four times NASA's budget. They've got about two hundred kids between the ages of ten and sixteen living full-time in a cosmonaut city. Boys and girls, training to live up there. Kids who are fifteen years old understand physics on a senior college level."

And this country? George wondered. I don't know where the hell we're going.

"We need a space station—the incentive to stimulate the country and get space commercialization going.

"Mr. President, actions speak more eloquently than words. We at Grumman firmly believe that a national commitment by this administration to establish a manned space station by the turn of this decade is urgently needed. It would send a powerful message to this country's industrial community that commercial activity in space can be planned for and undertaken on a major scale. We must remain preeminent in space—both scientifically and operationally as well as commercially. The time is now. I say we should go for it!"

EXCERPT FROM PRESIDENT REAGAN'S STATE OF THE UNION ADDRESS, January 25, 1984

A sparkling economy spurs initiatives, sunrise industries—and makes older ones more competitive. Nowhere is this more important than our next frontier, space. Nowhere do we so effectively demonstrate our technological leadership and ability to make life better on Earth. The Space Age is barely a quarter century old, but already we've pushed civilization forward with our advances in science and technology. Opportunities and jobs will multiply as we cross new thresholds of knowledge and reach deeper into the unknown. Our progress in space, taking giant steps for all mankind, is a tribute to American teamwork and excellence. Our finest minds in government, industry, and academia have all pulled together, and we can be proud to say we are first, we are the best, and we are so because we're free. America has always been greatest when we dared to be great. We can reach for greatness again. We can follow our dreams to distant stars, living and working in space for peaceful economic and scientific gain. Tonight, I am directing NASA to develop a permanently manned space station, and to do it within a decade. . . .

And here we go again.

BUZZ ALDRIN, astronaut (*Gemini 12, Apollo 11*), lives in Laguna Beach, California. He is president of Starcraft Enterprises, a company that supports the establishment of a permanent base on the moon. In 1996, having developed an interest in deep ocean exploration, he became a member of the second expedition team to achieve a successful landing on the deck of the *Titanic*. Charles Pellegrino was present when Aldrin entered the record books as "the man with the most ups and downs" (250,000 miles into space and 2.5 miles to the bed of the Atlantic). Not knowing quite what to tell him before his descent, Pellegrino (opting for the last word on some historic first words), echoed the same good luck message George Skurla had given him on another summer morning, at another launch site, some twenty-seven years before: "Don't get your feet wet." (The phrase, borrowed from Apollo, has become somewhat of a standard among deep ocean explorers.)

APOLLO ARTIFACTS continue to have interesting fates. Although no moon rocks were ever "officially" given to astronauts and engineers, no fewer than three pieces of lunar basalt (complete with hypervelocity impact scars visible all the way down to resolutions attainable by electron microscopes) were donated to museums after their owners died. A fourth rock was tossed in a garbage pail by mistake (ironically, at a place called Stony Brook University). The now-famous blue plaques, each autographed by the *Apollo 13* crew and bearing piece of *Aquarius*, can fetch prices as high as $10,000. In 1994, only a few weeks before Ron Howard's classic film, *Apollo 13*, premiered, these same plaques were available through Long Island's *Pennysaver* for as little as $20. At that time, the *Apollo 13* command module—"the moon mission that never made it to the moon"— was still being listed among *National Lampoon's* "100 stupidest tourist traps in America," and actual slides photographed during the voyage of *Apollo 13* were discarded on account of "having come from a failed mission of no scientific value." In 1984, the majority of Grumman/NASA's Lunar Module construction logs (excerpts from the LM-5 log appear in Chapter 39) were buried in Long Island's Oceanside landfill. At about the same time, Charles Pellegrino rescued Lunar Module parts (including the LM-15 descent stage, designated for *Apollo 20*) from a similar fate and began shipping the pieces to New Zealand's National Observatory, where even the smallest Apollo artifacts had already proved worthy of near-worship. The arrival of the first LM landing leg strut, however, almost touched off an international incident. After a long decision-making process over how to best classify a LM leg ("Model spacecraft? But *no*—we can't check that box, it's the real thing!"), New Zealand Customs officials eventually listed it as a "used aircraft part." As it turned out, without special approval (in advance) from the Ministry of Transport, the importation of "secondhand items . . . for use in flying machines" was almost as illegal as the smuggling of cocaine. "At this stage," recalls astronomer Frank Andrews, "I told them what they could do with the bloody thing—and I hoped it gave them piles." At this stage, the Comptroller of Customs stepped in and, after the proper heads had been rolled, established New Zealand's Pellegrino Rule ("Henceforth, any space hardware shipped by Charles Pellegrino to the National Observatory shall enter the country with no questions asked."). In very short order, a Hercules cargo transport was assigned to airlift the last remnants of Apollo hardware (which no U.S. museum, at that time, wanted). In equally short order, New Zealand's declaration that its waters were a nuclear Free Zone and that

nuclear combat ships would no longer be allowed near, pro-
voked President Ronald Reagan to declare New Zealand "no
longer an American ally." The Apollo airlift was cancelled and
LM-15 was ordered buried in the Oceanside landfill (where it
will probably be found perfectly preserved, along with most
of the LM construction logs, about 4000 years from now).
Meanwhile, a spare moon rock hammer (carved by computer-
guided tools from a solid block of titanium), having been used
for years to hammer nails at Grumman's Plant 5, was found
to operate more efficiently as a lobster hammer. After the flight
to Crater Copernicus was cancelled, the unfinished *Apollo 18*
Lunar Module (LM-13) was stored at Grumman for several
years before being transferred to Long Island's Cradle of Aviation Museum. In 1997, Tom Hanks and HBO, under the
guidance of museum curator Joshua Stoff, finished the construction of LM-13, and filmed it for re-creations of the Grumman Clean Room and the lunar voyages in Mr. Hanks's epic
mini-series, *From the Earth to the Moon*. LM-13 now resides
at the Cradle of Aviation Museum, having finally completed
its mission (albeit on a Hollywood set), nearly 28 years after
Tom Kelly watched it leave Plant 5.

NEIL ARMSTRONG, astronaut (*Gemini 8, Apollo 11*), is chairman
of Computing Technologies for Aviation Incorporated, which
supplies computer programs to commercial airlines. Though
on the boards of several aerospace corporations (including AIL
on Long Island, New York), he lives on a farm in Ohio and
rarely makes public appearances.

ISAAC ASIMOV, best known for his science fiction, was also a com-
petent biochemist and astronomer. He was a major contributor
to design concepts for large-scale solar arrays on the moon
(using self-replicating robot technology). When the engineers
and physicists made a mathematical error—which he immediately pointed out—he suggested that if and when they finally
built the thing right, they could call it the Asimov Array. "We

could?" one of the scientists said. "I insist on it," he replied; and we have been calling it that ever since. Dr. Asimov died in 1992.

TOMMY ATTRIDGE, LM-3 vehicle supervisor, test pilot, and interface between Grumman and the astronauts, retired from the space program to manage a cemetery in Queens, New York. He died in 1997.

AL BEAUREGARD, LM-5 supervisor who worked under Ross Fleisig, retired after an "eventful" stint in Iran with Grumman's F-14 program.

BILL BISCHOFF, advance systems planner, was vice-president and chief engineer of Grumman Aerospace when he retired in 1987. He lives in New Hampshire.

ARTHUR C. CLARKE, whose 1951 book, *The Exploration of Space*, was presented by Wernher von Braun to President Kennedy (as a means of showing the president, in lucid English, that a landing on the moon was possible), continues to provide humanity with profiles of the future. For Arthur, this is nothing short of a long habit. On July 19, 1939, he and his colleagues at the British Interplanetary Society (of which Wernher von Braun was an honorary member, despite the fact that while aiming for the stars he would sometimes hit London), posted a lengthy letter to H. G. Wells detailing their design for "a rocket ship which we honestly believe could reach the moon and return." What they described was, in all essentials, the ancestor of Project Apollo, complete with a mother ship to remain in lunar orbit and a smaller ferry craft to actually land on the moon. "We are going on," added BIS president Bill Temple, "despite non-cooperation and non-sympathy from almost everyone, because we think it's worth going on." The reply came three days later, from Mr. Wells's secretary, stating that Mr. Wells had "duly noted" the letter, and politely suggested that Mr. Clarke's group refrain from bothering him in the future. And so it went: the visionary of the nineteenth century responding to the visionary of the twentieth century.

CLAUS'S, NAGY'S, BRIGGS'S, AND UREY'S "ORGANIZED ELEMENTS" in carbonaceous meteorites remain a mystery. Subsequent work by Folsome, Pellegrino, and Stoff suggests that they are "microfossils" of protocells, representing a pre-living chemical evolution in ancient hydrothermal environments that froze in mid-stride on the path to life—more than 4 billion years ago, inside very large asteroids. In 1967, word that such structures might be remnants of extraterrestrial life inspired a young medical student, who had the "crazy" notion that he could finance his education by writing "the great American techno-thriller." The novel he had in mind was *The Andromeda Strain*, and the student was Michael Crichton.

MICHAEL COLLINS, astronaut (*Gemini 10, Apollo 11*), continued to work for LTV Aerospace and Defense Co., and was also active in the Space Shuttle Program. He retired in 1992 and lives in Maryland.

JOHN COURSEN, assistant project engineer for LM ground support equipment, was program manager of Grumman's Rotary Launcher Proposal at the time of his retirement and Grumman's acquisition by Northrop. He lives on Long Island.

MANNING DANDRIDGE, rocket engineer, remained Grumman's manager of design engineering. He died in 1996.

JOHN DICKENSON, rocket engineer, was promoted to deputy director of Grumman's Environmental Planning and Control Program. He is now retired and living on Long Island.

"DOC" DZIALZKIEWICZ, foreman of Grumman's detailed parts department, designed prototype tools for building LMs during the mock-up phase of construction. After retirement, he restored ancient armor and cannons for museums until his death in 1998.

Bob Ekenstierna, supervisor of LM descent stage construction, retired to restore ancient armor full-time. He died in 1994.

Max Faget, chief assistant to the Space Task Group and a principal designer of the Mercury capsule, retired from NASA in 1982. Now living in Houston, he is president of Space Industries, Inc.

Artie Falbush, welder, stayed on as a welding engineer for Grumman. Retired, he continues to live on Long Island.

Ross Fleisig was Grumman's project leader for space trajectory, guidance, and control system analysis and one of the key people in charge of LM-5 (*Apollo 11*). He continued to serve as Grumman's engineering manager for advanced programs, until his retirement in 1990. He remains active in space advocacy.

Joseph Gavin, LM program manager, became president of Grumman Corporation. (Retired April 1985.) He lives in Massachusetts, and lectures at Amherst.

Robert Gilruth, director of the Manned Spacecraft Center in Houston, worked for NASA until 1986. He lives in a nursing home in Virginia.

Thomas Gold was and is still a professor of planetary sciences at Cornell University. After Apollo, he formulated a controversial (yet probably correct) theory that most of the Earth's oil reserves originated as organic material in carbonaceous meteorites. His equally controversial lunar ice theory was confirmed by space probes in the 1990s.

GRUMMAN AEROSPACE CORPORATION is now Northrop Grumman. The Plant 5 Clean Room, birthplace of the Lunar Module, remained essentially unchanged through 1998, in spite of the fact that the space shuttle's wings were built there. In 1998 and 1999, the room was being used as storage for old machinery (including F-14 parts) prior to disposal by the new parent company. The room itself, considered briefly for purchase by Steven Spielberg (as one of the worlds largest platforms for interior movie sets) was scheduled for demolition in 2001. Apollo veteran George Skurla lamented, "Grumman always had an affinity for the shadows." (Even during the heyday of Apollo, when he told people that he worked for Grumman, the place was often confused with the famous Chinese theatre in Los Angeles.) Skurla makes a valid point, but at least the world's largest flying saurian—*Quetzalquatalus northropi*—is now properly named. When the paleontologist who first unearthed the huge fossil realized that it had a wingspan as large as the F-14 Tomcat, he decided to name the species after the company that built the F-14, which he mistakenly (or prophetically) credited to Northrop, not Grumman—and we've been calling that thing *northropi* ever since.

LEON GURINSKY, rocket engine technician, works for IBM on Long Island.

TOM GWYNNE, consulting pilot, retired from Grumman in 1996. He is now administrator of the Cradle of Aviation Museum on Long Island. "Amazingly," he reflects, "the Apollo program was very short-lived. It represented an almost complete opposite to its fiscal competitor, the war in Vietnam—creative vs. destructive, uniting vs. separating, inspiring vs. degrading. When money ran short, it turned out to be easier to cancel the Apollo program than to extricate ourselves from Southeast Asia. NASA has never again been able to capture the same level of public imagination and support for its projects. Perhaps in the not too distant future, Mars exploration will again inspire the world to reach out."

FRED HAISE, astronaut/engineer (*Apollo 13*), piloted the Space Shuttle *Enterprise* from the top of a 747 to the first Shuttle runway landing, then left NASA to become president of Grumman Technical Services, where he was in charge of the Shuttle software turnaround. He retired from Northrop Aircraft Services in 1995.

PEGGY HEWITT, director of LM checkout at Cape Kennedy, died in January 1984.

MYRTICE HOLLAND, electrician, became assistant foreman at Grumman's Great River Plant. She is now retired and living on Long Island.

JOHN C. HOUBOLT, NASA engineer who pushed for adoption of the Lunar Orbit Rendezvous plan, is designing twin-fuselage aircraft at Langley, Virginia, where he is NASA's chief aeronautical scientist. Though officially retired in 1985, he remains an active consultant.

JOHN HUSSEY, who worked in the LM flight-simulation program, worked as project leader on Grumman's Space Station Program until his retirement in 1990.

BILL KAISER, airship pilot and history professor, retired to become head curator at the Cradle of Aviation Museum, Mitchel Field, Long Island, which now displays the world's largest collection of LMs (including MOLAB), all in various stages of construction. He died in 1986.

TOM KELLY, LM program engineering manager, was promoted by Grumman to vice-president of engineering. He is now retired on Long Island, but like Houbolt remains on NASA's "active" list. Among his most recent assignments: a report on "Space Station Orbital Debris Hazards."

JOE KINGFIELD, Grumman quality control manager, became Grumman's vice-president of quality control. He is retired and living on Long Island.

SERGEI KOROLEV, "Chief Designer" of Soviet spacecraft, died in 1966.

CHRIS KRAFT, director of NASA flight operations, retired as director of NASA's Johnson Space Center in 1983. He lives in Houston.

BOB KRESS, who worked in the LM flight-simulation program, retired from Grumman as assistant to the vice-president for business development.

KUPZYK, Grumman technician, works for Grumman on the JSTARS program in Melbourne, Florida.

JOHN LOGALBO, welder, is retired.

JAMES LOVELL, astronaut (*Gemini 7, Gemini 12, Apollo 8, Apollo 13*), is president of Lovell Communications, Lake Forest, Illinois.

GEORGE LOW, assistant to NASA administrator James Webb, died in 1984, several weeks after seeing his son, George Low, Jr., named a Shuttle astronaut.

FRANK MESSINA, Grumman production supervisor, served as Grumman's vice-president of manufacturing before retiring to South Carolina.

Bob Mullaney, Grumman's first program manager on the LM, became vice-president of Grumman International, South America. He is retired and living in Florida.

Al Munier, advance systems planner, spent much of the 1980s trying to get Princeton's Tokamac fusion reactor started. He also participated in brainstorming sessions at Brookhaven National Laboratory on the next seventy years in space, including a manned flight to the Alpha Centauri star system using antimatter annihilation propulsion. Known as Project Valkyrie, it gave rise to a viable means for triggering fusion with streams of antiprotons. Al died in 1994.

Rocco Petrone, director of Cape Kennedy launch operations, having served as president of Rockwell Space Transportation System, is now working to get the Alpha Space Station on line.

Lynn Radcliffe, base manager of Grumman's White Sands rocket facility, is retired.

Milt Radimer, Bob Ekenstierna's manager in charge of LM descent stage construction, is retired and lives in New Hampshire, in the home he and his wife designed and built.

Eberhard Rees, assistant to Wernher von Braun, is retired. He divides his time between Huntsville and Germany.

Chet Senig, supervisor in charge of LM ascent stage construction, is retired. He lives on Long Island.

Joseph Shea, Apollo spacecraft manager, served as vice-president in charge of engineering at Raytheon Corporation, which manufactures missile components in Lexington, Massachusetts. He returned to NASA in 1993, as assistant deputy administrator for Space Station Analysis.

HOWARD SHERMAN, preliminary design engineer in charge of crew systems, was Grumman's team leader on "Crew (Space Station) Technology Thrust" at the time of his retirement (in 1992).

GEORGE SKURLA, director of Grumman Kennedy Space Center Operations, served as president of Grumman Corporation, which, along with Lockheed, won the 1983 Space Shuttle turn-around contract. He was always an anomaly among America's corporation presidents, for he did not merely "fly behind a desk." During the conflict in Lebanon, George Skurla visited squadron leaders and Grumman representatives directly on the aircraft carrier *Robert F. Kennedy*, then took a backseat ride during a two-hour reconnaisance mission along the Lebanon coast. "I believe in going where our hardware is," he explained. "I want to see how it works in the environment it was built for." Now retired from Grumman, Skurla is a trustee for the Cradle of Aviation Museum, the Astronaut Memorial Foundation, and the Center for Space Education at Kennedy Space Center. He is one of the people responsible for Apollo era hardware finally being rescued from Florida junk yards, cleansed of graffiti, and put on proper display. Since his meeting with President Reagan, and the declaration of the Station Alpha Program, space really did become a story of: *And here we go again.* "The loss of the *Challenger* in 1986 was a tremendous wake-up call to the reality that spaceflight is still far from being routine," says Skurla. "I like to believe space is going to be part of our life through the next fifty years. I like to believe that our involvement will grow larger and larger. I like to believe that the space station, if it proves itself, will fortify the fact that the outside world—the envelope world around the Earth—is going to be built more and more into the lives of people on the ground. But we must make sure that the machine is literally perfect before it flies, to the fullest human ability to make it perfect. I remember talking with [astronaut] Pete Conrad in Tokyo, just before the *Challenger* exploded, and I asked him what he thought of the program, and he told me that he was 'getting goosey.' He felt that they were not running enough tests on the shuttle, and they were accepting things too readily. Overconfidence and arrogance—again. It will jump up and get you every time. That same sort of thinking, the sort that gave Pete Conrad goosebumps, goes back to the *Apollo* 13 Service Module, when, prior to launch, their test equipment registered a subtle indication that there was something [odd] about that oxygen tank—the one that exploded—and they could not figure it out; and they wrote it off as a 'one time anomaly'; and they went with it; and it caught up with them two-thirds of the way to the moon. And of course *Apollo* 1 before that . . . I saw the ship afterward, all the bad wiring that had been approved, under the assumption that nothing could go wrong. I hope we've learned our lesson, thrice and for all time. I hope we never have to learn it again. I hope so, but I really don't think so."

MIKE SOLAN, engineer, LM flight simulator, became the flight-control project leader on Grumman's X-29 forward-swept-wing aircraft. He died in 1995.

TOM STAFFORD, astronaut (*Gemini* 6 and 7 rendezvous, *Gemini* 9, *Apollo* 10, *Apollo Soyuz*), is now developing the Oklahoma Air and Space Museum after retiring as brigadier general, in charge of the Vandenburg Air Force Base. He is vice-president of Stafford, Burke and Hecker, Inc.

JOHN STRAKOSCH, designer, stayed on with Grumman as director of vehicle engineering.

ERNST STÜHLINGER, assistant to Wernher von Braun, is currently designing a new generation of heavy-lift airships (dirigibles). As Senior Research Scientist at the University of Alabama, Huntsville, he became one of the original designers of the Hubble Space Telescope.

JACK SWIGERT, astronaut (*Apollo 13*), died in 1982.

JOEL TAFT, who built the last lunar module (for Japan), became special projects supervisor, Grumman Kennedy Space Center Operations. He is now retired and living in Florida.

GEORGE TITTERTON retired as Grumman senior vice-president. He died in 1998.

RALPH "DOC" TRIPP, engineer and LM program manager, retired and continued to serve as a consultant to Grumman Aerospace, until his death in 1992.

HAROLD UREY, Nobel Prize-winning chemist and exobiologist, died in 1982.

JESCO VON PUTTKAMER, engineer on Wernher von Braun's Huntsville team, is NASA's director of long-range planning and was scientific adviser to Gene (*Star Trek*) Roddenberry.

HARRY WALTHER, quality control inspector who worked under Joe Kingfield, is retired. As a volunteer at Long Island's Cradle of Aviation Museum, his current projects include restoration of the original Lunar Module simulator.

BOB WATKINS, support manager for the LM program, became manager of Grumman's St. Augustine, Florida, operations. He retired in 1988.

JAMES WEBB retired from NASA in 1968 and lived in the Washington, D.C., area until his death in 1992.

ARNOLD WHITAKER, an engineer who specialized in rendezvous, became the flight-control-system project engineer on Grumman's X-29. He is retired and living on Long Island.

OZZIE WILLIAMS, manager in charge of LM Reaction Control System (the small direction control rockets that protruded from the sides of the ascent stage), became vice-president of Grumman International, Africa. Now retired, he lives in Queens, New York.

HOWARD WRIGHT, a Grumman engineer chiefly responsible for the design of the LM fuel lines ("plumbing"), is director for projects at NASA's Langley Research Center, Virginia. After LM, he participated in descent-phase design of the *Viking* Mars lander.

Adornato, Rudolph J., and Ross Fleisig. "Manual Orbit Rendezvous Analysis." Houston, Texas: TRW Systems, 1967.

Aldrin, Edwin E. *Return to Earth*. N.Y.: Random House, 1973.

Anderson, Frank. *Orders of Magnitude: A History of NACA and NASA, 1955–1980*. Washington, D.C.: NASA, 1981.

Armstrong, Neil; Michael Collins; and Edwin Aldrin. *First on the Moon*. Boston: Little, Brown, 1970.

Asimov, Isaac; Tom Kelly; Christopher Kraft, et al. "Men on the Moon: A 10th Anniversary Report." Long Island: *Newsday*, July 15, 1979.

Baker, David. *The History of Manned Space Flight*. N.Y.: Crown, 1981.

Basenov, V. I. *Landing Cosmic Apparatus on Planets*. Moscow: Mashinostroyenive Press, 1978.

Benson, Charles D., and William B. Faherty. *Moonport: A History of Apollo Launch Facilities and Operations*. NASA SP-4204.

Bergaust, Erik. *Wernher von Braun*. National Space Institute, 1976.

Brooks, Courtney G.; James M. Grimwood; and Lloyd S. Swenson, Jr. *Chariots for Apollo: A History of Manned Lunar Spacecraft*. NASA SP-4205, 1979.

Buwalda, P.; W. J. Downhower; P. K. Eckman, et al., "Man-to-the-Moon and Return Utilizing Lunar-Surface Rendezvous." JPL TM 33-53, Jet Propulsion Laboratory, Pasadena, Calif., August 3, 1961.

Clarke, Arthur C. *The Exploration of Space*. N.Y.: Harper and Brothers, 1951.

Cortright, Edgar N. *Apollo Expeditions to the Moon*. Washington, D.C.: NASA SP-350, 1975.

Eldredge, N., and Ian Tattersall. *The Myths of Human Evolution*. N.Y.: Columbia University Press, 1982.

Enzmann, Robert D., ed. *Planetology and Space Mission Planning*. Annals of the New York Academy of Sciences, vol. 140, Art. 1, pp. 1–683, December 16, 1966.

French, Bevan M., and Stephen P. Maran, eds. *A Meeting with the Universe: Science Discoveries from the Space Program*. NASA, 1981.

Gatland, Kenneth. "The International Space Arena." *Sky and Telescope*, October 1982.

Gatland, Kenneth. *Space Technology*. N.Y.: Crown, 1981.

Gibbons, Ralph. "Soviet Man-Around-the-Moon Programme: Outline Plan and Sequence of Events." *Spaceflight*, vol. 19, no. 11, November 1977.

Gilruth, Robert R., and Maxime Faget. "The Manned Lunar Mission." Paper presented before the American Rocket Society, Cleveland, Ohio, July 17–19, 1962.

Gorman, James. "The Righteous Stuff: How Astronauts Find God." *Omni*, vol. 6, no. 8, May 1984.

Gould, Stephen Jay, and Elizabeth S. Vrba. "Exaptation: A Missing Term in the Science of Form." *Paleobiology*, vol. 8, no. 1, Winter 1982.

Grahn, Sven. "A Soviet Lunar Spaceship?" *Spaceflight*, vol. 15, no. 10, October 1973.

Grissom, Betty, and Henry Still. *Starfall*. N.Y.: Crowell, 1974.

Grissom, Virgil "Gus." *Gemini: A Personal Account of Man's Venture into Space*. N.Y.: Macmillan, 1968.

Grumman *Plane News. Apollo 11*. Vol. 28, no. 14, July 28, 1969.

Grumman *Plane News. Apollo 17*. Vol. 32, no. 2, January 29, 1973.

Haggerty, James J. *Spinoff 1980, An Annual Report*. NASA Office of Space and Terrestrial Applications, Technology Transfer Division, April 1980.

Hartford, J. *Korolev: How One Man Masterminded the Soviet Drive to Beat America to the Moon*. N.Y.: Wiley, 1997.

Hartman, W. K. "The Moon's Early History." *Astronomy*, vol. 4, September 1976.

Heppenheimer, T. A. *Countdown: A History of Spaceflight*. N.Y.: Wiley, 1977.

Houbolt, John C. *Manned Lunar Landing Through Use of Lunar-Orbit Rendezvous*. (2 vols.) Langley Research Center, Hampton, Va., October 31, 1961.

Irwin, James. *To Rule the Night*. Philadelphia, PA.: A. J. Holman Co., 1973.

Jastrow, Robert. "Doorway to Space: Why We Need a Manned Space Station." *Science Digest*, vol. 92, no. 5, May 1984.

Johnson, Nicholas. "Apollo and Zond: Race Around the Moon." *Spaceflight*, vol. 20, no. 12, December 1978.

Khrushchev, Nikita. *Khrushchev Remembers: The Last Testament*. Boston: Little, Brown, 1974.

Lebedev, L.; B. Lyk'yanov; and A. Romanov. *Sons of the Blue Planet*, NASA TT F-728 (translated by Mrs. Frema Pande), 1973.

Lewis, R. S. *Voyages of Apollo*. N.Y.: New York Times Book Co., 1974.

Lindbergh, Anne Morrow. *Earthshine*. N.Y.: Harcourt, Brace and World, 1969.

Low, George M. "Notes from Visit to Soviet Union, May 17–23, 1975." NASA, June 5, 1975, pp. 1–17.

Low, George M. "The Spaceships." In *Apollo Expeditions to the Moon*. NASA SP-350, Washington, D.C., 1975.

McCurdy, H.E. *Space and the American Imagination*. Washington, D.C.: Smithsonian Institution Press, 1997.

Nagy, Bartholomew. *Carbonaceous Meteorites*. Elsevier. 1975.

NASA. *The Apollo Spacecraft: A Chronology*. (3 vols.) Washington, D.C.: U.S. Govt. Printing Office, Washington, 1974.

NASA. *Apollo 13: "Houston, We've Got a Problem."* NASA Release EP-76.

NASA Space Task Group. "A General Description of the Apollo 'Bug' Systems." Hampton, Va., September 11, 1961.

National Air and Space Museum. *Apollo to the Moon: A Dream of Centuries*. Smithsonian Institution, 1982.

National Geographic (for excellent coverage of the space program dating from the first V-2 rocket tests after World War II to the present).

Oberg, James. *Red Star in Orbit*. N.Y.: Random House, 1981.

Oberg, James. "Russia Meant to Win the 'Moon Race.'" *Spaceflight*, vol. 17, no. 5, May 1975.

Oberg, James. "Soyuz 1 Ten Years After: New Conclusions." *Spaceflight*, vol. 19, no. 5, May 1977.

O'Donnell, Bill. "NASA Modifying Saturn—Apollo Equipment, Disposing of Some." NASA Release No. 76–206, December 16, 1976.

Parkinson, R. C. *High Road to the Moon*. London: British Interplanetary Society, 1980.

Pellegrino, C. R., and Jesse A. Stoff. *Darwin's Universe: Origins and Crises in the History of Life*. N.Y.: Van Nostrand Reinhold, 1983. 2nd ed. Tab, 1986. 3rd ed. (in preparation).

Pellegrino, C.R. *Time Gate*. Blue Ridge Summit, Pa.: Tab, 1985.

Pellegrino, C. R. "The Trouble with Nemesis." *Evolutionary Theory*, vol. 7 (December 1985), pp. 219–221.

Pellegrino, C.R. and James R. Powell. "On Self-Replicating Solar Pond-Building Machines, Lunar and Mercuran Power Production, Antihydrogen Propulsion, and Other Things." *Analog*, September 1986.

Pellegrino, C. R., Harrison Schmitt, James Powell, et. al. "Living with Our Enemies in Space." AAAS 1987 Symposium.

Petrovich, G. V. *Homeland of Cosmonauts*. NASA Technical Translation, NASA TT F-11. Washington, D.C., 1968.

President's Science Advisory Committee. *The Space Program in the Post-Apollo Period: A Report of the President's Science Advisory Committee*. February 1967.

Riabchikov, Evgeny. *Russians in Space*. Moscow: Novosti Press, 1971.

Ridley, W. "Petrology of Lunar Rocks and Implication to Lunar Evolution." *Annual Review of Earth and Planetary Sciences*, 1976.

Sagan, Carl. *Cosmos*. London: Macdonald Futura Publishers, 1981.

Sheridan, David. "The Daring Contraption Called LEM." *LIFE*, vol. 66, no. 10, March 14, 1969.

Stoff, Joshua. "Where Have All the Spacecraft Gone?" (IN PRESS).

Thomson, Andrew. "Space and Superpower Rivalry." *Spaceflight*, vol. 21, no. 7, July 1979.

Time-Life Books. *Life in Space*. N.Y.: Alexandria, Va., 1983.

U.S. Govt. Printing Office. *Soviet Space Program: 1966–1970*. Washington, D.C., 1971.

Urey, Harold C. "Biological Material in Meteorites: A Review." *Science*, vol. 151, January 14, 1966.

Vick, Charles. "Russia's Moon Plan?" *Spaceflight*, vol. 21, no. 10, October 1979.

Vick, Charles. "The Soviet Super Boosters." *Spaceflight*, vol. 15, no. 12, December 1979.

Von Braun, Wernher; Ernst Stühlinger; and Heinz Koelle. "ABMA Presentation to the National Aeronautics and Space Administration." ABMA Report D-TN-1-59, Huntsville, Ala., December 15, 1958.

Von Braun, Wernher, and Frederick Ordway. *History of Rocketry and Space Travel*. N.Y.: Crowell, 1966.

Von Puttkamer, Jesco. "Humanization Beyond Earth: The New Age of Space Industrialization." In *Life in the Universe*. AAAS Selected Symposium, vol. 31, 1979.

Von Puttkamer, Jesco. "The Next 25 Years: Industrialization of Space: Rationale for Planning." *Journal of the British Interplanetary Society*, vol. 30, no. 7, July 1977.

Von Puttkamer, Jesco. "Reflections in a Crystal Ball: Science Fact vs. Science Fiction." In *Science Fiction and Space Futures*, Eugene M. Emme, ed., Advances in the Astronautical Sciences History Series, vol. 5, 1981.

Von Puttkamer, Jesco. "The Sleeping God." In *Star Trek: The New Voyages* 2. N.Y.: Bantam, 1978.

Von Puttkamer, Jesco. "Space, a Matter of Ethics: 'Toward a New Humanism." *Futurics*, vol. 5, no. 4. N.Y.: Pergamon Press, Winter 1981.

Wolfe, Tom. *The Right Stuff.* N.Y.: Farrar, Straus, 1979.

Woods, D. R. "A Review of the Soviet Lunar Exploration Programme." *Spaceflight,* vol. 18, no. 7, August 1976.

Woods, D. R. "Lunar Mission Cosmos Satellites." *Spaceflight,* vol. 19, no. 11, November 1977.

GRUMMAN AIRCRAFT ENGINEERING CORPORATION DOCUMENTS

Basic Orientation for Aero-Space Environmental Areas (Clean Room), 1965.

LM Cabin Contamination Control Plan, Grumman LPC-27-312 A.

Log Flight of Apollo 13, recorded at MSC by William Bischoff, John Strakosch and Gray Smith, 1970.

Lunar Module Structures Handout, LM-3, Grumman Aerospace, for MSC structures course, NASA, July 1968.

Lunar Module 10 Through 14 Vehicle Familiarization Manual, LMA 790-2, Grumman Aerospace, Bethpage, N.Y., November 1969.

Lunar Module Subsystems Assembly and Installations, GAEC, December 1967.

Orientation Study Guide: Lunar Module, Grumman Aerospace, NASA contract NAS 9-1100, LM subsystems briefing, MSC, January 1969.

Project Apollo Feasibility Study Summary, PDR-279-2, Bethpage, N.Y., May 15, 1961.

Proposals for Lunar Module Program, Grumman Aerospace, Bethpage, N.Y., 1961.

Studies of Lunar Logistics System Payload Performance, Grumman Project 344, Summary Report. Prepared for NASA, February 14, 1963.

Copies of taped interviews with principal characters listed in this book are available through the Northrop Grumman History Center, Bethpage, New York.

INDEX

ABOUT THE AUTHORS

Dr. Charles Pellegrino wears many hats. He has been known to work simultaneously in crustaceology, paleontology, preliminary design of advanced rocket systems, and marine archaeology. Stephen Jay Gould has described Pellegrino as a space scientist who occasionally looks down, and Arthur C. Clarke has called him "the polymathic astro-geologist-nuclear physicist who happens to be the world's first astropaleontologist." He was, with James Powell, Harvey Meyerson, and the late Senator Spark Matsunaga, a framer of the U.S.-Russian Space Cooperation Initiative (which included, among its designs, an International Space Station and joint Mars missions). With Jesse A. Stoff he proposed the first models predicting oceans (possibly life-bearing) under the ice of certain Jovian and Saturnian moons. He is, with Brookhaven physicist James Powell, a co-designer of the Europa ("ice-melt") probe and the Valkyrie interstellar rocket.

Through his work on ancient DNA Pellegrino hopes to one day redefine extinction. His hope—and his "recipe" involving dinosaur cells that may be preserved in ninety-five-million-year-old-amberized flies—became the basis for the Michael Crichton novel/Steven Spielberg film *Jurassic Park*.

Dr. Pellegrino has published twelve books of fiction and nonfiction, including the *New York Times* bestseller *Her Name, Titanic*. He lives on Long Island, New York.

Joshua Stoff is the author of eleven books on aviation and space history on such wide-ranging topics as pre–World War One aviation, Charles Lindbergh, and American aircraft production during World War Two. He is currently the curator of the Cradle of Aviation Museum in Garden City, New York, a major new air and space museum set to open in the Spring of 2000. The collection features over sixty-five air- and spacecraft, nearly all of them locally built, including two original Lunar Modules. He has served as the historical adviser on several projects, and assisted in obtaining historically accurate spacecraft for HBO's production *From the Earth to the Moon*. He lives with his wife and children on Long Island, New York.